THE DEVELOPMENTAL PSYCHOLOGY Of THE BLACK CHILD

by Amos N. Wilson

Africana Research Publications
2580 Adam Clayton Powell Jr. Blvd.
New York, New York 10039

First Printing/January 1978
Second Printing/April 1978
Third Printing/July 1978
Fourth Printing/November 1978
Fifth Printing/October 1980
Sixth Printing/January 1987

Cover Illustration: NAT EASTON

*Dedicated to my Mother and Family
and my Students*

ACKNOWLEDGEMENTS

My special appreciation is extended to those authors and publishers whose works I have incorporated into my own. Grateful acknowledgement is made to the following authors and publishers for their permission to quote sections and the use of other materials from their books.

Markham Publishing Company for PSYCHOLOGICAL FACTORS IN POVERTY, edited by Vernon Allen; Random House for BLACK ENGLISH: Its History and Usage in the United States by J. L. Dillard; Prentice-Hall, Inc. for THE MYTH OF THE DEPRIVED CHILD; Poor Children's Intellect and Education by Herbert Ginsburg; Collier-MacMillan Ltd. for RACE AWARENESS IN YOUNG CHILDREN by Mary Goodman; McGraw-Hill Book Co. for CHILD PSYCHOLOGY: A Contemporary Viewpoint by Mavis Hetherington and Ross Parke; McGraw-Hill Book Co. for SOCIOLOGY by Paul Horton and Chester Hunt; McGrawHill Book Co. for CHILD DEVELOPMENT by Elizabeth Hurlock; Simon and Schuster for THE CULTURE OF POVERTY: A Critique edited by Eleanor Leacock; McGraw-Hill Book Co. for A CHILD'S WORLD: Infancy Through Adolescence by Diane Papalia and Sally Olds; MacMillan Company for CHILDREN: Development and Relationships by Mollie Smart and Russell Smart; and Rand McNally College Publishing Co. for LANGUAGE AND POVERTY: Perspectives On A Theme edited by Frederick Williams.

CONTENTS

INTRODUCTION

There is a large and influential segment of the black community and of the community of developmental and social psychologists, social workers, sociologists, etc, who assume without question that except for skin color and economic differences, the black child is the same as the white child. In other words, the black child is a white child who "happens" to be painted black. This unexamined assumption when carried to its logical conclusion, as it has so often been, implies that what is good for the white child (particularly the white middle class child) is equally as good for the black child. It further implies that the middle class white child represents all that is superior and that the black child would profit by the close imitation of his white counterpart. Consequently, the mental and physical developmental patterns of the white middle class child have become the optimal standard by which the black child is to be measured.

The ultimate outcome of such reasoning is that blacks will achieve socioeconomic equality with whites if and when their children are given the same opportunities and are reared the same as white children. The 1954 Supreme Court decision with all of its resultant social, political, economic and educational ramifications was and is based on this assumption. Black children are bused far away from their neighborhoods so that they can receive the "same" education as their counterparts. They are "culturally enriched" by going to the same cultural events and establishments attended by white middle class children, they are fed the same food which have been found maximally beneficial for white children, they are subjected to special reading programs so that they may read at the same level as white children and they are pushed into "headstart" programs so that they may not enter grammar school "behind" their white counterparts. And yet, all these efforts have not appreciably closed the wide social, psychological and educational gap which separates black and white children. Why is this the case?

Our first attempt to answer this last question involves our questioning the validity of the assumption that except for group social and economic differences, the black and white child are the same and what differences there are between them can be removed by subjecting them to the same treatment contingencies. Is the black child a white child who "happens" to be painted black? A careful examination of scientific, historical and sociopsychological evidence points to a negative answer to this question. Each of the chapters of this book seeks to examine areas of critical differences between black and white children. In chapter one we show that detrimental prenatal influences are proportionally greater for the black child and that there exists substantial birthweight differences between the black and white infant, the black child averaging the lower birthweight. The infant prematurity rates, infant mortality and maternal mortality rates for blacks is also shown significantly higher than that of whites. The long term effects that these and other facts have on black mental, behavioral and educational development are assessed and shown to be negative. In chapter two the central issue revolves around the fact that regardless of class or economic background, the black child's physical development differs markedly and significantly in advance of that of the white child's. The difference is such that a need for nutritional standards developed specially for the black child is indicated. Facts such as the inability of a majority of black children to digest milk, the staple of the American diet, after age two and such as the possibility that the symptoms of sickle cell anemia which plagues black children may be diet related and the fact mentioned in the previous sentence are fully analyzed as to what they imply for black social psychological, behavioral and educational development. It is possible that elements of the typical American diet may work against the mental and physical development of black children. What genetic, evolutionary or selective forces have been at work or are currently at work which make for the differences in black-white psychomotor development?

Chapter two concerns itself with the effects of early child malnutrition and its influence on physical and mental development. The unique and advanced physiological development of black children is discussed along with studies of infant intelligence which indicate a general equality for the black child for the first 2½ years as compared to white children. The schizoid nature of black existence, the frustrated nature of black life and the restricted nature of the black world and their influence on the personal development of black children during the first crucial two years of life are discussed in considerable detail. Black parental attitudes and their children's physical characteristics are also analyzed here.

The mainstream of child psychology concerns itself with the influence of class differences, opportunity structure and in particular, parent-child relations on the child's mental, emotional and general personality development. These are considered the major variables whose interaction determine whether the child will fulfill his intellectual and personal potential. Race and race awareness is usually not considered as an important variable and is virtually never studied in its own right as a chief determinant of the child's intellectual and personal style. Far more so than any other ethnic child the shape of the black child's intellect and personality is determined by the concept of race, race awareness and race politics, economics, propaganda, etc, and psychology which fails to treat these items as major personality and mental variables is not adequate to deal with the black child. This has been the greatest failure of American developmental, educational and clinical psychology. Consequently, the American psychological and educational establishment has not been able to offer any practical solutions to black educational, behavioral, emotional and motivational problems. American psychology which is based on studies of white children by white psychologists whose only use for the black child is as a deficit model has been a colossal failure when dealing with the black child. White based educational psychology has not been able to teach the black child how to read. The obvious reason for this is the failure of American psychology to consider black child studies as a unique and important area of specialization. In American psychological literature the black child is treated as an after-thought, as a contrast to the white child, never as a subject matter in its own right. To ignore race and its many ramifications when dealing with the black child's educational problems, emotional problems or whatever is tantamount to ignoring the child himself and yet this is exactly what American psychology does and the price paid is too familiar to mention.

Around the age of three years the child begins to become aware of his ethnicity and this awareness begins to have a very definite effect on many areas of his personality including his self-identity, self-esteem, self-confidence and assertiveness, attitude toward his own and other ethnic groups. The dynamics of why black children exhibit remarkably high levels of self and group rejection, lowered self-esteem and an inordinate affinity toward whites are fully discussed in chapter 3.

In 1972 Ashley Montagu set forth the concept of "sociogenic brain damage". He thereby proposed that the normal growth and development of the brain may fail to occur due to the lack of proper and adequate social stimulation. In chapter four we present a similar view which we refer to as "psychogenic brain damage." The admittively speculative view proposes that the failure to properly program a vital area of the brain during two critical periods of the child's development produces behavioral problems which closely resemble those resulting from actual physical damage to the same area. We also consider in this chapter the relationship between hemispheric specialization of the brain and the general sociocultural behavior of a large percentage of ghetto black children.

Chapter 5 deals with the role of play in the black child's development. How much and in what ways the black child's play activities enter into his intellectual and personality development has not been considered in the literature and points to another gross oversight of the

American developmental and educational psychological establishment. There is some indication that the black child's play activity may be schizoid in nature, is more filled with elements of frustration and restrictiveness which adversely affects his preparation to deal effectively with the world into which he is entering. What effects the reading of comics, the viewing of T. V. and movies and the listening to of radio, have on the personal and mental development are discussed and it is demonstrated that these activities may subtley negate a significant portion of his growth potential. Standardized infant intelligence scales scores indicate a general equality of the black child up to age 2½ years. Why this trend is later reversed is explained from an angle not commonly used in psychology.

In chapter 6 the mythology of "intelligence" and of "intelligence" tests are fully discussed. The fact that there is no consensual definition of the term "intelligence" is emphasized. The differing average scores of classes and ethnic groups on IQ tests are presented. A detailed attempt to demonstrate beyond doubt that "intelligence" as measured by IQ tests is a function of environmental adaptation is also made. Data relating IQ change to institutionalization, to the rearing of black children in white homes, to migration, to class membership, and to ethnic social history and socialization practices are presented to in support of an adaptational hypothesis of intelligence.

In chapter 7 the biological and sociocultural basis of language behavior of all distinct language groups is outlined. This is done to show that infants of all ethnic and language groups in their acquisition of spoken language follow basically the same developmental patterns. An effort is made to demonstrate that black english is a language in its own right and that the problems black children have in learning to speak and use standard English are essentially the same as those of children from other non-english speaking cultures. Efforts are made to show why black english should be considered a legitimate primary language and standard English as a second language as far as the black child is concerned. A brief history of the black dialect is given along with some structuring differences between standard and black English. Black English and the linguistic conflicts of the black child are discussed here.

Enslavement of black people was not just physical but more importantly it was mental. Blacks suffer from a "slave mentality" which is the result of the most massive and successful behavioral modification and brainwashing program in history. The socialization of black people in slavery and since has very definite and measurable influences on black behavioral and cognitive behavior. The way black mothers socialize their children is directly related to the historical and current ways

9

black people were and are treated in American society.

In chapter 8 a discussion of the parental functionality of the lower and middle class black mother is undertaken. The class lifestyle of these mothers and their related socialization practices are considered at length and the concept of "locus of control" also as it relates to black children's social and intellectual behavior is analyzed. We also consider the question of the effect of fatherlessness on the growth and development of the black child and the results of achievement motivation in the black child and its relationship to socialization, feelings of powerlessness, intellectual and academic performance is given a detailed presentation.

A review of the above paragraphs should make it obvious why this book was written. All the educational, social, economic, personal, crime, community organization problems which confront the black community and the black child motivated the writing of this book. It has become obvious that psychology and the social sciences as they are presently constituted are unable to meet the challenge that black people in America present. This book is an attempt to help strengthen the power of these fields and the workers in them to meet more successfully the challenge of black people. So it follows that this book is aimed at professional psychologists, social scientists and concerned others who wish to aid and/or understand the black child. But most of all this book is written to black people and especially black parents. The solution of black problems must begin in the black family and within the black community.

We wish to acknowledge here the kindness, patience and expertise of Mr. Kofi Quaye who spent many hours proofreading this work.

Amos N. Wilson
Hostos Community College
CUNY. N. Y.

ABOUT THE AUTHOR:

AMOS N. WILSON is a graduate of More-house College, Atlanta, Ga. and the New School For Social Research, New York City. He currently teaches in the Social Sciences Department at Hostos Community College of the City University of New York. He is pursuing further studies in General Theoretical Psychology at Fordham University of New York City. He has authored a series of articles and read a number of papers in the area of The Developmental Psychology of the Black Child before many interested lay and professional organizations.

THE PRENATAL PERIOD

During the prenatal period, the nine month preparatory period before the American black child is born, or is conscious, even in a primitive way, of its existence in the world, let alone what kind of world he is to be born into, he is much more a victim of that world's adverse effects than is any other ethnic American child. The unfortunate effects of slavery, past and present racial discrimination and cultural deprivation, make themselves felt during this period when the very foundation of life is being laid. From the beginning of his creation, the black child suffers both the emotional and physical consequences of the "Black condition" in America.

Black life, like all human life, in many obvious and subtle ways reflects the influences of its prenatal existence. And the prenatal existence in turn, reflects the wholesome or unwholesome nature of the maternal prenatal intrauterine environment, her mental and physical life history which includes that of her ancestors, and her prenatal mental and physical lifestyle and attitudes while carrying her child. This being the case, we can logically conclude that the generally culturally deprived conditions of black existence are represented in the black mother's prenatal intrauterine environment and adversely influences her child's basic physical and mental development. Consequently, her ability to produce optimally healthy, fully potentiated babies is seriously handicapped. The prevailing socioeconomic-emotional environment surrounding the majority of black mothers exposes them to factors which adversely influence the development of their unborn children. Such factors include poor physical health, inadequate diet, poor prenatal medical care, unfavorable age and parity, unhealthy emotional attitudes concerning the self, others (including the fathers), the world and the unborn child, and finally, an unwholesome lifestyle which often leads to the chronic or overingestion of harmful chemical agents, drugs, substances and residues.

12

Maternal Health: A fairly broad spectrum of disease and disorders which may negatively affect the health of the expectant black mother may, in turn, negatively affect the health, growth and development of her child. The adverse effects of maternal disorders and diseases can be catastrophic. For example, maternal hypothyroidism, an endocrine disorder which results in a deficiency of the thyroid hormone which is so essetial for the regulation of body metabolism and growth, may produce cretinism in the child. In this instance the bones and cartilage of the child fail to develop, its stomach will be large, flabby and protruding, its skin rough and coarse, the hair shaggy and its intellectual functioning far below normal. Other endocrine disorders may also cause microcephaly, mental deficiency accompanied by a small, pointed skull, and mongolianism, subnormal mental functioning accompanied by slanted eyelids.

Infectious diseases such as syphilis, gonorrhea, poliomyelitis, rubella, smallpox, chickenpox, measles, mumps, scarlet fever, tuberculosis, if acquired by the expectant mother during the early months of pregnancy, may lead to still births, miscarriages, blindness, deafness, mental deficiency, microcephaly, motor disorders, or deaf-mutism in her child (29). Maternal health conditions such as high blood pressure and diabetes may also seriously destroy the child's development or prove fatal to it's life or the life of it's mother.

It goes without saying that the group or groups containing the largest number of mothers suffering from such disorders, infections and health conditions enumerated above will produce the largest proportion of babies with health problems, developmental irregularities, abnormalities and deviations. Overcrowded, poverty-stricken sociocultural conditions as well as the absence or lack of adequate prenatal medical care add to that larger proportion. At least twice as many blacks suffer from disease such as meningitis, measles, encephalitis, diptheria, whooping cough, scarlet fever, nephritis, influenza and pneumonia (27), than do whites. Consequently blacks as a group produce proportionately more children with nervous system damage which may lead to lowered intellectual functioning, and various types of developmental malformations, irregularities, abnormalities, deviations, and with greater susceptibility to fall victim to childhood diseases and infections. Black mothers who have tuberculosis and infections of the urinary tract produce more children with birth defects than normal mothers (42). It is possible for syphilis bacteria to enter the embryo and cause spontaneous abortion which may be the more fortunate event, when one realizes that a child born of a syphilitically infected mother may suffer from congenital syphilis itself (9). Measles, mumps, smallpox, chickenpox and scarlet fever are all capable of being transmitted from the mother's body to that of her child's. This means that the unborn child may suffer from any of these diseases and possibly die in the womb. It is at least probable that viral infections can cause chromosomal breakage and induce mongolianism and other genetic abnormalities (39). The greatest percentage of children born of diabetic mothers require special diet

13

and insulin treatment at birth. In spite of such special efforts 21% of these children may die in the womb or soon after birth (40). Serious lower-limb malformation occur more often in children born of diabetic mothers than to normal mothers. High blood pressure is directly responsible for increased rates of spontaneous abortions, infant deaths and maternal deaths among black people. Even if the unborn black child is not exposed to maternal diseases and infections while in the womb, he is far more likely than his white counterpart to contract these diseases and infections during child and adulthood. Thus, we can see that the relatively high rate of infections, diseases and poor health conditions among blacks operate against the life chances of black children as well as reduce their mental, physical and social functioning. A great percentage of black potential is destroyed in the wombs of black mothers as a result of the "black condition" in America.

Drugs: The "black condition" not only induces a high incidence of infections, diseases, health problems and other conditions yet to be discussed among black mothers, but also is greatly responsible for the relatively higher ingestion by black mothers of harmful or potentially harmful drugs such as alcohol, barbiturates, heroin, morphine, methadone, nicotine and other stimulants and depressants of various types. In her efforts to cope with environmental stress, personal problems, peer group pressures and sociocultural traditions brought on by the "black condition" in America, the black mother may become dependent on alcohol and/or increase her intake of drugs and substances with the objective of finding temporary or permanent respite from the effects of such stress, problems and peer group pressure and as a means of accomplishing peer group approval and social acceptance.

Alcohol: The maternal bloodstream is the source of fetal nourishment, growth and development. Substances which may acutely or chronically upset the healthy constituency of the maternal blood and impose a strain on her physiological resources and functioning, directly or indirectly impose a burden on the fetus's physiological resources and functioning and thereby poses a threat to the fetus's normal mental and physical development. Even if the consumption of alcohol by expectant black mothers is low or nonexistent, the threat of this drug to their unborn children would still be present due to the relatively high consumption of alcohol by black fathers. The presence of alcohol in the father's bloodstream may weaken the potential of his germ cells before fertilization takes place (29).

While the effects of the moderate intake of alcohol during pregnancy are unknown, it is known that the excessive drinking of alcohol during this period can bring on a "fetal alcohol syndrome" (32). The symptoms of this syndrome are retarded physical development, which never attains its full genetic potential, retarded motor development, subnormal intelligence, heart abnormalities, small heads with concomitant facial defects and deviations in the structure of the joints.

Addictive Drugs. The taking of various barbiturates and other stimulants and depressants by the expectant black mother may virtually immobilize her unborn child (25). The heavy or continued intake of certain barbiturates may asphyxiate the fetus and damage its brain. Despite the relative lack of media attention currently, the addiction to morphine or heroin is still quite extensive in black communities. The social-cultural disruption caused by addictive drugs is well known. However, less well known is the developmental disruption addictive drugs cause in the children born of addicted mothers. These babies are often themselves addicted to heroin. They exhibit a number of withdrawal symptoms such as unusual sleep patterns, restless sleep, great variability in heart-rate, a relative high rate of rapid-eye movement—all indications of central nervous system disturbance (43). In addition such symptoms as hyperirritability, convulsions, fever, vomiting, trembling, shrill crying, rapid respiration, sneezing and hyperactivity may be present (51, 54, 52). Two to three days of careful medical attention are required to aid the neonate in recovering from the withdrawal symptoms of heroin addiction. In a number of cases the heroin affected baby will die while trying to cope with demands of withdrawal. The surviving infants will be more prone to develop illnesses than will normal babies due to the fact that they are more often born premature and of low birthweight which ill prepares them to deal with the traumatic ordeals of withdrawal (14). The longer the mother has been addicted to heroin the more severe the symptoms suffered by the newborn. Drug-addicted mothers tend to develop premature menopause as well as lowered fertility thereby increasing the probability of giving birth to low birthweight or premature babies when they do conceive (14).

In many drug rehabilitation programs methadone is used as a substitute for heroin since it does not bring on the less desirable physical and social side-effects of the drug it replaces. However, there is evidence that methadone, when utilized by pregnant women, may lead to more severe withdrawal symptoms in the newborn of women who have been addicted to heroin (23). Marijuana which is not an addictive drug, has no demonstrated effect on the fetus.

Nicotine. Nicotine is a potent narcotically poisonous drug. The nicotine enters into the fetal circulatory system and adversely affects many parts of its body including its heart, vascular system and other organs which diminshes the fetus's supply of oxygen and nutrition. Smoking generally reduces the expectant mothers appetite and consequently may reduce her intake of proteins and other vital nutrients needed for proper fetal development. Depending on the individual fetus the fetal heart rate may be greatly accelerated, up to 39.6 beats per minute faster than normal or decelerated by 16.8 beats per minute slower than normal, by maternal smoking (48). These reactions by the fetal cardiac and related vascular systems may lay

15

the basis for future cardiac and circulatory disorders in adulthood (34). It has been firmly established that maternal smoking produce more premature, low birthweight infants, more miscarriages, stillborn infants and infants who die soon after birth (49). Other things held constant, the frequency of premature births are in almost direct proportion to the amount of smoking done by pregnant mothers. Mothers who smoke more than 10 cigarettes per day (heavy smokers) have the highest prematurity rate; mothers who smoke 1 to 10 cigarettes per day (light smokers) have a lower rate, and the lowest rate is maintained by nonsmoking mothers. Mothers who are heavy smokers produce nearly twice the number of premature births as do nonsmoking mothers (49).

Maternal Malnutrition. Since the fetus obtains its nourishment from its mother's bloodstream it is essential that the mother's diet provide the necessary nutrients if the fetus is to attain its full genetic, mental and physical potential. An adequate supply of the following nutrients should be present: proteins for tissue growth, repair and building; fats for fat tissue formation, body fuel, and as a stored reserve; carbohydrates for strength and energy; vitamins and minerals for growth and for maintaining the body in optimal physical condition and working order (29).

Maternal malnutrition can either be qualitative or quantitative or a combination thereof. Qualitative malnutrition exists when there is a lack of essential nutrients in the maternal diet. Quantitative malnutrition exists when the maternal diet contains the essential nutrients but in insufficient amounts. Of the two forms of malnutrition, qualitative malnutrition is more life-threatening. In prolonged or severe qualitative hunger a vitamin deficiency occurs which becomes harmful to the fetus. The fetus of the quantitatively hungry mother, provided she eats foods containing the necessary nutrients, will get its share of nutrients even if it is at the mother's expense. However, prolonged or severe quantitative and/or qualitative hunger is physiologically dangerous or life-destroying.

There are an estimated 23 million persons who may be suffering from malnutrition in America alone (47). Worldwide, a billion or more people suffer from malnutrition. This amounts to a third of the human race. Almost all children born to poor parents in the underdeveloped nations suffer some degree of qualitative or quantitative malnutrition. The degree of malnutrition for millions of these children can only be described as severe (39).

Returning to the U.S., as we have noted, malnutrition is quite extensive—especially among poor blacks and whites. The number of women of childbearing age living in poverty-stricken circumstances approximates 5 million, more or less. Poverty almost certainly insures poor diet. Sixty-seven percent of households in America with incomes beyond $10,000 have good diets—diets containing an adequate amount and variety of the essential nutrients. Below $5,000 and $7,000, 53% of the households have good diets.

Only 37% of families with incomes $3,000 have a good diet. The larger percentage of black family income falls under the $5,000–$7,000 category. The nutrients most often missing in poor diets are calcium, vitamins A and C. All too frequently the B vitamins are also missing or are present in inadequate amounts.

PER CENT OF HOUSEHOLDS WITH DIETS AT THREE LEVELS OF QUALITY BY INCOME

Income	Good Diets [1] (%)	Fair Diets [2] (%)	Poor Diets [3] (%)
Under $3,000	37	27	36
$3,000–4,999	43	33	24
$5,000–6,999	53	29	18
$7,000–9,999	56	32	12
$10,000 and over	63	28	9

1. Good diets: meet Recommended Dietary Allowances (1963) for 7 nutrients.
2. Fair diets: ⅔ R.D.A. for 7 nutrients but below R.D.A. for 1–7.
3. Poor diets: ⅔ R.D.A. for 1–7 nutrients; is not synonymous with serious hunger or malnutrition.

Source: *Dietary Levels of Households in the United States,* Spring 1965. Agricultural Research Service, USDA.

Maternal malnutrition in combination with other deleterious physiological and environmental factors are related to numerous mental and physical defects in children. Severe dietary deficiencies, particularly in a number of important vitamins and protein, in the diet of expectant mothers are related to relatively increased rates of abortions, prematurity, stillbirths, infant mortality, physical and neural defects in infants. Malnourished mothers generally produce children that are smaller in length and weight when they are born. Some of the physical abnormalities and mental deficiencies which may develop from serious malnutrition are rickets, general physical weakness, lethargy and apathy, cerebral palsy, epilepsy, nervous instability and neuro-psychiatric disabilities, learning and behavioral disabilities.
Poor pregnant black mothers who suffer from protein deficiency produce more children of lower birthweight and of small skull volume (possibly indicative of a smaller number of brain cells) than black mothers not suffering from this deficiency (5). A definite relationship between low birthweight and mental retardation has long been established. We shall have more to say about this later. The percentage of fully healthy babies increases directly

with increasing intake of proteins.

A study of four hundred pregnant poor women demonstrated that vitamin supplementation of the mother's deficient diet during the last half of pregnancy increased the intelligence of their children, at least for the first four years of their life, at which time socio-cultural factors may overwhelmingly work against the children's intellectual development (19). Thus, vitamin deficiency may have an adverse effect on intellectual development—particularly, vitamin B deficiency. It has been established that expectant mothers suffering from vitamin B deficiency are more likely to produce offspring whose intelligence has been adversely affected or retarded during their early years (29). A niacin deficiency may cause personality and behavioral changes similar to apathy and even psychosis.

An experiment where in the diets of a group of low-income expectant mothers were supplemented during pregnancy and lactation while another group of low-income expectant mothers were not supplemented, demonstrated that the children born to the "supplemented" mothers had, in early childhood, significantly higher IQ's than those of the "non-supplemented" mothers.

Prolonged malnutrition during pregnancy is one of the most common causes of fetal and infant mortality and of irretrievably damaged children. Poverty-stricken families produce an infant mortality rate two to three times higher than middle-class families. Malnutrition in childhood seldom exists as a free-standing entity. It is often accompanied by other medical and disease complications or leaves the child defenseless before the onslaughts of infections. A malnourished child is more likely to suffer from various illnesses than is a well-nourished child.

Malnutrition is bad enough by itself, but it almost never occurs alone . . . In places such as Africa, where malnutrition is a common childhood experience, measles is a killer . . . Furthermore, repeated bouts of infection can intensify and aggravate malnutrition . . . In many poverty-stricken regions of the world, infant diarrhea and respiratory infections in the young are the leading over-all causes of death . . . The alarm is over those who die . . . The combined assault of poverty and its social deprivations, along with the lack of good nutrition, both before and after birth, can leave a young child permanently handicapped virtually from the start of life.

The world is producing literally hundreds of thousands of children who will be at risk of poor mental development later on. These are the very countries that are underdeveloped and can least afford to have many of their 20-year-olds retarded 20 years from now (51).

". . .Today's malnutrition may already be shackling tomorrow's generation of adults (44)."

18

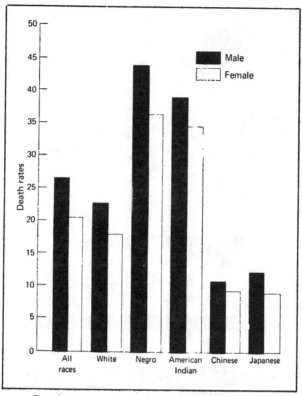

Death rates under one year per 1,000 live births.
(From Heterington and Parke, 1975)

The results of a number of studies indicate that all stillbirths, all cases of infants dying during the first few days after birth, excepting those with major genetic defects, were products of poorly nourished mothers or mothers who maintained a poor, inadequate diet during pregnancy (35). It was found that 94% of the infants born in good or excellent condition were born to mothers who maintained good or excellent diets during pregnancy (36). A follow-up study indicated that those mothers whose diets became poorer during the intervening three years, and who also became pregnant again, produced poorer maternal records with the later child. The trend was reversed with mothers whose diets had improved.

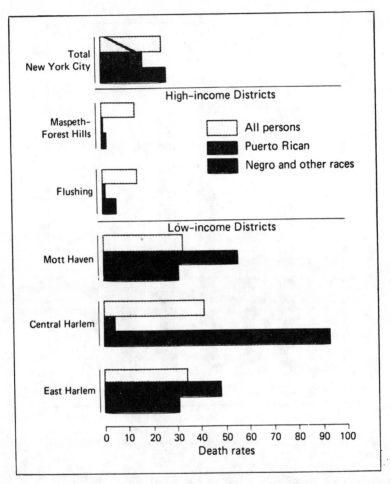

Infant death rates per 1,000 live births by race or national origin in selected health districts in New York City: 1966 - 1967.
(Adapted from Hetherington and Parke, 1975)

Maternal Malnutrition and Mental Retardation. Subnormal or below average intellectual functioning which begins during the developmental period and which is associated with impaired adaptive behavior is referred to as mental retardation (20). This term also covers such concepts as feeblemindedness, mental subnormality and moronity.

Mental retardation may arise from a large number of problems, diseases and medical syndromes. The genetic contribution to mental retardation adds up to at least 40% (52). Not much is known of the hows and whys of the genetic basis of subnormal intellectual functioning. Pathological, abnormal or mutant genes determine cerebral, structural and metabolic abnormalities which contribute significantly to mental retardation and other physiological deviations. They may do this by interfering with or destroying various metabolic processes involving the utilization of proteins, carbohydrates and fats for normal mental and physical growth, development and functioning. The possibility remains that the contribution of abnormal or malfunctioning genes may be smaller than current estimates would indicate and that "genetically" determined retardation is more the result of the interaction between the genes and the prenatal intrauterine environment.

The brain increases in size very rapidly during the prenatal period, particularly during the second trimester of pregnancy (3rd - 6th month). During this period there is a rapid multiplication of brain nerve cells (by means of cell division) coupled with a rapid growth in the size of these cells as well. Consequently, this rapid increase in brain growth occurs at the time it is especially sensitive to nutritional deprivation. Adequate nutrition must be readily available in order to support the phenomenally rapid cerebral growth. Apparently malnutrition can bring about a decrease in the number and size of brain cells. Autopsies performed on malnourished children in Uganda and India indicated that the brainweight of these children were up to some 36% lighter than normal (23). Similar autopsies performed on malnourished lower-class American children showed an average brainweight deficit of 15% when compared to middle-class American families (47). Churchhill (5) reported that autopsies of all the infants he studied who had died of malnutrition had a subnormal brain cell count.

If the evidence from animal studies can be extrapolated to human beings it could be firmly stated that diets low in proteins may produce babies whose brains are light in weight, protein content and number of cells. There is evidence that severely malnutritioned children tend to have smaller than normal head circumferences, indicating possibly abnormally smaller brains (45).

It has been clearly demonstrated that the intellectual development of children is related to prenatal nutrition. A growing preponderance of evidence points to strong positive correlates between prenatal malnutrition and later mental retardation. A study of malnourished children from underdeveloped countries showed them to be impaired in intelligence and sensory-motor coordination, to be generally apathetic and limited in learning ability (38). A study of 4-year-old American children who were the offspring of mothers who had an inadequate amount of protein in their diets during pregnancy. exhibited significantly lower IQ scores than the 4-year-old offsprings of mothers who had an adequate amount of protein in their diets.

Maternal Age and Parity. Studies have indicated that on the whole, the optimal childbearing age for women is between 21 and 28 years. Before 21 the female's reproductive apparatus has not fully matured and hormones necessary for reproduction have not attained their full potential. After 28 and with increasing age until menopause in the forties, reproductive and hormonal changes drastically increase the chances of the mother producing miscarriages, stillbirths and infants with a variety of serious developmental irregularities.

Figure 1. Number of Maternal deaths for each 100,000 live births, given for non-white and white women (United States 1963 - 1965), by age.

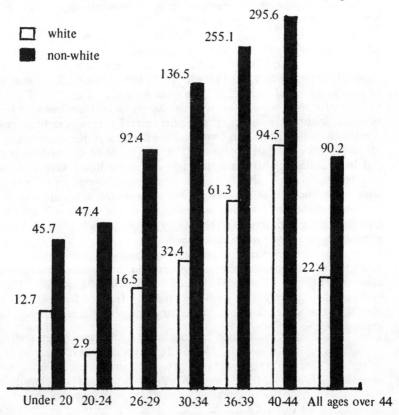

Source: Date from *Statistical Bulletin,* Metropolitan Life Insurance Co., December, 1968

The mother aged 35 or older, particularly if she is having her first child will be in labor an average of an hour and a half longer than normal. The highest rates for stillbirths occur among mothers 35 or older. The rates are lowest for mothers between the ages of 20 and 24 years old. Mothers aged 20 years or under and who have given birth to a number of children and older mothers who've also had a number of children, produce the highest proportion of infants that will die during their first month of life. The number of infant deaths between the ages of 1 month to 1 year increase directly with increasing parity (the number of children already born to a particular mother). Generally speaking, very young and/or older mothers produce more defective children than do mothers between those two age groups. Fifteen to nineteen-year-old mothers and even more so, mothers 35 and over, who are having their first child, produce the greatest proportion of premature infants (31). For a mother not yet thirty the chances of her producing a mongoloid child is about 1 in 1000; for a mother at 40, 1 in 100; for the mother at 45, 1 in 45 (10).

Maternal death rates generally follow the trend of the infant mortality rates. White mothers 20 and under and white mothers 25 and over produce the highest maternal death rates. Beginning at age 20 and under and with inreasing age the maternal death rate of black mothers increases by leaps and bounds (see figure 1). In studying maternal mortality in terms of race one can see most clearly the negative effects of the added dimension of being black in America. The number of black mothers who may die while giving birth to a child is anywhere from 3 to 16 times the number of white mothers who may die while giving birth.

Black mothers tend to have children at a significantly younger age (though this trend has reversed in the last few years) and at later ages than their white counterparts. A significantly larger number of black mothers produce a larger number of children. These factors lead to a higher infant mortality rate, a higher infant abnormality (in general, but not in every particular) rate, and a higher maternal mortality rate among black mothers. Black mothers have a higher frequency of multiple births (the birth of two or more babies within a few hours) than do their white counterparts. There are significantly more mental defectives among twins than there are among singletons. Twins who must share the maternal placental blood circulation may receive far less nourishment per fetus than would be the case if only a single fetus occupied the womb. Twins born to malnourished black mothers are obviously in greater danger of suffering from the negative effects of malnutrition and other prenatal problems than are single children born to malnourished black mothers.

Family Size and Intelligence. The family size, the length of time between births of children, and whether the births are single or multiple, have been shown not only to be related to the increased possibility of maternal and infant mortality or giving birth to infants who may suffer some physical handicap, but also has been shown to be related to reduced IQ. Generally, children in large families, from families with short time intervals between births, or children who are a part of multiple births, tend to have lower IQs than children from the opposite circumstances. Regardless of class, sociocultural or ethnic background, the most intelligent children come from the smallest families and from families where the longest time intervals exists between births (54).

Babies born within one year of previous gestation were matched with controls born two to five years after the previous gestation. Matching was done for sex, race, hospital of birth, and socioeconomic status. Their gestation ages were equal, but the babies produced in rapid succession averaged significantly smaller birth weights, lower scores on the Bayley tests at 8 months, and lower Stanford-Binet IQs at 4 years. At 1 year of age, the average baby in the experimental group had a smaller head and delayed motor development (Holley.24).

Baird conducted a survey in Scotland in 1969 along the lines of the study just quoted (1). He reported that "it is clear that the woman who has five or more children—no matter what class she belongs to officially—is likely to have children with IQ scores well below average."

Over three times as many black families have 6 or more children than do white families. It has been estimated that over six times as many black families produce children in rapid succession (children born within one year of each) than do white families (4). The implications projected by these facts are clear. It is obvious that the black intellectual potential is reduced by the black family situation. When the other negative factors resulting from the black condition in America are accounted for it's remarkable that the black intellectual potential is as strong as it is.

Maternal Emotions. When we measure stress in terms of marital problems, severe housing problems, economic problems, etc., we find that there is a definite relation between severe stress on the pregnant mother and pregnancy and birth complications, prenatal and postnatal problems in the child (17). Stress on the pregnant mother can be harmful at various developmental stages between fertilization and implantation of the ovum, possibly harmful enough to create abnormalities in the fetus or lead to its abortion (42). The mother's emotional state also affects the fetus at later stages of development. When the mother experiences negative emotions, even of a brief duration, the fetus may continue to react in response to the mother's emotional behavior for quite some time afterwards. Mothers with a higher than normal level of autonomic nervous system activity such as heart and respiration rate, blood pressure. gavanic skin response, body temperature, etc. -- all the usual signs of emotional stress -- also show higher than normal fetal activity (33). The mother who evinces a general state of moodiness, psychological depression and over-dependency is more likely to have physical complications during child birth (21). New born babies born to mothers who have suffered from severe and prolonged tension tend to have a greater than normal rate of postnatal adjustment difficulties (15, 16, 17). Poor postnatal adjustment may begin a "vicious circle" in which the mother, in reacting to her difficult child, sets up a neurotic or emotionally distorted relationship with it and vice versa which, in turn, may result in behavioral upset or deviant behavior in her child leading to lifetime problems. Thus, "women who are not happy about their pregnancies, because pregnancy interferes with the pattern of their lives or brings economic hardship, often experience continued emotional tension." (29).

How does the mother's emotional state affect the child which has no direct link to the mother's vascular or nervous system? Maternal emotional states are converted into embryonic and fetal emotional states through a rather complex series of actions and reactions wherein the autonomic segment of the central nervous system activates the endocrine glands to facilitate the particular emotional state by secreting hormones directly into the bloodstream. The hormone epinephrine (adrenalin), is an especially important factor in this respect and acts to produce many of the symptoms found in emotional states. During emotional states the endocrine secretions often reach the fetus through the placental barrier and consequently produce many of the symptoms of the emotional state in the fetus. Hormonal and other endocrine imbalances caused by the maternal emotional state can under certain circumstances, harm the fetus. For instance, cleft palates and harelips are partially or fully the result of maternal emotional stress.

Hyperactivity of the maternal adrenal glands during the seventh and tenth week of pregnancy may cause a deviation in the development of the palate bones which are forming at this time. Adrenal hyperactivity releases hydrocortisone, a hormone which may interfere with the normal development of the palate, thus causing cleft palate. If this hormone interferes with the development of the upper jawbone, a harelip may be produced (29). Emotional stress may cause mental retardation if the hormonal imbalance which results from that stress occurs during the time the brain is developing (29).

What effect and how serious the effect of emotional stress will be on the fetus depends on mainly when the stress occurs, how intense it is, how long the stress lasts and the particular chemistry and physiology of the mother's body. If the stress comes about early in the pregnancy and is intense, of long duration and sufficient enough to cause endocrine imbalance, it will be more injurious to the fetus than if it were to come during the latter part of the pregnancy. Chronic fatigue states may produce developmental deviational conditions similar to those conditions produced by severe emotional stress

Birth difficulties and infant mortality, which are significantly higher among black mothers, have been found to be related to black maternal emotional upset (8). The constant stress of being black in a racist society, the ongoing struggle with identity problems, inferiority complexes, double-consciousness, the stresses brought on by economic problems, marital problems, broken homes (nearly half of black families are headed by females), teenage motherhood, unwed motherhood, etc., which are highly prevalent in the black community, create a state of chronic emotional stress in black mothers and this stress affects many of their children in the form of physical, mental, emotional and behavioral problems. The psychosocial atmosphere of the ghetto created by poor economic circumstances, poor housing and all which that implies, such as inadequate heating, hot water, poor sanitation and ventilation, high insect and vermin infestation, and the continuing fear of being mugged, attacked or harassed, or robbed negatively affects the black mother's emotional wellbeing. The struggle for survival of the larger percentage of black mothers creates an emotional state of mind not conducive to childbearing or rearing. The economic hardship, regardless of familial support, institutional support such as welfare agencies are responsible for a large share of black maternal emotional stress. The black mother is far more likely to work late in her pregnancy and is therefore more likely to suffer from fatigue harmful to her child. Because she is more likely to receive inadequate financial support from the father of the child, her family, from social institutions, the black mother suffers most from adverse emotional stress and strain and physical exhaustion, thereby reducing the life-chances of her unborn child.

The frequent forming and breaking of emotional-romantic attachments, and/or the continued exploitation or feared exploitation of the black mother by unscrupulous males, add to her emotional problems. For the maritally abandoned mother, the unwed and teenage unwed mother (of which black mothers form the largest number), the absence of a supportive, extended family, the absence of or lack of emotional support by the baby's father or others can create a damaging psychological state of mind which may be physically or behaviorally harmful both before and after birth. Illsley (31), in a sociological study of reproduction, shows that mortality rates for both mothers and babies are higher for illegitimate pregnancies. Low birthweights and prematurity rates are also higher in this group of mothers. Similar rates are also established by mothers who work late into prgenancy and who may be under 20 years old.

Prematurity. Hurlock defines prematurity as "a condition in which the newborn infant is relatively unfit for extra-uterine life because of a lack of development or a retardation in development caused by a shortening of the fetal period" (29). Premature birth is life threatening to the neonate — seriously or fatally damaging to neonatal health, growth and development, both in a physical and psychological sense.

The length of the gestation period, i.e., the length of time the newborn has spent in the uterus prior to birth, and the birth size (weight of the neonate as well as the neonatal birth weight in relation to neonatal body length), are the criteria most often used to determine prematurity. If the newborn has a gestation period of less than 37 weeks or his weight is 5½ pounds or less, it is called premature. Taken by themselves — gestation period, because it cannot always be estimated accurately, and birth weight, which has also been proved not to be the most accurate indicator of prematurity - these two criteria leave much to be desired as accurate determinants for labeling the newborn as premature. However, taken together they provide a more useful prognostic tool for indicating the newborn's chances of survival and what measures should be taken to assure its survival and development. The measure of the head circumference provides the best single measurement for determining gestational age (11). Generally, a head circumference of less than 33 centimeters and crown-rump length of less than 32 centimeters may be used as additional evidence for prematurity (13). Probably a combination of measures we have already mentioned plus neurological, electro-encephalographic data and records of motor performance, provide the most reliable means of determing maturity.

Brain Damage and Prematurity. More neonatal deaths are caused by prematurity than by any other conditions. Premature infants are especially vulnerable to brain damage during birth. This is due to the fact that at birth, the skull of the premature infant is not well developed enough to shield it s delicate brain tissues from the physical stresses and pressures of the birth process. If the birth process is long or complicated, stress on the brain may be increased to such a degree that hemorrhages may occur both in and around the brain. These may be severe enough to cause permanent brain damage which may be reflected in the infant's future mental, physical or emotional behavior.

Other parts of the nervous system besides the brain may be damaged during the birth of the premature infant. Physical stress during the birth process on other parts of the body may cause the fracturing of a bone, which in turn may damage nearby nerve centers or sense organs such as the eyes and ears (29).

Far more threatening to the premature infant's brain than damage due to cranial pressure are anoxia — the complete interruption of the oxygen supply to the brain and asphyxia — the disruption of the normal working of the respiratory system. Anoxia is now recognized as the more common cause of brain injury than cranial pressure. An anoxic state lasting for a few seconds (sometimes less than 18) or more can cause temporary or permanent brain damage or even death of the neonate. Premature infants are especially susceptible to brain damage because they often have serious problems in establishing proper respiration thereby depriving their brains of needed oxygen. Due to the fact that premature births often are complicated and last longer than normal, they face increased chances of suffering brain damage due to oxygen deprivation.

The combination of low birth weight and short gestation period generally point to serious postnatal adjustment and survival, especially immediately after birth. This usually means that the premature newborn must stay longer in the hospital and incubator, requiring intensive medical attention.

Prematures who have relatively longer gestational period but significantly lower birth weight than prematures of a higher birth weight and shorter gestational period are five times more likely to have serious congenital abnormalities (46).

When birth weight is 2 pounds, 3 ounces or less, neonatal survival is relatively rare. Above this weight there is a direct relation between survival chances and birth weight. The 3 pound, 5 ounce infant has four times the survival chances than does the infant of 2 pounds, 3 ounces or less (12). Overall, newborns of birth weights less than 3 pounds, 5 ounces, have a mortality rate as high as 45% or higher. The mortality rate is generally rather high for all infants 6 pounds and under.

Among those low birth weight infants who do survive, about half will suffer from neurological damage ranging from mild to severe mental deficiency. One third of prematures suffer from cerebral palsy. Generally prematures suffer more severe handicaps, physical illnesses during early childhood, score lower on developmental scales in infancy and on intelligence scales in childhood than normals. The low birth weight child is more likely to show impaired reading and academic achievement relative to grade level than normals (50). Prematures besides having a greater tendency to be mentally retarded and handicapped physically also are more prone to have behavior disorders and social and emotional problems. Paradoxically, prematures may seem better adjusted socially in early infancy and childhood than later. Their tendency to be more shy, more closely attached to their mothers, and more dependent than their full-term counterparts may tend to make them seem more endearing and socially adjusted in their early years. However, during the preschool years their behavior is more likely to become problematic. This trend is continued into the early elementary school years, but on the whole, in adolescence, prematurely born children show poorer social adjustment. They are generally either overly or inappropriately submissive, passive or overly aggressive.

Race and Prematurity. Prior to this point we have spoken of the problems of prematurity in general terms. However, a more detailed picture requires that a separate set of norms be studied in terms of sex and race. The infant mortality rate for male prematures is twice that for female prematures. Prematurity is also more likely to occur in multiple birth cases than is the case among singletons.

The infant mortality rate for blacks is almost twice that of whites and this is largely due to the deaths of premature infants. It is well established that poverty and its attendant problems such as malnutrition, correlate positively with prematurity and its attendant problems such as infant mortality, reduced intelligence, social and behavioral problems, etc. The lower the mother's socioeconomic status the greater her chances of having a premature infant.

Malformations which are the result of brain damage are more common among blacks than among whites (29). This is mainly due to the fact that black mothers receive less medical attention during pregnancy than do white mothers. According to statistics contained in the report, "Health United States 1975", only 52% of black mothers received medical attention during their first three months of pregnancy while 75% of their white counterparts received such attention. This lack of medical attention is one of the major reasons that birth complications with their attendant injuries to the infant, are more prevalent among blacks than whites.

Table 4. Infant mortality Rates by Birth Weight and Color in the United States of America

Birth Weight	Total	White	Non-White
1000 grams or less	919.3	929.3	893.6
1001 - 1500	548.5	575.6	478.1
1501 - 2000	206.6	219.9	171.8
2001 - 2500	58.4	58.2	59.4
2501 - 3000	19.0	17.3	25.3
3001 - 3500	10.1	8.9	17.4
3501 - 4000	8.0	8.9	17.0
4001 - 4500	8.3	7.0	21.0
4501 - or more	13.3	11.2	28.0
Average	25.1	22.2	41.4

Table 4 indicates that though black mothers produce more low birth weight babies than do white mothers, up to 4 pounds, 6 ounces, black infants have a higher survival rate. McKinney (a personal communication) uses this data to propose that "Although there is not sufficient evidence to support such a thesis, one possible explanation for this is that medical factors may be a primary cause of low birth weight among white mothers, whereas social factors, e.g., poor nutrition, lack of adequate medical care, which do not have the lethal effect as early as the medical factors, may be more important causes among non-white mothers."

The paucity of prenatal medical care among black mothers also directly increases the number of cases of prematurity. In the District of Columbia, in the early sixties, among women who had at least some prenatal care, the prematurity rate was 10.4 percent. However, among women who had no prenatal care the prematurity rate was 22.7 percent (26). The problems of maternal malnutrition, infant malnutrition and other health problems are all directly or indirectly related to the quality of health care received. It is well known that the quality of health care received by blacks is substantially substandard and is thereby a major contributor to black health problems. No matter how one looks at it the overall health condition of blacks in America is decidedly inferior to that of whites. While 83.7 out of 100,000 black and non-white mothers die giving birth only 21.0 white mothers die under similar circumstances. In 1960 the predominantly black community of Watts, which comprised 17% of the Los Angeles population, produced 100% of the cases of polio and diptheria. Highest percentages of other diseases were also produced by this community. In 1965 the life expectancy of white males at birth was 6.5 years longer than black males (67.7. vs 61.1). This difference in life expectancy is essentially the same today. The average white female can expect to live 7.3 years longer than her black counterpart. While medical science and medical care has made tremendous progress against disease this progress has not been exceptionally beneficial to blacks in general. For instance, the differences between the maternal and infant mortality rates of blacks and whites have widened during the past twenty years. Differences in other health areas have either widened or remained the same over the past years.

Hereditary Birth Defects and The Black Child. The incidence of birth defects, including those caused by genetic abnormalities, occurs in approximately 7 to 14 babies out of every hundred (1).It has been estimated that every year 1,400,000 children are born with one or more significant birth defects throughout the world, some 250,000 or more of these in the United States (1).

Many hundreds of thousands of eleborate and complicated genetic interactions must take place according to a very precise timetable and blueprint in order that a normal human being be born and develop as he should.

Any errors, whether small or large, made in meeting the requirements of the genetic timetable and blueprint can result in any sumber and kind of birth defects. By the end of the first three months of prenatal life most birth defects have already been irreversibly established in the unborn infant. This does not mean however, that all significant birth defects are diagnosed or detected at or just after birth. This is true for only 50% of birth defects. Only by the end of the first year of life are nearly all birth defects uncovered. But a significantly small percentage of birth defects do not become apparent until later in the individual' life. For example, hereditary diabetes may not be detected until age 10 or 30 years. Huntington's Chorea, another hereditary disease which severely affects the muscles as well as the minds of its victims, may not actively produce symptoms until between the ages of 30 to 50 years. It may not be until the child is well into the first two years of school that learning difficulties which are the result of genetically caused brain dysfunction becomes apparent. There is growing evidence that certain personality traits such as temperament, level of activation and emotional disposition may be significantly influenced by hereditary components.

Birth defects are known to occur at all social, economic, educational levels, in all countries and among all races and ethnic groups. However, certain groups of people are more susceptible to particular kinds of birth defects than other groups. For instance, Cystic Fibrosis which affects twice as many whites as blacks is almost non-existent among Orientals. Muscular Dystrophy occurs with a much higher frequency among boys than girls. Tay-Sachs disease, which progressively destroys the brain of its victims and ultimately sends them to an early grave, affects primarily infants of Jewish parents of eastern European descent (1).

Sickle Cell Anemia. The birth defect which is limited almost exclusively to blacks is referred to as sickle cell anemia and sickle cell trait. This is a painful disorder which starting before age two or at any age may be the cause of many problems such as swelling of the fingers and toes, thickening of the bones of the hand and feet, pneumonia and respiratory infections of all kinds, headache, lethargy, convulsions, paralysis and coma, jaundice, gallstones, miscarriages in the expectant mother as well as possibly her death, the birth of premature or stillborn infants, and severe abdominal pains similar in some cases to those of appendicitis. Half of the victims of sickle cell anemia die by age 20 and few live beyond age 40 (1).

Some 8 to 10% of black Americans carry the sickle cell trait, i.e., they are carriers of the disease but are rarely victimized by its symptoms. Some 50,000 black Americans suffer from sickle cell anemia and 3 out of every 1,000 black American babies are born with the disease. What is the origin of this malady and why does it affect blacks almost exclusively? The generally accepted answer to these questions was described by Apgar (1) in the following way:

31

The single abnormal gene (which is the basic cause of the disease) is common among those of African ancestry because, in Africa, it offered an evolutionary advantage—protection against malaria. In that region, individuals who inherited two abnormal genes from sickle cell anemia usually died of that disorder. Those who had two normal genes often succumbed to malaria. But those who had one abnormal gene and one normal gene had a slight difference in their blood which prevented malaria parasites from multiplying. These individuals survived, produced offspring and passed along the genetic abnormality to their descendants. Scientists have discovered that the prevalence of sickle cell trait in areas of Africa parallels that of malaria.

It has been estimated that some 40% of the population in the malarial regions of central Africa carry the sickle cell trait. In the United States if two individuals who are carriers of the sickle cell trait marry and produce children chances are one in four that each of their children will inherit sickle cell anemia.

Fortunately, in 1971, researchers at New York's Rockefeller University began developing a hopeful new chemotherapeutic approach effective against the effects of sickle cell anemia. This approach makes use of a drug termed sodium cyanate which seems to modify the abnormal sickle cells and make them function more normally. The approach is currently undergoing clinical evaluation.

An intriguing report concerning the prevalence of sickle cell anemia in Africa was presented by Gonzalez (2) which in part stated that:
. . .Blacks in Africa, our true cousins with the same blood we have, simply do not suffer from sickle cell anemia.
As long ago as 1950, a prominent epidemeologist by the name of Dr. A.B. Raper noted that only 100 cases of sickle anemia had been reported in all of Africa between 1925 and 1950 . . . doctors recently working in Africa have recently demonstrated that our African cousins are indeed immune to deadly anemia which claims the lives of so many American blacks.

Gonzalez went on to report that the factor which seems responsible for protecting the Africans against the lethal effects of sickle cell anemia is diet. It appears according to research in this area that yams and cassava which make up a large part of the African diet are the richest sources of thiocyanate. This substance seems to be the effective ingredient in the African diet which neutralizes the effects of sickle cell anemia. It was reported that there is evidence that the amount of cyanate consumed by Africans in their daily diets approximates that used by the Rockefeller researchers in their therapeutic treatment of sickle cell anemia. Africans consume 40 times the amount of thiocyanate found in the typical American diet (2). It seems then, that the absence or low level of the chemical in the American diet consumed by blacks may possibly leave susceptible individuals unprotected against the effects of sickle cell anemia.

Lactose Intolerance. Milk is central to the American diet. It has been dubbed as "nature's most perfect food" due to its vitamin, mineral and protein content. It is generally recommended that children drink plenty of milk daily and regularly drunk for health and pleasure by American children and adults alike. However, it has been known that certain individuals have trouble digesting milk and may become ill as a result of its ingestion. Only relatively recently has evidence been presented which seems to indicate that a large percentage of blacks—some seven out of ten—may not have the ability to properly digest milk (3). This inability may cause various reactions when milk is consumed by vulnerable individuals such as chronic indigestion and other digestive problems which may be misdiagnosed as colitis or other medical problems, diarrhea, gas, abdominal pains and other physical ailments. What is also very interesting is that psychological effects as the result of the ingestion of milk have been reported. Ingestion of milk by lactose intolerant children may cause irritability and confusion. A study done by the Johns Hopkins medical school in 1971 indicated that 58% of the black children tested were unable to digest milk properly. Only 16% of the white children tested showed a similar inability to digest milk (3). Gonzalez (3) pointed to the source of the problem when he stated:

The source of the trouble is a complex sugar found in milk, called lactose. In order to break this sugar down in the digestive tract, the body must produce an enzyme, lactase. While all babies, regardless of race, do make lactose, most Blacks will stop lactase production at about age two.

Without lactase, this sugar simply passes down the intestine without being absorbed, and actually ferments right in the body, producing noxious chemicals . . . The problem of lactose intolerance has grave implications world wide, as well as in our own community . . . Of course, for many of us milk has been a source of several important nutrients, including calcium. A daily intake of about one gram of calcium is necessary to guarantee strong bones and teeth, and much of that calcium in the American diet comes from milk . . .

An adequate amount also guards against overanxiousness and insomnia.

The information presented above though somewhat tentative in nature nevertheless is substantial enough to prompt us to question the common assumption by many that except for skin color the black child is the same as the white child. It has been glibly assumed that what has been shown to be nutritionally good for the white child is equally as good for the black child. This assumption completely ignores the fact that the evolutionary impact of the African environment on native Africans and their American descendants may have been such the dietary needs of descendants of white Europeans cannot serve as a model of what is nutritionally sufficient for non-European descendants - including black Americans. We have seen in the two instances discussed above that the standard American diet may be the cause of physical and psychological problems in black Americans. In the next chapter we will show that the psychomotor development of the black child is such that different nutritional standards than those developed for the white child are recommended by the American Academy of Pediatrics. The developmental characteristics of black children have been shown to be genetic in nature and therefore the result of their evolutionary African past.

In light of the fact that evidence has been gathered which shows that hyperactivity in some children may be caused by diet it may be quite pertinent to ask if elements in the standard American diet may not be the cause of psychological problems in black American children. Hyperactivity or hyperkinesis or minimal brain dysfunction is a group of symptoms that can have a number of causes - diet being possibly only one of them. The hyperactive child may exhibit behavior that is driven, uncontrolled, and that is unresponsive to discipline. He may also show sleeping difficulties, learning problems, a short attention span and throw temper tantrums. Some of these reactions may be present throughout the child's day, at certain times of day or night, or after meals (3). An inability of the body to tolerate and assimilate glucose (sugar), a prediabetic condition which may be aggravated by a high carbohydrate intake, and a deficiency of calcium in the body are some of the things which cause hyperactivity (4).

It has been demonstrated that mental problems as well as physical problems may be caused by diet and the intake of substances such as food additives. It is incumbent on every person who is truly concerned with the health and wellbeing of black children ask himself the question could it be possible that some significant percentage of black children could be the mental and behavioral victims of food additives in the American diet to which they may be allergic as a consequence of their African heritage. We fully agree with Gonzalez (2) when he states:

Unfortunately, little research is being done in America to study the particular dietary needs of Blacks, even though so much past work indicates we do have unique biochemical needs. Needs which arose from living for so many generations on that "dark continent."

Implications and Recommendations. The survey of evidence we have presented has clearly demonstrated that the black child does not escape the reach of racism even while snugly enclosed in its mother's womb. The evils of American racist, economic, social and psychological practices against its black citizens begin to eat away the hereditary potential of black people before they are conscious of their very existence or are in a position to defend themselves against such practices. Silently, as a thief in the night, American racism steals precious mental and physical treasures away from the child while it sleeps unknowingly in its mother's body. By means of poverty, lack of brotherly concern and their evil consorts such as malnutrittion, drug abuse, infectious diseases, inadequate medical care, the absences of family planning, emotional stress, etc, the yet-to-be-born black child's normality, health, intelligence, or worse still, its very life may be irreparably damaged or totally destroyed. The prenatal period is the very foundation of further physical and mental development. It goes without saying that if the foundation is not securely anchored then the superstructure which is built upon it will be weak, unstable and unable to fulfill the function for which it was designed. In our efforts to achieve the maximum self-actualization of black people we must not forget that the establishment of a healthy prenatal environment is the first and most important step to be taken in that direction. Our destination is the full realization of the black potential. However, starting out on the wrong foot, i.e., an unhealthy prenatal period, would be like a man beginning a 1000 mile journey on a lame horse without hope of exchanging it for another. It would be well nigh impossible for him to ever reach his goal. What is to be done? Well, some things have been done such as the distribution of food stamps and the passage of bills in Congress allowing for the supplementation of the diets of poor pregnant mothers. Yet cut-backs in the former program and the poor administration of the latter program leave much to be desired. Unsympathetic bureaucrats and civil servants, the racist attitudes of the majority of white Americans do much to sap the strength of such governmental programs. Consequently, it is incumbent on black will and leadership to see to it that the governmental programs are carried out as intended. No less an effort than that required to integrate lunch counters in the '60's is required here and the object is by far more important. We therefore recommend the following:

1. Increased pressure on the government and governmental agencies to carry out the intent of programs already established to nutritionally and medically aid pregnant black mothers, shoud be mounted.
2. New legislation should be introduced and passed to further improve the prenatal health of our children.
3. We must resist more vigorously efforts to cut-back on vital services to our communities which adversely affect the health and wellbeing of our mothers and children and the black community in general.
4. We must educate our mothers about the tremendous importance of the prenatal period. A thorough knowledge of what occurs during this period must be made available to our mother: potential and actual. This can be done by various means such as the introduction of developmental courses in the grade and high schools and adult education classes.
5. Our would-be mothers should be educated in the matters of nutrition, drugs, emotional stress, infectious diseases, etc. and their effects on the fetus.
6. The deleterious effects of drugs in the streets, poverty, crime, unstable family structures, teenage pregnancy, out-of-wedlock births, must become the focus of sustained black civil action.

7. The black church which has played a vital role in black civil rights progress can play a vital role in this area also. Perhaps a church or an organization of churches could provide free prenatal medical care for their members or their community. Many need only to persuade expectant mothers who may or may not be members of their congregations to attend health stations already established by their governmental agencies. Perhaps courses which provide nutritional education can be offered in addition to those which provide religious guidance.

8. Courses, seminars, etc, specifically designed to deal with the mental health of black men and women should be offered by various institutions and organizations so that a healthy love of self, knowledge of self, a confidence in self, can be fully developed.

9. Yearly check-ups for malnutrition among black girls should be made during the late grammar and high school years.

REFERENCES
FOR
Heredity Birth Defects and The Black Child

1. Apgar, V. and Beck, J., *Is My Baby All Right?* New York: Pocket book, 1974.
2. Gonzalez, N., Sickle Cell Anemia — Scientists Say: What We Eat Could Curb Disease: In the New York Amsterdam News, January, 1976.
3. Gonzalez, N., Milk: White Poison For Young Black: In the New York Amsterdam News, February 5, 1977.
4. Walker III, S., Drugging The American Child —We're Too Cavalier About Hyperactivity. Psychology Today, December, 1974.

REFERENCES

1. Braid, D. in Smart, M., & Smart, R., **Children: Development and relationships.** New York: Macmillan, 1972.

2. Brazelton, T.B. Effects of prenatal drugs on the behavior of the neonate. **American Journal of Psychiatry, 126,** 1970.

3. Caldwell, D., & Churchill, J. Learning ability in the progeny of rats administered a protein-deficient diet during the second half of gestation. **Neurology,** 1967.

4. Chance, Paul. Race and I.Q.: A family affair? **Psychology Today,** January 1975.

5. Churchill, J.A., et al. Relationships of maternal amino acid blood level to fetal development. **Obstetrics and Gynecology, 33,** 1969.

6. Churchhill, J. In the New York Times, July 28, 1968

7. Cohrinik, P.W., et al. Effects of maternal narcotic addiction on the newborn infant. **Pediatrics, 24,** 1959.

8. Davids, A., et al. Anxiety, pregnancy, and childbirth abnormalities. **Journal of Consulting Psychiatry, 25,** 1961.

9. Dippel, A.L. The relationship of congential syphilis to abortion and miscarriage and the mechanism of intrauterine protection. **American Journal of Obstetrics and Gynecology, 47,** 1945.

10. Eastman, N.J., & Kellman, L.M. **Williams obstetrics.** (13th ed.) New York: Appleton-Century-Crofts, 1966.

11. Eichorn, D.H. Biology of gestation and infancy: Fatherland and frontier. **Merrill-Palmer Quarterly of Behavior and Development, 14,** 1968.

12. Eichelaub, J.E. The premature. **Today's Health,** December 1956.

13. Ellis, R.W.B. Assessment of prematurity by birthweight, crown-rump length, head circumference. **Archives of Diseases of Childhood, 26,** 1951.

14. Erikson, M., et al. Drugs and pregnancy. In H. Osofsky (ed.), **Clinical obstetrics and gynecology:** High risk pregnancy with emphasis upon maternal and fetal well being. Vol. 16. New York: Harper & Row, 1973.

15. Ferrira, A.J. The pregnant woman's emotional attitude and its reflection on the newborn. **American Journal of Orthopsychiatry, 30,** 1960.

16. Grossman, H., & Greenberg, N. Psychosomatic differentiation in infancy. **Psychosomatic Medicine, 23,** 1961.

17. Grimm, E.R. Psychological tension in pregnancy. **Psychosomatic Medicine, 23,** 1961.

18. Grimm, E. Psychological and social factors in pregnancy, delivery and outcome. In Richardson, S., & Guttmacher, A. (eds.), **Childbearing–Its social and psychological aspects.** Maryland: Williams & Wilkins, 1967.

19. Harrell, R.F.E., et al. **The effect of mother's diets on the intelligence of the offspring.** New York: Teacher's College, Columbia University, 1955.

20. Herber, R. Definition of mental retardation. In Rothstein, J. (ed.), **Mental retardation.** New York: Holt, Rinehart & Winston, 1963.

21. Heinstein, M.I. Expressed attitudes and feelings of pregnant women and their relations to physical complications of pregnancy. **Merrill-Palmer Quarterly of Behavior Development, 13,** 1967.

22. Henly, W.L., & Fitch, B.R. Newborn narcotic withdrawal associated with regional enterisis in pregnancy. **New York Journal of Medicine, 66,** 1966.

23. Hetherington, E., & Parke, R. **Child psychology: A contemporary viewpoint.** New York: McGraw-Hill, 1975.

24. Holley, W.L., & Churchill, J.A. Effects of rapid succession of pregnancy. In Smart, M., & Smart, R., **Children: Development and relationships.** (2nd ed.) New York: Macmillan, 1972.

25. Hooker, D. **The prenatal origin of behavior.** Kansas: University of Kansas, 1952.

26. Hunt & Huyck . . . 1965 in Knowles, L., & Prewitt, R. (eds.), **Institutional racism in America.** New Jersey: Prentice-Hall, 1969.

27. Hurley, L. The consequences of fetal impoverishment. **Nutrition Today, 3,** 1968.

28. Hurlock, E.B. **Child development.** (4th ed.) New York: McGraw-Hill, 1956.

29. Illsley, R. The sociological study of reproduction and its outcome. In S.A. Richardson & A.F. Guttmacher (eds.), **Childbearing–Its social and psychological aspects.** Baltimore: Williams & Wilkins, 1967.

30. Jones, K.L., et al. Pattern of malformation in offspring of chronic alcoholic mothers. **Lancet,** 1(7815), 1973.

31. Jost, H., & Sontag, L. The genetic factor in autonomic nervous system function. **Psychosomatic Medicine, 6,** 1944.

32. Montagu, A. **Human heredity.** New York: Harcourt, Brace & World, 1959.

33. Montagu, M.F.A. **Prenatal influence.** Springfield, Illinois: Thomas, 1962.

34. Montagu, M.F.A. **Life before birth.** New York: Signet, 1965.

35. **New York Times,** October 6, 1974.

36. Nichols, W.W., et al. Measles–associated chromosomal breakage: Preliminary communication. **Heriditas, 48,** 1962.

37. Papalia, D., & Olds, W. **A child's world infancy through adolescence.** New York: McGraw-Hill, 1975.

38. Parke, R., O'Leary, S., & West, S. Mother-father-newborn interaction: Effect of maternal medication, labor and sex of infant. **Proceedings of the American Psychological Association, 7,** 1972.

39. Richardson, S.A., & Guttmacher, A.F. (eds.) **Childbearing–Its social and psychological aspects.** Baltimore: Williams & Wilkins, 1967.

40. Pasamanick, B., & Knobloch, H. Retrospective studies on the epidemeology of reproductive causality: Old to new. **Merrill-Palmer Quarterly of Behavior and Development, 12** (1), 1966.

41. Schulman, C.A. Sleep patterns in newborn infants as a function of suspected neurological impairment of maternal heroin addiction. Society for Research in Child Development, Santa Monica, California, March 27, 1969.

42. Scrimshaw, N.S., New York Times, October 6, 1974.

43. Scrimshaw, N.S. Malnutrition, learning and behavior. American Journal of Clinical Nutrition, 20, 1967.

44. Simpson, G.G. The meaning of evolution. New Haven: Yale, 1949.

45. Smith, W. New York Times, October 6, 1974.

46. Sontag, L.W., & Wallace, R.I. The effect of cigarette smoking during pregnancy upon the fetal heart rate. American Journal of Obstetrics and Gynecology, 29, 1935.

47. U.S. Department of Health, Education, and Welfare. The health consequences of smoking. Washington, D.C., 1973.

48. Wiener, G. Scholastic achievements at age 12-13 of prematurely born infant. Journal of Special Education, 2, 1968.

49. Winick, M. New York Times, October 6, 1974.

50. Yannet, H. Classification and etiological factors in mental retardation. Journal of Pediatrics, 50:2, February 1952.

51. Zajonc, R. Dumber by the dozen. Psychology Today, 19, 1975.

THE BLACK CHILD—THE FIRST TWO YEARS

An overview. The child develops and changes rapidly during the first two years. Its first task immediately after being delivered is to learn to survive in and adjust to a new and alien environment. Assuming that it is born healthy and receives peri- and postnatal care this task should be accomplished without much difficulty. In order to successfully cope with the new environment the newborn must learn to trust it. This can be accomplished if the environment, which includes his caretakers of course, responds to its needs in a consistent, satisfying way and if that environment is safe and relatively stable. If this is the case the child learns to trust the environment and to have confidence in his ability to influence it to meet his needs. This trust lays the basis for healthy, prosocial personality development. Otherwise, mistrust of the environment leads to a lack of confidence in itself to influence that environment, which then lays the basis for unhealthy, antisocial personality development.

Trust is developed through the baby's feeding, physically comforting, aural-tactile stimulative relations with its mother or other caretakers. If these relations are consistent, responsive and satisfying to the needs of the child, then the child will begin to trust in itself and its environment. If the child is fully affirmed by having his emotional-physical needs fulfilled he begins to develop into a confident and secure being and comes fully prepared to cope with the next developmental task.

The next task, which has existed simultaneously with the first but which becomes increasingly more prominent as the child approaches his second year, involves the integration of the many individual reflexes he was born with into larger, more complexly coordinated, voluntarily controlled, movement, and behavior. The consequence of such integrative efforts on the child's part is that he becomes automotive, i.e., self motivating, instead of being carried around by his caretakers. He becomes increasingly autonomous, as in the beginning of the second year he learns to "stand on his own two feet" mentally and physically. He constantly tests his swiftly developing physical, mental and linguistic prowess on the environment. The child tests himself to limits of his capacities and also tests the limits the environment and those who are a part of it. He does this basically of his own free will. Consequently his interactions with environment may enhance or negate his autonomous or independence strivings depending on the nature of its reactions to these strivings.

The overprotective mother may often negate her child's autonomous strivings by not allowing it to safely explore and learn of its environment and to test, develop and perfect its abilities to cope with various demands made by the environment. The underprotective mother may stunt her child's independent strivings by allowing it to experience too many hazardous and unsafe consequences of its environmental probings thus creating in the child a fear of the environment and a withdrawal from its exploration and also leading to a retardation in its testing, development, and perfecting of coping abilities. The underprotected child like the overprotected child may develop an insecure personality which fears that autonomous, independent actions on its part may lead to trouble, anxiety and shame. These children do not learn the clear limitations of their environment or behavior. Clearly appropriate caretaker behavior during this period involves striking a golden mean between these two extremes—allowing the child to safely express its autonomous strivings and perhaps encouraging them but at the same time establishing clear and rational limits on these strivings especially when they may result in dangerous consequences. The mother who encourages and affirms the child's reasonable autonomous actions lays the groundwork for future motivations to achieve and make independent and original decisions.

Not all of the child's attention is focused on mobility, integration, coordination, manipulation and exploration during this period. He is also developing attentive, cognitive and, linguistic abilities and a knowledge of self. The mother's role in the development of these abilities is an important one. Her ability to supply the optimal psychological support and environmental stimulants is a very important contribution to the baby's physical and mental development. One of the most important things to take place in the life of the two-year-old is the beginning development of communicative-linguistic abilities. These are obviously some of the most important abilities. They are highly influenced by the environment, the economic, social, educational level of the family and culture as well as the emotional, intellectual quality of the home and the general mass of experience the child is exposed to. We shall enter into a detailed discussion of this highly important and controversial topic later.

Infant Malnutrition. Up to its pre-school years the child may frequently get ill, necessitating careful physical care. Respiratory infections cause the most frequent type of physical illness experienced by children in this society. Gastrointestinal upsets are also very frequent. As during the prenatal period the greatest threat to the poor black mother's child is malnutrition, especially protein malnutrition. The second phase of brain growth occurs during the first two years of child development. Consequently malnutrition during this period may cause mental retardation or in a number of ways impair mental and physical development. In underdeveloped countries protein malnutrition may lead to death. The tremendous brain development taking place during this early period is demonstrated by the fact that "The two year old needs about 70 percent more calories and three times as much protein as an adult" (19).

In its severe forms malnutrition may produce two crippling diseases, marasmus and Kwashiorkor. The wasting away of the body tissues is symptomatic of marasmus. Also symptomatic of this malady are gross underweight, muscular atrophy, wasting away of cutaneous fat. Kwashiorkor causes swelling of the face, legs and abdomen due to the retention of water in the body tissues. Also body growth is retarded and the child suffers from a general, pervasive apathy. This syndrome most frequently occurs in 1 - 4 year-olds who are protein malnourished. Both liver and brain damage may occur as a result from this cause.

All over the world, including the United States of America, poor children are suffering from insufficient protein, often along with insufficient calories. Their physical and mental growth and health are being depressed now and for the future (18).

Malnourished children are more likely to succumb to all sorts of infections and to suffer more therefrom. Infections aggravate the state of malnutrition by suppressing the appetite and making excessive demands on nitrogen and other essential nutrients (18). The malnourished child's condition is worsened by infection and the body lowers its resistance to new infections. Malnutrition reduces the body's ability to manufacture antibodies. Growth is retarded since the body's store of nutrients is insufficient.

Poor hygiene is often the result of poverty. This factor along with poor diet leads to the spread of disease.

. . . poor quality, unsanitary food introduces disease organisms causing infections, diarrhea, and parasite infestations. Widened social contact introduces viral diseases such as measles and other childhood diseases. Pneumonia is a frequent complication of measles (19).

In this country, illiteracy and ignorance of basic hygienic methods and nutrition, combined with the inadequacy of governmental food programs and medical care most often have the most important adverse influence on the baby's health and growth.

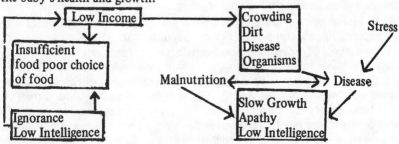

The interrelations of causes and results of malnutrition and disease (after smart).

44

Physiological Development and Race. There are a number of distinct differences in the rate and distribution of physiological development between ethnic groups particularly between blacks and whites. For instance, the time at which the teeth first erupt in infancy differ markedly between the two ethnic groups. Generally, nonwhites tend to erupt earlier than do whites (5). Some have interpreted this to mean the "the least favored groups seem to have the most advanced eruption time" (19). Thus, since blacks erupt earlier than whites the assumption is that since blacks are "least favored" then the eruption must be due to the generally low socioeconomic status of blacks and their concomitant poor diet. However, a ten-state survey conducted by the American Academy Of Pediatrics indicated that when corrected for socioeconomic status, the permanent teeth of black children are established significantly in advance of white children, reached maturity earlier, and tended to be larger. One of the general conclusions drawn by the Academy are of interest here—

"Both on an absolute basis, and when corrected for income level, black boys and girls in comparison to white and Spanish-American children, tended to have skeletal advancement (ossification), dental advancement (age at permanent teeth eruption), and earlier maturation and some tendency toward greater body size, notwithstanding lesser body fat through adolescence. Black boys and girls evidenced a greater mass, both on a group basis and on an income corrected basis. Therefore, genetic factors outweighed economic factors in explaining differences in skeletal and dental development. *These findings suggest the need for different standard for blacks and white children when assessing nutritional status during growth.*" (underlining by the author).

The genetic difference in physiological development alluded to in the above study may not be of much importance except when we consider that many black mothers use white nutritional standards, and when we recognize the psychosocial advancement of black children during early childhood and the relationship of these advanced states to learning readiness. The use of white-based nutritional standards may not actually be in the best interest of the developing black child.

Psychomotor Development and Race. An impressive number of studies of variances between black and white child psychomotor development have shown consistently that up to at least the first two years black children are significantly more advanced than are white children. Though this variance is most marked by black children's definitively established motor superioritv the base measures are *psycho*motor measurements, i.e., childhood motor behavior involving mental and intellectual components. Therefore, when we speak of motor development in this section we are in no way implying that we are speaking of "purely" motor behavior and that this behavior is without intellectual input or of no importance in intellectual growth.

It has been noted that "Whenever motor differences between white and black American infants have been noted in the research literature, the black babies have been advanced in comparison wih the whites" (19). We may note here that this is also the case with black children of other nationalities, particularly of African origin. In a comparative study of the psychomotor development of African and European children, Geber concluded that "The results of tests showed an all-round advance of development over European standards which was greater the younger the child" (6). A look at some comparisons listed by Geber in this study may give a better idea of the differences between these groups.

Comparison of African-European Psychomotor Development

1. 9 hours old, being drawn up into a sitting position, able to prevent the head from falling backwards (Euro. - 6 wks).
2. Two days old, with head held firmly, looking at face of the examiner (Euro. - 8 wks).
3. 7 weeks old, supporting herself in a sitting position and watching her reflection in the mirror (Euro. - 20 wks).
4. 5 months old. holding herself upright (Euro. - nine months). Taking the round block out of its hole in the form board (Euro. - 11 months)
5. 5 months old, standing against the mirror (Euro. - 9 months).
6. 7 months old, walking to the Gesell Box to look inside (Euro. - 15 months).
7. 11 months old, climbing the steps alone (Euro. - 15 months).

In reviewing Geber's studies Papalia and Olds (16) came to the conclusion that "The African babies actually seemed to have been born at a more advanced stage of development, since many of their activities as less than a week corresponded to those performed by European children aged four to eight weeks."

Tronick, Koslowski and Brazelton (20) compared the neonatal behavior of urban Zambian and American infants. Despite the fact that on the first day the Zambian children reacted less than the American children, within five days they had caught up and in ten days had surpassed their counterparts, becoming more attentive and responsive. Etta Walters (22) tested babies on the Gesell developmental schedules within three days of their 12-week, 24-week, and 36-week birthday. These children were divided according to black-white ethnic origins and according to low, middle and high socio-economic status. She found that the black children were motorically superior up to age 12-weeks at which point the differences were not significant except that at 36 weeks the black high socioeconomic group was superior. Finally, in an extensive study of 1409 babies between the ages of 1 month and 15 months, and located in 12 urban areas representative of various areas of the United States, Bayley (1) found "a general trend toward superiority in the Negroes." The averages of the black children were higher at every age except 15 months. Bayley's 1409 infants included 55% white, 42% black and 2.3% other. The Black infants were superior on all sixty test items of the Bayley scales.

Though cultural, prenatal-postnatal environmental factors, evolutionary and nutritional (one writer implied that a protein deficiency may be responsible for the black advancement in motor development) explanations have been invoked to explain the differences found by the above mentioned studies, most of the writers on this matter incline toward a genetic explanation. Thus it would appear that the psychomotor precocity of black children is genetically determined. It is indeed very interesting that despite the many prenatal insults that the black child has to suffer, as noted in the first chapter, he still is psychomotorically more advanced than his more prenatally fortunate white counterpart. We shall see that the psychomotor advancement of the black child is paralleled by   similar advancement in I.Q. or more accurately, D.Q. (Developmental Quotient).

Intelligence and Race. Many of the studies mentioned above also tested the mental capacities of black and white children. The vast majority of them used one of the two most popular infant developmental scales—Bayley's Scales of Infant Development or the Gesell Developmental Test. The Bayley scales consist of two major components, a mental and motor scale. The scales together yield an I.Q. score. These scales were factor analyzed in one study to test the functions of eye-hand manipulation, object-relation, imitation-comprehension, vocalization-social contact, and active vocabulary (11). Thus the Bayley scales were definitely designed to measure more than motor development. These scales measure development from birth to fifteen months. The Gesell schedules are principally standardized observations used to measure four major areas of development covering the ages of 4 weeks to 6 years. The four areas covered by this test include motor behavior, adaptive behavior, language behavior and personal- social behavior. The schedules yield a D. Q., which is obtained by dividing the child's overall score, termed a mental age, by the child's chronological age and multiplying by 100. A final figure of 100 indicates that the child has scored equal to his or her age level. Above 100 indicates that the child has scored better on some items than 50% of children of the same age level. Below 100 indicates the obverse.

Utilizing the Gesell scales Etta Walters in the study mentioned above concluded that ". . . The only statistically significant differences between the two groups was in favor of the Negro infant in motor development at 12 weeks . . . However, the mean scores for the Negro group were higher than the white mean scores for the Negro group were higher than the white mean scores for all test areas of development at 12 weeks; after that, the means were comparable. " Geber, in her 1958 study quoted above also used the

Gesell scales and concluded—". . . precocity was not only in motor development: it was found in intellectual development also. It is not always realized that intellectual development is displayed very clearly in the use of the Gesell material. To take an elementary example, the child who merely looks at the cubes and then picks them up is demonstrating a series of intellectual processes and for the building of a tower with the cubes, more complex processes are needed, in addition to the greater manual dexterity. . . . Although most of the African children had never seen anything resembling the test material, they used it in the same way as European children and succeeded in the tests earlier than those children. Their interest was lively, and their personal-social relations excellent. They made very good contact with the tester, turning and "talking" . . ., smiling . . ., and trying in every way to communicate . . . ." A study by Knoblock and Pasamanick (10), also using the Gesell scales, it was found that the black American infants had "superior motor scores and similar adaptive, language and personal-social scores, as compared with white through age 2 years." Bayley's previously quoted study indicated that ". . . it is clear that there are no differences in the mean scores of these three samples of babies (black, white, Puerto Rican) at any period of development in the first 15 months. . . . It is clear that for the kinds of developmental behavior we are able to designate as mental during the first 15 months, there are no differences between the Negroes, the Whites and the small subsample of Puerto Ricans we have tested." Bayley goes on to conclude that "It would appear that the behaviors which are developing during the first 15 months of life, whether they are motor skills or the early perceptual and adaptive forms of mental abilities, are for the most part unrelated to sex, race, birth order, geographical location, or parental ability. The one possible difference is in motor development in which the Negro babies tend to be more advanced than the whites during the first 12 months . . . a genetic factor may be operating. . . ."

Before we deal with the implications of these studies a quotation from Jensen (9) is of interest—"It has also been noted that brain wave patterns in African newborn infants show greater maturity than is usually found in the European newborn child . . .This finding especially merits further study, since there is evidence that brain waves have some relationship to IQ . . ., and since at least one aspect of brain waves—the visually evoked potential— has a very significant genetic component, showing a heritability of about .80 (uncorrected for attentuation) . . . ."

Let us summarize our data thus far mentioned—
1. All the studies showed the black child to be significantly advanced over the white child in motor development up to at least 2 years when the trends tend to disappear. The consensus of the researchers in this area is that these differences are genetic.
2. The scales established that the black child was intellectually above or equal

to, but not less than, his white counterpart. Strangely enough, a genetic explanation for this advancement or equality was not invoked by the researchers.

3. Generally, it would appear that the differences between black and white infants disappear between the ages of 1½ to 2 years and the equality of their mental and motor functioning begins to reverse in favor of the white child at around age 3. We think that it is no coincidence that black intellectual functioning as compared to that of whites, as measured by standard IQ tests, begins to fall during the period beginning with the acquisition of language (starting somewhere around 12 to 18 months) and the formation of a stabilized personality structure (from 3 to 5 years).

4. For the first 2 to 3 years at least, it appears that the black child approaches the Greek ideal of a sound mind in a sound body. However, the ravages of racial prejudice and poverty destroys and distorts much of this wonderful potential.

Reliability of Infant Intelligence Tests. Due to the extremely low predictive correlation between the intelligence scores of early infancy and later childhood and adulthood some psychologists tend to regard the infant intelligence tests as unreliable or to assume that they are not measuring intelligence. We think it would be expecting too much for tests which essentially measure preverbal subjects, relatively unacculturated subjects, subjects whose personality and cognitive styles are still relatively unformed, to correlate well with tests given as close as a few months later, let alone years later when culture, environment and traumas have added or subtracted so much to or from the whole.

Interpreting data collected by Bayley (2), Ginsburg (7) stated that "Infant test scores during the first year of life are nearly useless for predicting scores at later ages. . . . Infant scores during the second year of life (months 13, 14, and 15) are moderately correlated with scores during the third year of life (months 27, 30, and 36), but are poorly correlated with scores after that point. Scores during the period from about the third year of life to 5, 6, and 7 are fairly stable, showing a correlation of .70. After the age of about 5, the scores are highly stable. For example, the correlation between the average scores at age 5, 6, and 7 and the corresponding score at years 17 and 18 is .86." It is important to note that the correlation between IQ scores and later ones begin to become increasingly reliable from the period of rapid language acquisition, when the basic foundations of personality are being laid, when a child's culture is beginning to have a most marked influence on his mental functioning and when the child is becoming consciously aware of his ethnic category. In light of this, it may be that infant intelligence scales which are relatively unaffected by sex, birth order, parental educational level and geographical residence, may be more reliable than the more culturally biased IQ tests of late childhood and adulthood. What-

49

ever the case, whatever the infant scales are measuring, the black child is on or above par with his white counterpart. Even in their unreliability for predicting later IQ scores, the infant scales reliably show black children to be of at least equal potential as white children. In terms of the influence of parental educational level, geographical residence, cultural background, etc, a statement by Papalia and Olds is relevant here (16).

Although socioeconomic status does not appear to be related to infant mental or motor development, it is a good predictor of the direction of DQ change from infancy to preschool age. The test scores of children in middle-class and superior working-class homes increases after infancy; children from culturally deprived working-class homes increases after infancy; children from culturally deprived working-class homes show a decline...As the child grows, then, the home environment assumes more and more importance...This can be seen in the rising level of racial differences in DQs as children grow older...Even when there are considerable disparities in the amount of education of the children's mothers, the children's DQs do not reflect this. By three years of age, though, the picture is very different. White children score better, even when the mothers of both white and black babies have similar amounts of education.

In racist American society the black middle and upper classes are also deprived. Racism with its tendency to breed chronic anxiety, lack of self-confidence, self-knowledge, and self-love, its tendency to restrict black children of all economic levels from optimally potentiating environments and with its tendency to produce neurotic-schizoid adaptive mechanisms in blacks takes a measurable toll from black personal-social-cognitive functioning. In a society where a "smart nigger" is seen as a threat and an athletically adept one is seen as an asset, cognitive brilliance among blacks is seen as threatening and may even be punished in various ways and athletic brilliance is highly rewarded, it is no accident that black intellectual functioning tends to decline with age and black physical functioning does not tend in the same direction or may actually become more advanced.

There is evidence that it may not be physical home-institutional deprivations that are so damaging to cognitive and other emerging skills as psychological cognitive-motivational functional deprivations. It is well established that motivation and intellectual functioning are inextricably bound together. Motivational systems such as the one alluded to in the previous paragraph are without a doubt dysfunctional for black cognitive development in the full sense of the word (24).

In spite of the quite extensive number of prenatal dangers the black child must face as compared with the white child, he generally begins life a step ahead of, or at least on equal footing with his white counterpart in all of his physical and mental congenital possibilities. We have seen that the black child is in no way born inferior to the white child.   Apparently the "cognitive-cultural lag" which the black child begins to manifest in his second and third years are the result of psychosocial factors, the cognitive-motivational-functional deprivations that he is subject to by belonging to the out-group in a racist society. Granted that poor pre-, peri- and postnatal environments take their negative toll of the black potential, it is the prevailing poor psychosocial conditions under which the black child is reared that are pre-eminently responsible for whatever cognitive-behavioral problems he may display. Though the dominant white society with its racist policies and beliefs laid the basis for such poor psychosocial conditions it is black parents who are ultimately responsible for not training their child to successfully cope with such circumstances. During the first 2–3 years it is black parents who represent the negative psychosocial world to their children and consciously or unconsciously socialize their children in terms of that world. We are all aware of the nature of the white created negative psychosocial world which engulfs black people. What we wish to know is what is it in the nature of the psychosocial world of black parents which causes them to socialize such a large number of their children to become dysfunctional in both black and white society? In an effort to answer part of this broad question we will briefly discuss what we think are the three major variables which, operating through black parents, adversely influence the development of the black child during his early years − (1) the schizoid nature of black existence, (2) the chronically frustrated nature of black life, and (3) the restricted nature of the black world.

The Schizoid Nature of Black Existence. Black people in America do not belong to any one functional, coherent, cohesive culture. They belong to neither the white culture nor to one they can call their own. Culturally speaking, blacks exist between "the devil" of the dominant white world to which he is not premitted to fully belong, and " the deep blue sea" of the currently dysfunctional black world to which he also is not permitted to belong. He is victimized by both worlds and has thus far found no positive way out of this crushing dilemma. The black man of today is only part black. The other part of him is white. These two parts which more often than not pull against each other, which contradict each other and which are "out of synch"with each other, make up virtually the whole of the black body and mind. Thus, the black man is a "split personality," a schizoid personality which tries to operate with two sets of mutually incompatible needs, drives, impulses, values, cultural traditions, ways of thinking, etc, simultaneously. W.E.B. DuBois (3) poignantly describes this "black condition" when he states that—

... the Negro is a sort of seventh born with a veil, and gifted with second sight in this American world — a world which yields him no true self-consciousness, but only lets him see himself through the eyes of others, of measuring one's soul by the tape of a world that looks on in amused contempt and pity. One ever feels his two-ness — an American, a Negro; two souls, two thoughts, two unreconciled strivings; two warring ideals in one black body, whose dogged strength alone keeps it from being torn asunder.

The history of the American Negro is the history of this strife-this longing to attain self-conscious manhood, to merge his double self into a better and truer self. In this merging he wishes neither of the older selves to be lost. He would not Africanize America, for America has too much to teach the world and Africa. He would not bleach his Negro soul in a flood of white Americanism, for he knows that Negro blood has a message for the world. He simply wishes to make it possible for a man to be both a Negro and an American, without being cursed and spit upon by his fellows, without having the door of opportunity closed roughly in his face.

Regardless of income, social or educational status, every black individual, group or family is haunted by this "double-consciousness" to which Dubois refers. It is an existential fact of black existence and its influence for better or worse, is pervasive in all areas of black behavior. Though effectively present at all class levels of the black community, as we have just implied, "double-consciousness" and its effects are not experienced psychologically with the same intensity or reacted to with the same defense mechanistic priorities by the various class levels. Generally, because of its similar values, educational background, income, occupational status and its desire to be fully accepted by the white middle class which it emulates and by which it evaluates itself, the black middle class experiences "double-consciousness" the most acutely when compared to the black working and lower classses. The black middle class is therefore the most schizoid of the classes. (Please note that the the term "schizoid" is used here in the social-psychological sense, not the psychopathological sense even though it can and does have psychopathological consequences). That segment of the black middle class which fits what Frazier (4) calls the "black bourgeoisie" is the most schizoid of all.

The hallmark of schizoid living is ambivalence, an ambivalence which enters into virtually every activity of the schizoid's life. His relation to himself and to others is marked by this same ambivalence.Thus, the schizoid black chronically maintains a fluctuating love-hate relation to himself, his people, other peoples (particularly whites). His life is characterized by a constant vacillation between two conflicting worlds of differing ethnic histories, lifestyles, values, etc. He has no fixed reference point which he can use with confidence to orient his life, values, goals, attitudes and behavior, and to stabilize his relations to himself as well as others. Consequently, his relations with himself and others are confused, labile, and ambivalent even though these may be smoothed over by a superficial order and harmony. The middle class, black or white, is particularly adept at maintaining "appearances."

From the above description one could logically conclude that the schizoid black parent's relationship to his or her child would be one marked essentially by ambivalence. This means that the child will be loved on one level and hated on another. The child may be loved because it was desired for personal and social fulfillment, because it represents the hopes of its parents. and hated at the same time because it bears the mark of oppression — its blackness (since blackness is hated by whites and is the source of black self-hatred. If one hates oneself because one is black then one hates others who bear the same hated color as the self — other blacks including one's black children). The schizoid black parent's relationship may be also marked by feelings of guilt stemming from the parent's awareness of the degradation his child will suffer as a member of the black race in racist American society and his or her having been responsible for bringing the child into such a society and exposing him to such degradation. Thus the schizoid black parent loves and rejects and fears for his or her black child at one and the same time. The feeling of guilt in the schizoid black parent will at times generate compensatory over-protectiveness, overindulgence, permissiveness toward the child and at the same or other times, along with the feeling of rejection referred to above, generate negative over-reactions, negligence, indifference, over-strickness toward the child. Because of their schizoid nature the parents can offer little or no consistent discipline, direction, unneurotic love, etc, to the child. They cannot establish consistent limits which the child can readily and easily comprehend and by which he can guide his current future behavior. Thus the child, in an effort to adapt to the behavior of his schizoid parents begins to develop a confused, powerless, contradictory, emotionally crippled, incompetent, ambivalent, and schizoid personality like that of his parents. In addition, he will begin to develop a poor self-image, a lack of self-confidence, self-love and self-knowledge. These personality factors early reveal themselves by their negative influences in the major areas of cognitive, personal and social functioning.

A study by Langner, et al, (12), can serve as a possible example of how pervasive the negative effects of "double-consciousness " which as we previously said affects all blacks, are. This study determined the prevalence of emotionally disturbed children in high and low income spanish, black and white families in the midtown area of Manhattan, New York City. One of the surprising findings of the study was that in terms of psychological impairment, there were no substantial differences between black low income children and black high income children. This goes against the general trend in these types of studies where the low income group usually has the significantly higher rate of psychological impairment. Langner, et al, interpreted this finding to imply that:

> . . . as Negroes attain higher incomes, various environmental forces such as prejudice and job discrimination, which in turn may have effects on family organization and relationships, prevent their children from obtaining a commensurate reduction in impairment.

Langner and his co-workers also imply that due to the fact that a very high percentage (81 –49%) of the high income black families' incomes were generated by both husband and wife working, maternal care have deteriorated, causing emotional impairment in their children, income notwithstanding. We believe that the schizoid nature of black existence in America as we described it above, which we also indicated is felt more acutely by the higher income blacks, was a major factor responsible for Langner's finding. Besides a number of other negative effects listed as resulting from the schizoid nature of black existence, one of the major effects of this kind of existence was the inability of black parents to offer non-contradictory consistent discipline, guidance, etc, to their children. We believe this additional interpretive factor is to a large degree validated by Langner's further finding that in the area of disciplining their children, high income black parents showed five times more disagreement over rearing practices than did low income black parents. In this regard Langner found that:

> There were equal proportions of fathers and mothers acting as "boss" among Negro families, while twice as many fathers were the boss among low whites, four times as many among high whites, and seven to eight times as many among the Spanish.

This "equality of authority" between black parents who are experiencing the negative effects of black schizoid existence, one of those effects being a lack of fixed values which are agreed upon by both parents and supported by the black community at large, is deleterious for their children. In such a family situation areas of authority are confused and the demands made on the children are contradictory and conflicting. Such a situation is a well established condition for the development of psychopathological behavior in the children.

It was also found by Langner that high income black parents are more apt to get their children to do things by threatening than low income black parents, that a higher proportion of high income mothers and, black mothers in general, "were about five times more likely to punish by depriving the children of things or privileges than white or Spanish mothers," and that generally, fewer high and low income black parents were likely to use hugs or kisses when their children were unhappy. He also found that a higher proportion of high income black children lacked pride in their fathers and mothers than did low income black children, that of three ethnic groups studied, the largest percentage of children expressing hostility for their mothers was among the high income black children. In terms of the mother's character structure, Langner combined several questions centering around the mother's "handling of the child or her own psychophysiological complaints." While problems in handling their children and their own problems, took the expected direction among high and low income white mothers, i.e., the low income mothers having the greater proportion of problems in both categories, ". . . the Negro ranks were reversed, so that high income Negro mothers had more problems on the average . . . than low-income Negro mothers." Langner goes on to conclude that:

. . . This finding alone makes us feel that a real elevation in impairment exists in high-income children, and that it may be partially accounted for by the emotional impairment and coping difficulties of their mothers. Body complaints, lack of understanding of the child, changeableness, dissatisfaction in general and lack of enjoyment of her child, and a poor self-image all contribute to a picture of poor mothering in this high-income Negro group. Behind this, we hypothesize, is the second-class citizenship, the ghetto, and its more devastating effects on the people who try to rise above it. Perhaps we are seeing in some small measure the price paid for upward mobility across what has been called caste, rather than class, lines.

In summary, there can be no doubt that our preliminary data show that low socio-economic status and minority ethnic background are associated with greater impairment in urban children. The information also suggests that an increase in family income at the expense of having both parents work full time, without improvement of parental education, or without social acceptance of the family in the wider community, is not enough to diminish the rate of impairment among Negro and possibly Puerto Rican children.

Langner's study being rather limited in geographical scope and possibly subject to a number of differing interpretations and criticisms, makes one hesitate to generalize its implications. However, its disturbing preliminary findings without a doubt point to a crucial need for more and broader studies of this type.

As was indicated by Frazier (4), the black middle class, which now includes almost half of the black families in America, is caught on the horns of a serious dilemma. In its effort to succeed according to white standards it has become increasingly alienated from its black roots and yet its rejection and non-acceptance by the white middle class whose acceptance it perceives as the necessary factor needed for authenticating its own existence, leaves it in a state of psychological limbo (this perception is also shared by the rest of the black classes even though generally experienced less acutely and striven against less consciously than is the case of the black middle class.

Therefore, the rest of the blacks classes still suffer the consequences of this perception accordingly). In this limbo the alienated black suffers from a double ambivalence—a love-hate relationship with members of his own race, including his own children, and the members of the white rejecting race. Because of this limbo the black family is disorganized and becomes a "tangle of pathology (15a)." The eminent student of the American family, psychologist, Urie Bronfenbrenner (2a) noted that;

Over the past three decades literally thousands of investigations have been conducted to identify the developmental antecedents of behavior disorders and social pathology. The results point to an almost omnipresent overriding factor: family disorganization.

Much of the same research also shows that the forces of disorganization arise primarily not from the circumstances in which the family finds itself but from the way of life that is imposed on it by those circumstances.

He goes on to indicate that those circumstances can be such that they;

. . . undermine relationships of trust and emotional security between family members . . . make it difficult for parents to care for, educate and enjoy their children. When there is no support for one's role as a parent and when time spent with one's family means frustration of careei, personal fulfillment and peace of mind, then the development of the child is adversely affected.

In this white dominated society, the higher the status of the black man or woman, the more insecure they may become. The fact that the white man can "make" them leads to the conclusion that he can also "break" them. The striving to overcome their feelings of insecurity engendered by the nature of white dominated society, the capricious nature of white power and the desire to be fully accepted by whites, a great number of blacks regardless of class, seek to overcome these feelings of insecurity by striving even more, using "white" standards as their measurements of progress. This question the part of these blacks bring on self-alienation, alienation from the ethnic group and the family. Though the black parents among these striving blacks may provide their children with all the material things they themselves never had when they were children and material things comparative to what white children receive from their parents, they may fail to give their children the emotional things they need to develop wholesome prosocial personalities.

The Chronically Frustrated Nature of Black Life. Continuous with and inextricably bound up with the schizoid nature of black existence is the chronically frustrated nature of black existence. The latter condition is to a large extent a direct function of the former.

Since blacks evaluate their worthiness and their self-regard, positively or negatively speaking, by use of the measuring stick of "white" standards and by their acceptance or rejection by whites, they value very much and/or seek after those material, social, psychological, economical, educational,

56

political things which the emulated white culture possesses and which that same culture has decreed must be possessed in order to be considered a "first-class citizen", to be fully accepted along with a sense of equality. Consequently, blacks are "pushed-pulled" toward those goals that the whites have achieved or are striving to achieve. Blacks have been told in so many ways that their acceptance by whites as equals demand that they achieve these goals and live according to the white lifestyle that these goals and goal-strivings make possible. However, the black possibility of attaining these goals or their possibility of attaining the necessary preparatory equipment for striving after these goals with a fair chance of achieving them are constantly blocked by inordinate and insurmountable white racist barriers and obstacles. As a result, blacks in America suffer chronic frustration and black life is generally characterized by the symptoms of frustration.

Frustration refers to the unpleasant feelings and/or state of mind resulting from the lack of satisfaction of a desire, the fulfillment of a wish and/or from being or having been delayed, misled from, or blocked from reaching a certain goal, and not possessing the power of being able to satisfactorily compensate for the subsequent lack of satisfaction or lack of fulfillment. The symptoms of black frustration are extremely debilitating to the black personality and the black community in general. Although frustration in both its conscious and nonconscious forms operate at all levels of the black community its effects are more readily observable and manifest their most vicious effects in the black lower classes. The black middle class, which by no means has escaped the pernicious effects of frustration, has been relatively more successful at reducing its effects in a superficially socially acceptable way through its material, social, educational, economical and political gains.

Among the many symptoms of frustration we shall at this time discuss the following (others are discussed in chapter (9); feeling of powerlessness, inability to delay gratification, apathy, fatalism, denial of the worthiness of social goals, low achievement motivation, ego-restrictiveness, high interest in diversive activities and unrealistic striving. The following table schematically illustrate the relationship between the symptoms of parental frustration and their concomitant parental attitudes and child-rearing practices.

Parental Frustration Symptoms	Parental Attitudes and Childrearing Practices
Powerlessness	Lack of interest in maintaining control over child, feels powerless to effectively control child's destiny, to control child itself, does not inculcate in the child a sense of control over its own destiny and circumstances, encour-

agees dependency in the child, teaches "learned helplessness", does not take deep and sustained interest in developing the child's inherent cognitive, social, physical potential, teaches the child to overexaggerate the power of obstacles in its way.

Inability to Delay Gratification

Tends to react with hostility toward child when it is perceived as a hindrance to parental pleasure, child is treated as a general nuisance and consequently rejected and neglected, child is treated as a "doll," an extention of the parental ego, not as a individual, fails to train child to control emotions and appetites, to concern itself about the future and about the future consequences of current behavior, overindulgence of the child.

Apathy

Fails to take deep interest in child's development, neglect of childs mental, physical, emotional wellbeing, fails to motivate child, to teach child how to overcome and solve problems, to inculcate a sense of duty in child, to teach the child to take a continuing interest in its self-improvement, teaches it to be satisfied with far less than it is realistically capable of doing, teaches it to accept low status uncomplainingly.

Denial of Worthiness of Social Goals

Not interested in being a socially acceptable model for child to imitate, shows disdain for social institutions, for the child's social striving, teaches the child that social mobility is "not worth fighting for."

Fatalism

Believes that child's growth and development is a matter of luck, believes that deliberate efforts in child-rearing are futile, teaches child that achievement is a matter of luck, encourages fantasy and magical thinking as solutions to problems, not realistic imagining and thinking, teaches the child to accept laconically what happens to it.

Low Achievement Motivation	Not highly motivated to achieve optimal circumstances for self development and the child's development, does not motivate the child to achieve, to be cognitively independent, personally and socially independent, does not teach child techniques for achieving, does not supply child with games, toys, books, etc,–the tools which lay the basis for high achievement motivation, does not encourage self-confidence, self-love, self-knowledge in the child, does not adequately repulse inferiority complex in the child.
Ego-restrictiveness	Parental self is the main source of interest, the child is secondary, the home is not child-centered, takes little interest in the child as an individual, encourages the child's interest in and concern for others, discourages child's identity with his racial group and the society in general.
High Interest in Diversive Activities	Interested mainly in "pasttime" activities, not problem-solving activities, which leads to child neglect, only interested in playing with or distracting the child as a means of dealing with its problems, teaches the child to engage in diversive behavior when faced with problems or to perceive such behavior as a solution to all problems, fails to train child to inhibit irrelevant impulses, how to complete a task once begun.
Unrealistic Striving	Parental unrealistic striving alienates self and child, leaves inadequate time for proper child-rearing, teaches child to pursue goals beyond its inherent, acquired and attainable talents, powers and means, imposing on child the parent's status strivings without regard to the child's own wishes.

59

The Restricted Nature of The Black World. That the black world in America is a restricted one both psychologically and otherwise is well-known and has been and still is much discussed. Therefore it will not be necessary for us to further elaborate on this matter here except to remind ourselves in a very general way, of its effects on the black child as mediated through black parents. The preceding two sections discussed what are essentially the products of the segregation of black people and their effects on black child-rearing practices and in turn on the development of the black child. In this section we merely want to crystallize what has already been implied.

The maturing and matured black individual to be functional in white dominated world, must learn and play by its game rules. The task of learning these rules must begin during the very earliest years of childhood and this learning is done under the tutelage of the parents or their substitutes. The task of teaching the child the rules of the "white" game is made difficult if not impossible if the parent has not learned in depth the rules herself or if the parent, knowing the rules, is prevented from successfully transmitting them to her child. by any number of social-psychological, economic-political factors. The restricted black world obviously breeds these two parental deficiencies. Black parental efforts to rear their child so that they can function equally with white children miss their mark because their child-rearing practices are often based on erroneous assumptions abstracted from their observations of superficial white behavior. They have little or no knowlege of the social-psychological, cultural infrastructure behind the white behavioral facade. Thus the restricted black parent may want her child to attain such socially valued goals as academic success, becoming a successful professional such as a doctor, lawyer, brilliant scientist, etc, but her lack of knowledge of what kind of early childhood training lay the best basis for such achievements, may doom her desires to disappointment. In sum, black parental aspirations for their children are as high as their white counterparts, but the restrictedness of their world cuts them off from the necessary psychosocial resources needed to lay a firm foundation for the success of their children.

One of the major foundational ingredients for succeeding in the white dominated world is the mastery of the language, the vocabulary of that world. This means a firm mastery in all of its variously related aspects, or the graphical (reading, writing), lexical (vocabulary), semantic (meaning), syntactical (grammar), expressive (speaking) qualities of the language. This mastery which is firmer the earlier it begins in life, (in the first two years) is the keystone in the cognitive, social-psychological superstructure of the individual. Generally, it can be safely intimated that the black parent has too little awareness of the immense importance of language and the grave importance of linguistic facility for the black child's success in white terms. It is principly "deficiencies" in linguistic functioning that are responsible for much of black cognitive and academic failure, other things held constant. We mentioned earlier in this chapter that the black child's mental development begins to fall behind that of the white child's at the point where language begins to influence significantly the personality structure. We are mindful that other important factors also contribute to this "lag" of the black child, in fact, our two previous sections dealt with some of those factors. But it is because language is the main vehicle for the transmission of these other factors that we are emphasizing it here. As the child develops language is the principal means by which he structures his relations to the world and to himself, it is the principal means by which he influences the world, is influenced by the world, and influences himself. The brain is the controlling computer of the body and mind and language and words are the cards which program the computer brain.

Analysis and generalization are the key elements in intellectual functioning. These processes are guided by the logical structure of speech. The same can, to a large extent, be said about behavior in general, of which intellectual functioning is but a part. The basis of speech and of ideas is word-meaning which which begins to develop in the first years of childhood (21) The "psychological structure of thinking as a whole" is word-meaning (13). Luria (14) underlines the importance of the word in early childhood when he writes:

Language, which incorporates the experience of generations or, more broadly speaking, of mankind, is included in the process of the child's development from the first months of his life. . . . This whole process of the transmission of knowledge and the formation of concepts, which is the basic way the adult influences the child, constitutes the central process of the child's intellectual development.

*   *   *

. . . the acquistion of a language system involves a reorganization of all the child's basic mental processes; the word thus becomes a tremendous factor which forms mental activity, perfecting the reflection of reality and creating new forms of attention, of memory and imagination, of thought and action.

We are terminating our discussion of language at this point because the subject will be more extensively discussed in chapter nine. However, since ". . . at about the age of two the curves of development of thought and speech, till then separate, meet and join to initiate a new form of behavior (21)," we felt it important to briefly discuss it at this point.

The restricted black world and the attitudes it generates effectively cuts the black parent off from the knowledge of the "white" linguistic structure and thus vitiates her attempts to transmit the necessary linguistic knowledge to her child, and blinds her to the vast importance of language in the development of her child's full potential, cognitive and otherwise. This same world also prevents her from obtaining a substantive, causal-content, knowledge of the mental, physical, social, economical, educational, behavioral pattern that are necessary for achievement and non-psychopathological adjustment in a white dominated world.

Note: The reader should not assume that the author thinks integration into the white world is the only or most desirable means by which a healthy psychosocial adjustment can be made by the black individual or the black community. This is most difinitely not the case. In fact, the reader would be nearer the truth if he assumed the opposite.

In our effort to answer the question of what is the nature of the psychosocial world of black parents, which includes of course, their children, which "causes" them to socialize their children to behave maladaptively in both black and white society, we have briefly discussed three possibly responsible variables, the schizoid, the frustrated and the restricted nature of black existence. We have seen that these variables, operating in dynamically changing combinations and permutations in the black parent causes that parent to "program" her child to emit cognitively, personally and socially inappropriate and dysfunctional behavior. One of the main characteristics each of the variables have in common is the inability to properly socialize the child due to the absence of a clearly established consistent and rational socio-culturally founded and supported system of attitudes, goals and values. Such a system if it existed could serve as a means by which the parent could conduct her behavior and that of her child's so as to reduce significantly the probability of permanently creating serious malfunctions in the child's cognitive-behavioral functioning. The vacillatory, dissonant child-rearing practices brought on by black schizoid existence, the reactionary child-rearing practices engendered by frustrated black existence and the ignorance of the "rules of the game," resulting from the restricted nature of black life, coalesce to produce fertile conditions for the aberrational growth of asocial, antisocial, cognitively deficient, self-denigrating, or at best, minimal "normal" functioning tendencies in the black child and adult.

Black Parental Attitudes and The Child's Physical Characteristics. Obviously the attitudes of the parents toward their child's physical characteristics is of great importance in parent-child relations and in the child's own psychological well-being. Leaving aside body structural characteristics, in America skin color does much to structure the relations between persons—including parent and child. A person is often accepted or rejected based on skin color.

The crucial nature of skin-based relations become quite apparent when we realize that the skin is the primary sense and communicative organ of the human infant. To achieve adequate physical and psychological growth the child must receive the appropriate amount of physical and affectionate cutaneous stimulation. Affectionate skin stimulation is the principal means by which the mother communicates her love to her child. Physically speaking, the early growth and development of the infant's nervous system is to a large extent dependent on the nature of the cutaneous stimulation it receives (15). Psychologically speaking, proper cutaneous stimulation gives the infant concrete feelings of security and reassurance in the face of strange new complexities. Too little or too much cutaneous stimulation, degrading comments about the child's skin color, may generate conflicts in the child, feelings of rejection, self-hatred and an inferiotiry complex in the child. Thus, the infant's skin (as well as that of the adult) is a very crucial part of his personality. To insult the child's skin is to insult the child itself. Warm cutaneous contact between parent and child develops parent-child emotional attachment and develops trust, self-confidence, self-love, and self-respect in the child.

Lloyd Warner, et al (23). confirmed three hypotheses about blacks and their attitudes toward skin color in their book, *Color and Human Nature:*

1. The systematic subordination of Negroes to white people in the American social system has a definite effect upon the development of Negro personality.

2. Evaluations of color and other physical traits made by Negroes themselves on their own group influence the development of personality.

3. Social-class position and occupational status in the Negro society have effects upon Negro personality formation.

Warner's first hypothesis is essentially what this book is about and the second is our present concern and the third which is basically beyond the scope of this book is briefly related to our discussion in chapter(8).Not surprisingly, Warner found that among blacks "personal appearance is a constantly recurring theme." He also found that most blacks "evaluate physical appearance in terms of caste contrasts or essentially according to white standards." During his interviews which were made in Chicago in the early 1960's, Warner confirmed the already well-known fact that there existed many expressions, almost of a proverbial nature, that placed a low value on dark skin color and a high value on light skin color. Color then, served as a caste determinant in the black community as it did in the white community. Warner quotes anthropologist, Melville Herskovits as asking—"Is it strange, then, that he (the Negro) should unconsciously glorify that which is like the traits of the group enjoying every opportunity that is denied him?"

Color evaluations which reflect the values, standards and attitudes of the dominant white society influence black self-awareness, self-concept, self-love and black interpersonal relations in a variety of ways — — most of them detrimental. It is the pronouncedly "Negroid" black that is the most rejected and the more "caucasoid" black that is the most accepted in the black community. This color based acceptance-rejection continuum may reveal itself operationally at the birth of the black child. Harrison-Ross, in her book, *The Black Child—A Parents' Guide* (8), points out that black parents look at their newborn differently than do their white counterparts. Black parents check the baby's color before assessing anything else about the infant's body. Other body parts are checked after the color is determined. This is unlike that of white parents who concern themselves firstly with the child's physical normality and health. According to Harrison-Ross, whites rarely ever mention skin color. She goes on to a crucially important statement:

This overwhelming concern with color is part of the special black dimension to childrearing. The color of the child can affect the quality of parental love and the child's position in the family. In my practice I have often had to help mothers change their attitude toward their children because they were favoring the lighter-skinned youngsters at the expense of the darker ones.

The black mother or father who consciously or unconsciously align themselves with the American color-caste value system are prone to reject or treat their children differently according to that system. This creates an unhealthy psychological atmosphere for the children involved. Under these conditions the child is looked on in terms of his or her superficial qualities and also related to in those terms. This practice of putting the child's basic humanness last destroys the possibility of the child's fulfilling it inherent potential. The black mother may signal her rejection of her dark baby in several ways: (1) by being overly annoyed by the baby's crying, eating problems, temperament and its unresponsiveness to her calming and soothing efforts (which are generally caused by her own problems), (2) by handling the child roughly, carelessly or neglectfully when attending it, (3) by refusing to talk, sing or play with it, and (4) by not responding to its apparent loneliness or sadness (8). The dark child brought up under such a regime will learn that is is unloved, unworthy and unwanted because it is dark and it will early begin to suffer from lack of self-confidence, self-love and self-respect. It will develop into a person who will have a difficult time trusting or loving others, particularly those of his own ethnic group because he first felt rejected by his parents who are members of this group.

Some of our readers may think that the current "Black Is Beautiful", "I'm Black And I'm Proud" movement has removed much of the relevance of what we have just finished discussing. We do not think so. While the new black consciousness has helped and is helping to reduce the problems discussed above the job by no means complete. In fact there is the danger of "reverse discrimination" against the light skinned black child. However, we don't think this danger will materialize significantly due to the historical color discrimination by blacks who because of their dependent relationship with whites will not change a system the whites support. The fact that such jingos as the ones we have quoted in this paragraph exists indicates that the struggle with the evaluative nature of skin color in the black community is a critical stage of development and is still unresolved. "Black Is Beautiful" was more of a statement used to convince the uncertain minds of the vast majority of blacks rather than a statement of conviction. Though it may be socially expected and consciously demanded of one another by blacks to make such positive sounding statements in public it is very doubtful whether ideas conveyed by such statements are actually personally and unconsciously believed by blacks. The belief in the truth of such statements is too tenuous in black minds to result in a confident, healthy attitude toward their children at this point in time. We must remember that today's black parents and grandparents were brought up under regimes where black was not beautiful and are still suffering from the psychological scars produced by their own upbringing. Under optimistic conditions in this area it will still take a number of generations for the black child to escape the curse of the "mark of oppression."

Implications and Recommendations. If the black child is to realize his full potential then his care and training should be pursued with as much accurate knowledge as is possible about his unique developmental qualities and vulnerabilities. We have seen that the black child in his psychomotor developmental rates is not just a white child painted black. Of course it is plain to all that the black child's psychosocial developmental career significantly differs from that of his white counterpart. Even though there are fundamental differences between black and white child development little or no complete programs have been promulgated to deal with the uniqueness of black child development and its attendant problems. In books on child development the black child is treated as an after-thought, used as a symbol of deprivation, treated as a footnote or just plainly ignored. It is necessary that the care and training of the black child, if it is to be maximally beneficial to the child himself, to the black community and the society in general, must be based on other than unexamined extrapolations from developmental care and training procedures based on studies of white children and developed mainly for the rearing of white children. Certainly there are many areas of overlap between child-rearing procedures used for the white child and procedures used for the black child, but the racial-historical background differences, the differences in the conditions under which they are reared and the essential differences in the futures they will face and problems they will have to endure, are wide and in demand that black child-training should be pursued along conscious, studied, informed, well-thought lines and not the haphazard, faddish, reactionary, contradictory, dysfunctional lines that characterize such training today. We therefore recommend the following:

1. that the black child should be the body of studies and books in child development and not treated as a mere appendage to the body of white child developmental studies.

2. that in light of the fact that the black child's average psychomotor development differs significantly from that of the white child's during the first two years of life, then nutritional and other socio-psycho-physical programs be developed that will answer to the unique needs of our black children.

3. that we educate our black parents to the fact that the black child is not naturally inferior to any other child and what "lag" there may exist between the black child and the white child is due to adverse psychosocial and politico-economical circumstances which prevail in the black community and that they can do much to allay the pernicious effects of such circumstances.

4. that the black parent, through reading, conversation, observation, imagination,etc, learns in depth the "rules" of the white-defined game in which her child will one day play and lay the foundations for the learning of those rules early in the child's life. This means training the child for flexibility, not for being "white". The child can be taught to deal cognitively and socially with whites without losing respect and love for himself and his racial group.

5. since the black child is virtually destined to be bi-cultural he must be taught from his early years how to function efficiently in both of the cultures he will have to deal with. This means he has to be taught to equally respect and handle efficiently his own "black English" as well as "standard English."

6. that the black parent be educated to guard against the negative child-rearing practices generated by schizoid, frustrated, restricted black existence.

7. that clear, rational, consistent, understandable (to the parent and child), community-supported values and limits be established and used by black parents to guide their child-rearing practices.

For the black parent who wishes to raise competent, independent, assertive, exploratory, self-determining, happy children who are also prosocial, we make the following recommendations (16).

8. Guide your child's activities along rational lines. Help the child to see that what is demanded of him should be done because "it is right" or the reasonable thing to do not because he may be punished or will lose your love.

9. Do not be afraid to exert control when necessary. The exertion of control will not be psychologically damaging to the child if the reasons behind such exertion are explained to him, if the child is allowed to have some input concerning parental policies.

10. Show your child that you expect him to have a will of his own but at the same time he is expected to conform to reasonable parental and social standards.

11. Have confidence in your ability to parent. However, do not let that confidence be such that you disrespect your child's interests, opinions and individuality.

12. Be a loving, consistent, demanding and respectful parent of your child's independent decision-making, but at the same time be steadfast concerning your own standards. Do not fear the use of limited punishment if necessary.

13. Expect your child to perform as well as he can.

14. Build in your child a sense of duty by assigning him family chores which he is required to complete. Teach him to fulfill reasonable commitments once he makes them.

15. Have fun with your child and at times let him be a part of the family decision-making process.

The combination of control with encouragement which we have tried to embody in the above recommendations will create in your child a feeling of security, of being loved and of knowing what is expected of them. The child will also experience the satisfaction of completing tasks, meeting responsibilities and successfully achieving goals. These things can be accomplished if you set reasonable goals and realistic standards for yours and your child's behavior.

67

REFERENCES

1. Bayley, N. Comparison of mental and motor test scores for age 1-15 months by sex, birth order, race, geographic location, and parents. **Child Development, 36,** 1965.

2. Bayley, N. Consistency and variability in the growth of intelligence from birth to eighteen years. **Journal of Genetic Psychology, 75,** 1949.

2a. Bronfenbrenner, U. **Scientific American,** August 1974.

3. Du Bois, W. The souls of black folk. New York: Avon, 1965.

4. Frazier, E. **Black bourgeoisie.** New York: Collier, 1962.

5. Garn, S., Lewis, A., & Kerewsky, R. Genetic, nutritional and maturational correlates of dental development. **Journal of Denatal Research, 44,** 1964.

6. Geber, M. The psychomotor development of African children in the first year and the first year and the influence of maternal behavior. **Journal of Social Psychology, 47,** 1958.

7. Ginsburg, H. **The myth of the deprived child: Poor children's intellect and education.** New Jersey: Prentice-Hall, 1972.

8. Harrison-Ross, P., & Wyden, B. **The black child: A parent's guide.** New York: Wyden, 1973.

9. Jensen, A. How much can we boost IQ and scholastic achievement? **Harvard Educational Review, 39,** Winter 1969.

10. Knoblock, H., & Pasamanick, B. Further observations on the behavioral development of negro children. **Journal of Genetic Psychology, 83,** 1953.

11. Kohen-Raz, R. Mental and motor development of kibbutz, institutionalized and home-reared infants in Israel. **Child Development, 39,** 1968.

12. Langner, T. , et al. Children of the city: Affluence, poverty, mental health. In **Psychological factors in poverty,** V. Allen (ed.), 1970.

13. Luria, A., **The working brain: An introduction to neuropsychology.** Maryland: Penguin, 1973.

14. Luria, A., & Yudovick, F. Speech and the development of mental processess in the child. Maryland: Penguin, 1971

15. Montagu, A. Touching: The human significance of the skin. New York: Harper & Row, 1972.

15a. Moynihan, P. The negro family: The case for national action. Office of Policy Planning and Research, United States Department of Labor, March 1965.

16. Papalia, D., & Olds, S. A child's world: Infancy through adolescence. New York: McGraw-Hill, 1975.

17. Provence, S., & Lipton, R. Infants in institutions. New York: International University Press, 1961.

18. Scrimshaw, N. The effects of the interaction of nutrition and infection on the preschool child. In National Academy of Sciences, Preschool child malnutrition: Deterrent to human progress. Washington, D.C.,: National Research Council, 1966.

19. Smart, M., & Smart, R. Children: Development and relationships. (2nd ed.) New York: Macmillan, 1972.

20. Tronick, E., et al. Neonatal behavior among urban Zambians and Americans. Biennial meeting of the Society for Research in Child Development, Minneapolis, Minnesota, April 8, 1971.

21. Vygotsky, L. Thought and language. Massachusetts: Massachusetts Institute of Technology, 1962.

22. Walters, E. Comparative development of negro and white infants. Journal of Genetic Psychology, 110, 1967.

23. Warner, L., et al. Color and human nature. New York: Harper, & Row, 1969.

24. Yarrow, L., et al. Dimensions of early stimulation: Differential effects on infant development. Paper presented at the meeting of the Society for Research in Child Development. Minneapolis, Minnesota. April 4, 1971.

THE BLACK CHILD — THE PRESCHOOL YEARS
The Effects Of Race Awareness

An Overview. At the end of the first two years the child has gained intelligent control of his musculature, has accomplished a fairly well developed sense of trust and autonomy, and has begun to use language as a cognitive-communicative instrument. From ages 3 to 7, the preschool years, and beyond, he perfects the coordination of his growing body and continues to mature intellectually by encountering and solving new problems. Personality-wise he continues to develop his senses of trust and autonomy and begins to develop a sense of initiative (2). The peoples and objects he interacts with in his ever-expanding environment greatly influence his cognitive, psychological and social growth. The preschooler builds his mental structures in wonderously complex ways through asserting himself, testing the limits of his abilities, and by testing and. exploring thoroughly his familial and environmental limits. He is rather "up front" in revealing his feelings, thoughts and behavior.

B. L. White (8) compiled a list of " competences" developed during the preschool years, assuming that all had gone well before:

Non-social abilities

1. Linguistic: grammatical capacity, vocabulary, articulation, extensive use of expressed language.
2. Intellectual: sensing dissonance, anticipation of consequences, ability to deal with abstractions, such as numbers, letters, rules, taking the perspective of another person, making interesting associations.
3. Executive: planning and carrying out multistepped activities.
4. Attentional: maintaining attention to a proximal task while simultaneously monitoring peripheral events.

Social abilities:

1. Getting and keeping adult's attention in socially acceptable ways.
2. Using adults as resources.
3. Expressing both affection and hostility to both adults and peers.
4. Leading, following, and competing with peers.
5. Showing pride in his accomplishments.

6. Taking part in adult role behavior or otherwise expressing a desire to grow up.

What happens in these years are of exceeding importance for the child's academic future which begins at their close. These are the "head-start" years, the years of establishing resilient personality and cognitive structures which will be the foundation of the child's future personal, cognitive, social style.

As we mentioned in the previous chapter prior to the preschool years the child is chiefly concerned with gaining mastery over his mind and body. His learning to walk during this period symbolizes his autonomous strivings, his efforts to "stand on his own two feet" both in the physical and psychological sense. His rapid mastery of the language extends his power of self-control and self-direction, thereby enhancing his sense of independence. This same mastery also extends his power of control and direction over others, but simultaneously it also extends the power of control and direction of others over him. We indicated that parental attitudes, standards and values as conveyed through their behavior and language .. crucial during this period in helping or hindering the child's intellectual and psychological growth. A child's autonomous behavior at about the age of 2½ years correlates positively with his cognitive style and nonverbal intellectual style at age six (5).

Initiative. As the development of the sense of autonomy is the hallmark of the child's first two years the development of the sense of initiative is the hallmark of the preschool years. Then the child becomes a full-fledged explorer, a curious adventurer and an incessant "activist." He takes great pleasure in trying new things just for the satisfaction of doing them, he also relates his new experiences to his old ones and re-interprets the old ones in terms of the new. His chronic questioning and talking may become the dread of his parents. Through his growing imagination he tries out various roles and gains new experiences through his creative use of his surrounding environment.

A fundamental part of the sense of initiative developed during this period is the child's aggressive pushing out into the world and assertive attack on obstacles in his path. This aggressiveness and assertiveness is inextricably tied up with the child's cognitive-intellectual-imaginative growth. This aggressiveness and assertiveness when left undisciplined and rationally uncontrolled or over-disciplined and over-controlled will work against his positive intellectual, personal and social growth. Measures of assertiveness are a reflection of the child's ability to interact with his environment and to master it. Since intelligence tests measure knowledge and mastery, the child who deals assertively with his world is more likely to score high on such tests (7).

It is during the preschool years that the child more effectively begins to distort and restrict his imagination and initiative through the introjection of parental attitudes, values, behavior patterns in general, and their prohibitions.

71

His behavior becomes less and less controlled by the fear of punishment and more and more under the control of these introjected attitudes, values, etc. Consequently, for the first time the child begins to experience feelings of guilt, pangs of conscience, and more importantly, begins to judge himself in terms of others. Additionally over-protection or over-restriction of the child's initiative strivings force him to choose from among several coping strategies which may become a permanent characteristic of his personality. The restrained child may choose to become withdrawn or socially psychologically and cognitively unassertive. He may choose to become difiant, to attempt to gain his way through the use of bravado or gile, to become destructive, compulsive, stubborn, rigidly conforming in an unreasoning, irrational way. This child may also become overwhelmed by and a chronic victim of feelings of shame, guilt, doubt and worthlessness. Permissiveness may lead the child to exhibit reckless, uncontrolled assertive behavior. It may cause the child to disregard the rights of others or may lead also to the development of the types of strategies listed above as used by the over-restricted child if the child from the permissive environment is allowed to let his recklessness lead into situations where he is hurt, severely rebuffed, shamed or brutally retaliated against by an offended environment or something or someone in the environment. Thus, in line with the recommendations listed at the end of our last chapter we say that authoritative caretaking which allows the child room enough to flex his physical and psychological muscles but which at the same time restricts reckless, uncontrolled, destructive, unreasonable behavior on his part best suits the development of healthy initiative, assertive behavior.

Initiative and The Black Child. Generally the average parent rears his or her child in terms of his or her own childhood training, past experiences and future expectations. The childhood training, the experiences of, and the expectations for the future of black parents raised in racist America and subjected to the negative operations of the three variables, schism, frustrationism and restrictivism, discussed in the previous chapter do not bode well for the development of the black child if they raise their own children in terms of these variables. Unfortunately this is the case. It is obvious even to the casual observer what the American experience has done to black people in general, including black parents. Some of the well-known results of the American black experience has been the crippling feelings of shame, guilt, doubt, fear, confusion, powerlessness, rejection, self-hatred, inferiority, and general inadequacy which characterize black psychic existence today. These feelings are passed on to their children by black parents whose consciousness does not allow them to conscientiously resist such tendencies in their families, communities and the nation at large.

The history of American racism has been the punishment of black initiative, assertiveness, originality, independence striving, self-confidence, belief in their equality with all men, self-love, self-knowledge, etc., and the reward of black docility, servility, and reward of the opposite of initiative, assertiveness, etc. Consequently, what was and is suppressed and repressed by the dominant whites in turn becomes suppressed and repressed by his own efforts in the dominated black. The history of this suppression and repression has been such that the black man has come to believe that he actually does not possess the repressed characteristics. The repressed black parent, in order to prepare her child to cope with and survive in the white world, "pre-represses" her child as is demanded by that world. This may be done consciously or unconsciously by the black parent. Even if a repressed black parent chooses not to "pre-repress" her child the effects of her own repression has been such that she will not know how not to do so. Her effort to raise a "man" or a "woman" may be frustrated by her self-doubt or lack of knowledge. Thus the healthy development in the black child of initiative, assertiveness, etc, and his resistance to feelings of shame, guilt, doubt, etc, are thwarted or left malnourished by his repressed black parents who in line with the racist history and current practices of America, wittingly or unwittingly inculcate an inferiority complex in their children. Independence, self-assertiveness, self-confidence, etc., in the black adult has been so viciously punished both overtly and covertly, by the dominant white society that in their efforts to ward off that punishment and to protect their children from it, to ward off white retaliative responses against black independence, self-assertiveness, etc, strivings and through a curious identification with and love for their white oppressors, that even within their own communities and families, blacks often become vehemently resentful and punish or fail to support independent, self-assertive activity among their own members and children.

The low expectations engendered by white racism coupled with the low expectations (and fear of failure) that blacks have of themselves combine in the black parent to vitiate the black child's initiative, self-confidence, etc. At best the black parent's expectations for her child are ambivalent, confused, uncertain and lacking in confidence. The black parent's own experiences and low expectations helps her to easily rationalize her lack of interest in encouraging and supporting her child's healthy assertive, confident strivings. It helps her to help her child to easily rationalize his failings and fear of competitiveness.

The introjected tendency of repressed black parents to be overly disturbed by (historically white-punished) assertive, self-confident strivings in their children causes them to create passive dependency in their children by punishing these strivings or simply by not rewarding them. Thus, the child early learns a lesson that his parents were taught in their youth, that being a "smart nigger" is dangerous or at best unrewarding. Thus, the black child soon abandons his efforts to be a "smart nigger" and learns to become imitative instead of creative, to fantasize instead of think, to switch instead of fight, to be destructive instead of constructive, to be consumptive instead of productive, to feel inferior instead of superior, etc.

73

Race Awareness in The Black Preschool Child. The black experience in America has traumatized the black psyche in a number of ways. For our purposes here we shall only list the following ones which we feel are the most important:

1. As a result of racist propaganda and of the "second class" experience in America the black man has come to believe that he is inferior to the white man.

2. This belief on the black man's part has robbed him of self-confidence, has made him feel powerless to determine his own destiny, has made him feel that he is incapable.

3. The black man has not come to have a practical confidence in his self-reliance and therefore abets a dependency relationship with the white-man. Despite his brutal mental and physical treatment by the white man, the black man still sees the white man as his main source of survival and has not sought to become independent as much as he possibly can from his slave master.

4. It is well-known that the black man suffers from self-hatred as a result of his American experience. One of the symptoms of this self-hatred is a strong wish to deny in various ways their blackness which they see as the source of their inferiority and the source of their degradation by whites.

5. The black experience in America has led many blacks to strongly desire to become totally identified with whites — to become "equal," to become for all practical purposes "white." They have come to believe that white culture represents a universal ideal for Mankind and that all men should strive to become identified with it. They see a merging with whites as their only salvation.

Other blacks,'who do not wish to "lose their skin" express a strong desire to possess the trappings of white culture and power without necessarily wishing to become "white" in the process.

7. The American black experience created in blacks the tremendous need to be accepted, approved, affirmed, and loved by whites. He feels that these actions by whites are necessary pre-requisites for his own self-acceptance, approval, affirmation, and love. In other words, since it was the white man who took him apart it is the white man who will make him whole again. Thus the black man does not see himself as the source of inspiration and orientation. He is therefore not self-directing but other-directed.

While the "black is beautiful" movement (essentially a fad) did much to neutralize some of the things implied in the above list their validity is still very, very substantial. Each of these statements do not apply equally to all segments of black society. For instance, while statements 1 — 4 may have general applicability, statements 5 and 7 are more representative of the black middle class orientation while statement 6 is more representative of black working and lower class orientations. However, these do not represent pure distinctions between the classes mentioned, they are merely where the orientations are strongest. Certainly orientations 5 and 7 are significant parts of the black lower class orientation and likewise orientation 6 is an essential part of black middle class orientation. The crux of the matter is that given any combination of orientations black life regardless of class is "white-centered." The orbital path of the black psyche is defined by its revolution around the central "white" star.

The world we have described above represents a very important part of the psychosocial world of both the black parent and the black child. The latter is socialized in such a world and matures to reflect the imprint of such a socialization process. It is evident that blacks have very serious difficulties facing their blackness and its realities. We agree with Harrison-Ross (4) when she says that:

> One of the realities many blacks have great difficulty in grasping is the most obvious, most personal reality: dark skin. They go to extremes to avoid facing it. Like the ostrich, they're scared.

Harrison-Ross prepared a questionaire about race and administered it to an informal sampling of New York City youths ranging in age from 5 to 18. They came from the black ghettoes as well as from the black upper class. To the questions, "What did your parents tell you about being black?" and "When did your parents tell you about being black?", typical of some of the answers were:

Boy, 12½: "I found out myself. I looked at my skin and looked at theirs and I came up with that conclusion."

Girl, 17: "They told me that as a black person we are originally from Africa, our mother country."

Girl, 5: They said it very hard   be black."

Girl, 10: "No."

Girl, 6: "Nothing."

Boy, 14½: "They didn't tell me anything. I learned it for myself."

Girl, 18: ""My parents never tell me about being black, I find out on my own."

Harrison-Ross concluded that most black parents do talk to their children about being black, but it seems that what is said about the subject is innocuous, virtually philosophically meaningless, platitudinous, or comes in the form of admonitions exhortations for the youngster to live up to white standards. She quotes a black mother as saying."My husband and I talked to both our sons about being black. We told them that blacks are just like anyone else, but that some white people still have to be shown and that it's up to us to always put our best foot forward in public."In other words the children were admonished not to "act like a nigger." Harrison-Ross rightly implies that black parents, in line with the dominant white society, make racism in American culture a "black problem," instead of the "white problem" it really is. Consequently, the burden of proof of acceptability falls on the black person. The prime requirement for gaining such acceptability is that the person becomes "other-than-himself," i.e., a "white-black" man, the schizoid to which we earlier referred (this is true despite what may appear as white acceptance of blackness). The first person to push the black child into this schizoid process are the black parents.

This parental tendency which results from nature of black existence which we discussed in chapter two creates discontinuities in the black child's personality and starts him on the road to schizoid living. These discontinuities perpetrates in the black child a set of chronically active, neurotic tendencies that will become a permanent part of the rest of his life. These discontinuities drive many blacks to distraction. The need to prove their acceptability to whites attains the characteristics of an obsessive-compulsion.

Black parental ethnic-cultural confusion and ambivalence toward blackness stands as an invisible, and often not so, barrier between parent and child. Consequently, the discussion of the reality of blackness with the child is often marked by fear, consternation, avoidance behavior, feelings of shame. guilt, inadequacy, embarrassment and other uncomfortable feelings in the black parent. The child does not miss the message that to deeply probe into "race" is a "no no." Harrison-Ross very cogently points out that black parents feel:

... uncomfortable themselves about being black. A great many parents feel the same way when it comes to telling their children about sex. In both cases parents tend to stiffen up when they talk to children about these subjects. The kids sense the uptight atmosphere and immediately absorb another lesson about race — not the one their parents are giving out loud. The kids learn that race and sex are very uncomfortable topics."These subjects are really loaded, too hot to handle." That's the silent message parents are sending. And that's the first one the youngsters absorb. Parent and child both are relieved when the lecture is over.

Some children do not verbally initiate racial discussions with their parents. However, this should not be taken to indicate that the child is not concerned about the matter. It may merely mean that the child senses the discomfiture of his parents in this area. Children, whose sensitivity is often under-estimated by their elders, can sense their parent's ambivalence and self-hatred in matters of race. This is the case even if a black parent who harbors these feeling consciously and publicly acts proud of their blackness.

Thus, by verbal and nonverbal means, through various other types of interpersonal reactions, and through the perception of racial, cultural and creedal differences, a foundation is laid for the learning about and the practice of racial prejudice in the preschool child as well as the adult. It is obvious that children learn social, racial and religious prejudices from their parents, peers, and influential others. These childhood prejudices are learned through observation, imitation, experience, through the rewarding of prejudiced responses and as the result of direct instruction. Even though the development of racial prejudice (which also implies prejudice about one's own race, e.g., the unfounded belief in one's own racial superiority or inferiority) is a gradual process, it makes its appearance early in childhood and its definitive effects can be observed reliably beginning at age 3. Children exhibit racial preferences at the kindergarten and first grade levels and express conscious awareness of the social-evaluative meanings of ethnic differences at this time also.

In his well-known "doll" experiment in a northern city, Kenneth Clark (1) found that 75% of black children around age 3 were conscious of the difference between "white" and "colored." By the age of 7 the percentage was virtually 100. Clark indicated that "There is no doubt that children learn the prevailing social ideas about racial differences early in their lives. Not only are they aware of race in terms of physical characteristics such as skin color, but also they are generally able to identify themselves in terms of race." It appears, according to Clark, that the dominant factor in self-identification for the black child between the ages of 5 and 8 is race. While less than half of the Jewish children, 30% of the white Catholic children and 27% of the white Protestant children in Clark's sample used religioun for self-identification, no black child identified himself in religious terms. Clark concludes, "In these tests, no Negro child identified himself in religious terms. This fact probably indicates that for the Negro child at these ages the dominant factor in self-identification is skin color. The impact of their minority status as determined by skin color is so great that it precludes more abstract bases for self-identification." During his experiment Clark made the following four requests of the children:

77

1. Give me the doll that you like to play with or the doll you like best.
2. Give me the doll that is the nice doll.
3. Give me the doll that looks bad.
4. Give me the doll that is a nice color..

In response to these requests a majority of the black children between the ages 3 and 7 preferred the white doll and rejected the brown doll.

In addition to the "dolls" experiment Clark gave his sample of children a "coloring test." The investigator conducting the test gave each child a sheet of paper with drawings of a leaf, an apple, an orange, a mouse, a boy, and a girl, plus a box of twenty-four crayons which included brown, black, white, yellow, pink and tan. Each child was tested alone and asked to color the leaf, apple, orange, and mouse. If the child responded correctly, it was assumed that he knew what colors things really are. If the child was a boy, the investigator then said: "See this little boy? Let's make believe he is you. Color this little boy the color you are." After the child responded, he was told: "Now this is a little girl. Color her the color you like little girls to be." Only those children between 5 and 7 seemed consistent enough to be analyzed. Clark found that all the very light skin black children colored the figure representing themselves with white or yellow crayon; 15% of the medium-brown skin children and 14% of the dark-brown children colored their figures white or yellow or some unusual color such as red or green. This occurred despite the fact that these same children accurately colored the leaf, the apple, the orange and the mouse. Clark interpreted this as an "indication of emotional anxiety and conflict in terms of their own skin color. Because they wanted to be white, they pretended to be." He also found that "When these children were asked to color the child of the opposite sex the color they preferred, 48% of them chose brown, 37% white, and 15% a bizarre or irrelevant color. It is significant that 52% of these children refused to color their preference either brown or black. This finding supported the conclusions of the "dolls" experiment, " ... in which 60% of these children preferred the white doll or rejected the brown doll." After administering the "coloring test" to southern black children Clark found that in marked contrast to their northern counterparts 80% of the southern children colored their preferences brown (36% for northern black children); 20% of the northern black children colored their preferences in a "bizzare" color as compared to only 5% of southern black children. The southern children seemed concerned with the prettiness or ugliness of a particular color while the northern children seemed concerned about the desirability of a particular color. It was noted that only among the northern black children were there open demonstrations of intense emotions in the reaction to the "dolls" and "coloring" tests. The southern black children were "much more matter-of-fact" in their reactions. Clark rejected the idea that the demonstrative behavior on the part of the northern black children indicated more personality damage for these children than it did for the southern black children. He viewed the demonstrative behavior of the northern children "... as an attempt on their part to assert some positive aspect of the self." He viewed the apparent emotional stability of the southern black children as "... indicative only of the fact that through rigid racial segregation and isolation he has accepted as normal the fact of his inferior social status. Such an acceptance is not symptomatic of a healthy personality."

We think Clark's last interpretation was specious. The northern black child who inhabited a far more "schizmic" world (re: our no. 1 variable in chapter two) due to its hypocritical, quasi-integrated nature, reflected the confusion and emotional upheaval brought on by such an existence. He reflected the "identity crisis" that is characteristic of such circumstances. The southern black child who lived in an almost totally black world and who having accepted segregation as a fact was logically more prone to accept his racial identity as a fact and to be less confused about it. The southern child it seems may have been far more realistic than his northern counterpart. To accept one's skin color does not mean that one accepts one's "inferior social status" anymore than to reject one's skin color means' the opposite. To be in emotional turmoil about one's racial identity, i.e., what color one is, is not necessarily a positive statement about one's personality. Despite what racial conditions inhere, not to know or to misconstrue one's skin color is not a sign of health. The knowledge and acceptance of one's physical self, regardless of how that self has been maligned, seems an assertion of some positive aspect of the self.

While Clark's study is by some standards "dated" (it was done in 1950) its implications concerning the effects of "schizmic" living vs. segregated living on black racial identity, is of enduring value. The fact that the kind of children studied by Clark are now young parents (the oldest being between the ages of 31 and 33 and the fact that the "black is beautiful" revolution did not become influential until the late '60s and early '70s) themselves, lends currency to his work. The "scared" children of Clark's study are the "scared" parents and young adults of today. Most importantly, Clark's interpretations of his findings made the healthy self-identity and self-acceptability by blacks contingent on the acceptance by whites of blacks and the full integration (with black becoming colorless) of blacks into white society. Thus black self-love could only be made possible through full white acceptability. It was these interpretations and implications in Clark's studies which contributed so much to the Supreme Court decision of 1954 which in turn led to the brutal (and in large number of cases futile) integration struggles that continue up to today. The point of view that black self-love and acceptance and black mental health in general can only or best be achieved through full white love and acceptance of blacks is still a potent view in the black community (re: the NAACP, a large segment of the black middle class and black integrationists in general).

The varying effects of "schizmic" living which we have indicated is more prevalent in the black middle class, and "restricted" living which we have indicated is more prevalent in the black lower classes, on racial identification and the differences between the "schizmic" northern black child and the segregated ("restricted") southern black child of Clark's studies on this same factor, are supported by a 1971 study by Judith Porter (6). Porter found that among black social classes the middle class black child showed a "high rate of rejection of both other blacks and either rejection or ambivalence toward his own racial membership." In terms of their own self-identification, Porter found that black working class (highest of all) and the black lower class (close to the working class score) manifest significantly higher brown preference when compared to the black middle class child. She also made the interesting finding that ". . . though the ADC (here representing the lower class blacks—author) subjects show almost as much white preference as the middle class, their self-identification results are more similar to those found for the working class."

The middle class results found by Porter's study can be explained by the black middle class's "schizmic" tendencies and its "without-group" orientation, i.e., the wish of this class to attain full acceptance and status outside its own group in the larger white dominated society. In addition to the wish this group tends to measure itself according to white standards and values and to compete directly against the whites (despite the anxiety-producing side-effects of such competition creates in such blacks). The failure of the black middle class to find full white acceptance and the obvious reason for this failure being their blackness makes the members of that class more prone to reject their color which is seen as the source of their failure. To a large degree the black middle class is dependent on the white middle class for affirmation of its status and for its self-acceptance.

The black working class because it is mainly dependent on the black middle and lower classes for affirmation of its status and self-acceptance is relatively independent of white middle class standards and values as a means of gauging itself. This "independence" permits this group to have a more positive self-identification and self-image than either of the other two groups (according to Porter, children from this group were more vocal in expressing hostility toward whites than the other groups). The black working class unlike the black middle-class is "within-group" oriented, i.e., it tends to affirm its status more within the black world than does the middle-class black group.

Because of its restricted living circumstances and its on-bottom position which forces it to intermingle and compete against the two black classes above it, the black lower class can little deceive itself about its racial identification. However, its powerlessness to attain status even within the black community let alone the white community makes "preferring to be white"

80

the only logical means of rising above the black middle and working classes and if desired, being fully accepted by white society. The apparent contra diction that Porter noted about the black lower class child may also be due to the possibility that the black lower class identifies ultimate power and status with "whiteness" (in this sense it is similar to the black middle class) and wishes to be identified with the power and status "whiteness" symbolizes without, as is the case with its more schizoid middle class counterpart, denying the reality of its skin color. The children of these three black classes reflect the orientations of the class from which they come.

Despite the class differences found by Porter we must remember that they are all relative. They are also differing by significant degrees "without-group" oriented. As we have stated before all blacks without regard to social status are "white-centered." As we shall see later on in this book this "white-centeredness" helps to maintain black feelings of inferiority, feelings of powerlessness in many areas of functioning including cognitive-academic functioning.

In regards to the without-group orientation of blacks a study by Mary Ellen Goodman (3) is of particular interest. (We should mention that Goodman in another study (3), which supported Clark's findings, found that black children between ages 3 and 4½, when asked questions about their racial identification, reacted with uneasy, tense, evasive behavior. Such was not the case among the white children studied.) In her study of the racial orientations of black and white children Goodman reached the following conclusions:

We found the Negro children to be basically out-group oriented—to share a "sense of direction" *away* from Negroes and *toward* whites. But the white children are in-group oriented; their basic orientation —their "sense of direction" is *around* within the orbit of the white world and quite without the racial self-doubt and self-concern which is in the Negro children . . .

The . . . Negro children showed their basically *out-group orientation* in an inclination toward out-group preference, friendliness toward out-group (coupled with *inclination toward in-group neutrality)* or even antagonism (author's emphasis), and inferiority (or neutrality), *but never superiority* (author's emphasis) vis-a-vis the out-group. Our white group presented a strikingly different orientational picture both generally and specifically.

The chart below schematically summarizes Goodman's findings.

Nature of Orientation in Negro and in White Children

Type of Orientation	Negro(%)	White(%)
In-Group Affinity	72	97
Out-group Affinity	28	3
In-group Preference	26	92
Out-group Preference	74	8
Superiority toward Out-group	0	48
Neutrality toward Out-group	43	52
Inferiority toward Out-group	57	0
Friendly toward Out-group	84	56
Indifferent toward Out-group	5	11
Antagonostic toward Out-group	9	33
Friendly toward In-group	56	93
Indifferent toward In-group	20	7
Antagonistic toward In-group	24	0

(adapted from Goodman)

Goodman also noted that "... for the whites growing race awareness and in group orientation brings a greater sense of security in their racial status." The whites were complacent about their racial self. This was not the case with the black children who showed a growing out-group orientation and a growing sense of insecurity in terms of their racial status, "*a heightened emotionality* and a greater sense of personal involvement and *personal threat*." (author's emphasis)

We believe Goodman's study of some twelve years ago still is valid today despite the "black revolution" (which for many blacks is a reaction-formation) due to the similarity of the American racial climate then and now, and due to the fact that black group disorganization, family disorganization, intra-group aggression, dependency orientation, academic problems, etc, have not changed significantly since that time. And it is now established that these factors just listed are in part the result of the feelings and attitudes studied by Goodman. Goodman's study clearly indicates that black children even at the age of four follow the racial out-group orientation of their parents and of black society in general. We must not overlook the crucially important fact that this out-group orientation is accompanied by feelings of insecurity emotionality, and other psychological factors which serve to vitiate smooth cognitive-personal-social functioning. We find most intriguing the total absence of feelings of superiority in the black children studied by Goodman. This finding would seem to imply that as a result of the current and historical repression by white people of black assertiveness and the racial brainwashing blacks have had and are receiving concerning their "inferior" abilities, that due to the fact that any real display of black equality with, let alone superiority to, whites has been and is met with white psychological, socioeconomic and physical violence (perhaps with the exception of these types of displays by blacks in sports and entertainment), the black parent has learned to repress such feelings within himself and consequently represses such feelings within his child. Parental repressing of racial superiority in their children is commendable but to "to throw the baby out with the wash water", i.e., to destroy the child's sense of equality is to commit a grievous error.

Implications and Recommendations. The history of the black man in America ·can easily be conceived as the history of the world's most massive and successful experiment in "behavioral modification" and "attitude change." Through a systematic program which punished or left unrewarded initiative, originality, independence, cohesiveness, and industry among black people, and which rewarded black servility, docility, self-abnegation, demonstrated belief in their inferiority, dependence, the love of "white" and belief in its inherent "rightness" and the hatred of "black" and belief in its inherent "wrongness." This punishment-reward system effectively developed a people and culture which fearfully avoids initiative, originality, independence, co-

83

hesiveness, and industry in terms of its own self-interest, a people in whom values have almost been completely extinguished. This system has affected attitudes of self-hatred, lack of self-confidence, etc., in black people. The consequences of such a thorough behavior modification program has been that the black parent, in an effort to socialize his child to survive in a "white" world, and as a result of his own "training", uses a similar behavior modification program to "train" his children. The "programmed" black parent programs his children in his image. Thus, the black child learns early in his life, as his parents learned before him, that self-interested and group-interested initiative, originality, independence, and industry, interests which when not placed in the service of whites is "dangerous" and unrewarding. He early learns the same thing about self-love, self-confidence, etc. He also learns that ideas, values, behavior patterns, beliefs, etc, which have not earned the "white seal of approval" are "invalid" and cannot be trusted. Thus, he comes to believe his own self-generated ideas are worthless and invalid unless approved by whites and he therefore learns to "look up" to whites and "look down" on himself. Consequently, early in his life the black child becomes out-group (white) oriented. This type of orientation is detrimental to blacks in every area of functioning. In an effort to more positively "re-program" our children we recommend the following:

1. Follow the outline of the recommendations made in the previous chapter.
2. The black parent should be educated concerning the white behavior modification program in depth and taught how to counteract its effects in themselves and their children. This requires diligent and thorough analysis as the methods and effects of our behavior modification have been and are very subtle.
3. Black children should be trained from the very early years for mastery.
4. The black child should be exposed to situations where black adults exert creative authority, knowledge, initiative and leadership.
5. Have no fear of talking to the child earnestly about race. Talk to him in a "man-to-man" fashion.
6. Teach the child to see the race problem as a "white" problem, as the result of white feelings of inferiority and the white need to subjugate blacks for their economic benefit. Enlist the child early in the battle against dominance by whites (without at the same time teaching race hatred) and emphasize that knowledge, initiative, independence, self-confidence, self-love, group-love and love of all Mankind are his major weapons against such dominance.
7. Do not degrade blackness, take it vainly, or permit anyone else to do it in front of your child. Do not permit your child to use the term "black" as part of invective or as a preface to a degrading statement about another black person.

8 Maintain consistent, positive cutaneous communication with your black child. Genuine, warm, supportive love which complements his blackness will go a long way in creating and sustaining self-love in your child.

9. Have your child understand that he is loved first of all for his own black self and will be loved unconditionally but at the same time reward signs of initiative, healthy assertiveness, originality, etc., and punish or do not reward or rationalize docility, self-doubt, feelings of inferiority, etc, which the child may have come to believe are the result of his being black.

10. Teach him to love his people and to seek them out as objects of his love and loyalty while at the same time teaching him to love and respect other ethnic groups and individuals.

11. To be pro-black is not to be anti-white. To love oneself does not mean to hate others. It must be understood clearly that the genuine love of one's own ethnic group is the basis for the love of oneself, for the love of others and the basis for a loving personality in general.

REFERENCES

1. Clark, R., & Clark, M. Racial Identification and Preferences in Negro Children. In *Readings in Social Psychology,* Maccoly, E., Newcomb, T., & Hartley, E. (eds.). New York: Holt, 1958.
2. Erikson, E. *Childhood and Society.* New York: Norton, 1950.
3. Goodman, E. *Race Awareness in Young Children.* New York: Macmillan, 1964.
4. Harrison-Ross, P., & Wyden, B. *The Black Child: A Parent's Guide.* New York: Wyden, 1973.
5. Pederson, F., & Wender, P. Early social correlates of cognitive functioning in six-year-old boys. *Child Development, 39,* 1968.
6. Porter, J. *Black Child, White Child: The Development of Racial Attitudes.* Massachusetts: Harvard, 1971.
7. Smart, M., & Smart, R. *Children: Development and Relationships.(New York: Macmillan, 1972.*
8. White, B. An overview of the project paper presented at the meeting of the society for Research in Child Development, Santa Monica, California,

PSYCHOGENIC BRAIN DAMAGE AND THE BLACK CHILD.

Psychogenic Brain Damage and the Black Child: ' The behavior of human. beings whether psychological, social, cultural, lingual or intellectual, is to a very great degree determined by the unique structure and organization of the human central nervous system. This system which consists of the human brain and spinal cord, is the true foundation of Man's superior standing above the other members of the animal kingdom. While the human brain and spinal cord, especially the brain which organizes and structures individual and group physical, social and intellectual behavior, are fundamentally the product of genetic interaction during various stages of development, we must not over-look the extremely important role played by non-genetic physical and social factors in these areas of human behavior. We've already discussed the effects of the physical prenatal and postnatal environmental factors such as adverse intrauterine conditions, genetic defects, ingestion of harmful substances during pregnancy, and malnutrition, on the development of the brain and the behavior it mediates. Therefore, after a brief review of the early development of the brain we will concern ourselves with the influence of psychosocial factors on the structure and organization of the system.

During the period of the 3rd to 6th months of prenatal life the size of the fetal brain increases very rapidly. This remarkable increase in brain size is due chiefly to the rapid multiplication of the number and size of the fetal brain cells. The structure and organization of the newborn's brain is very in-complete relative to its adult structure and organization. Though the new-born's brain size exceeds 10% of his entire body weight (as compared to approximately 2% of his adult body weight) it is not until "by the end of infancy, at about two years of age, the relative size and proportions of the brain and its sub-divisions are essentially similar to those of the adult brain (12)."

The brain of the newborn is more fully developed in its lower and posterior regions i.e., regions chiefly responsible for regulation of the body's autonomic and sensory functions respectively, than in its frontal or anterior regions which are roughly responsible for skilled motor and intellectual behavior. The brain undergoes a two and one-half to threefold increase in size during the first year, increasing from a weight of some 350 grams at birth to about 1000 grams at the end of that period. This rapid increase continues until about the age of 2 years after which its growth rate slows down (12). Noback is fundamentally correct when he states that:

The genetic code, acting through its biochemical control system, is instrumental in establishing the complex structural functional matrix of the nervous system as expressed in the patterning of the nuclei, pathways, circuits, and synaptic connections.

However, the growth of the human brain during its early years involves more than its construction according the genetic blueprint.

What then, does the growth of the human brain during its early years entail? Ashley Montagu (11) answers this question very succintly:

This growth entails the forming of connections between nerve cells within the brain, thus enabling messages to be sent from the brain to the muscles, telling them how to move; from the skin and the inner organs to the brain, giving it information about feelings; and from one part of the brain to another, making possible the integration of different kinds of information and consequently such human qualities of mind as language, visual imagery, verbalizable emotions, and so on. These neural pathways are not formed automatically; rather, they develop as a result of experience which provides input and therefore stimulation to the brain's growth.

In the last sentence Montagu quite properly alludes to the fact that the structural, organizational and functional aspects of the brain are not completely determined by the genetic code, that the brain is highly plastic in nature, i. e., it is to a very significant extent structured and organized by social and psychological experience.

One of the most important properties of the human brain during development is its plasticity, or ability to change and be molded under the influence of the external environment. It is able to receive and use stimuli from the outside during its exceptionally long developmental period. These stimuli can actually cause both structural and functional changes, which will then affect the way the brain will respond to the same stimuli in the future. This is one of the ways in which learning takes place (Shenour, 17).

There is a substantial amount of experimental evidence which indicates that the external environment and the individual's experiential interaction with it bring about definite changes in brain structure and biochemistry and play a significant role in the formation of functional contacts between nerve cells in the brain (15, 15, 16). **The Brain As A Statistical Unit.** The brain in executing its control over behavior neither functions as a total unit with all of its parts equally involved or equally contributing to the behavior taking place under its direction nor is relevant behavior completely controlled by some isolated, independent area of the brain. The brain operates on a statistical basis, i.e.,the occurrence of a particular behavioral act, whether physical or mental, is the averaged outcome of the coordinated input of any number of brain regions or cells. E. Roy John in 1972 proposed a theory of brain function which concisely expresses the concept of the brain as a statistical unit (6) His theory which he calls "statistical configuration theory" proposes that:

...sensory information is diffusely available to most if not all brain regions, and movements can be initiated from a wide variety of structures. Information is represented, not by activity in a specific neuron or a selected pathway, but by the average temporal pattern of firing in anatomically extensive populations of neurons. The activity of any neuron, ... is only significant insofar as it contributes to the average behavior of the ensemble, to the statistical process. The difference between brain regions is not "all-or-none" qualitative mediation of specific sensory, motor or other functions but the "graded" quantitative representations of different functions...

A. R. Luria (7) in a 1970 article in the Scientific American magazine titled "The Functional Organization of The Brain" develops concepts related to those of John's statistical theory. He notes that at least three-fourths of the cerebral cortex of the brain have nothing to do with sensory or motor functions. That is, the parts of the brain mainly responsible for perception and movement comprise only a small part of the cerebral cortex. He therefore concludes that in these non-sensory and non-motor areas must be located the systems responsible for the higher, more complex behavioral processes.

Luria conceives of the brain as consisting of three major functional units—the first unit which "regulates the energy level and tone of the cortex, providing it with a stable basis for the organization of its various processes" is located in the lower part of the brain. The second unit which plays the major role in analyzing, coding and storing information is located in the back half of the brain and the third unit is involved in "programming, regulating and verifying mental activity," is located in the front half of the brain. This unit which consists primarily of the frontal lobes is also "involved in the formation of intentions and programs for behavior." They accomplish this in part through the activation of the brain and the regulation of attention and concentration. Electrical studies of the brain indicates that whenever mental activity is engaged in a complex of electrical excitations occur in the frontal regions of the brain and that these excitations disappear when mental activity is ended. According to Luria the relationship between the three functional units of the brain and their constituents is such that —

It is clear that every complex form of behavior depends on the joint operation of several faculties located in different zones of the brain. A disturbance of any one faculty will affect the behavior, but each failure of a specific factor presumably will change the behavior in a different way... One should therefore expect that lesions of the structures involved might result in changes in the behavior, and that the nature of the change would vary according to the particular structure that is damaged.

Psychogenic Brain Damage. The principal concern of Luria's work to which we referred above was the effect of physical damage or malfunction in specific areas of the brain on behavior. We are not concerned here with the effects of physical damage of certain areas of the brain on behavior, but with the effects of psychological brain "damage" of these regions, particularly the frontal region, on behavior. For it is our contention that within certain sociocultural contexts, the presence or absence of certain psychological experiences can have the same effect on a person's behavior as actually physical damage to a particular area of the brain had occurred. In other words, poor programming of or socialization of the frontal regions of the brain produces behavior which is equivalent or similar to actual brain damage in the same regions.

The concept which we wish to develop here is similar to Ashley Montagu's (11) concept of "sociogenic brain damage" which he defines as follows:

Sociogenic brain damage refers to damage done to the maturation of the brain by depriving it of the social stimulation necessary for the development of those neural interrelations essential for successful mental functioning. By "successful" here I mean the ability to make the appropriately successful responses to the challenges of the social environment. It should be emphasized that by "damage" I do not mean that any nervous tissues are destroyed, but rather that normal growth and development of neural connections fails to occur in the absence of the necessary developmental stimuli. Just as in physical malnutrition nerve cells fail to grow and develop properly, so also in social malnutrition, where the physical nutrition may be quite satisfactory, there is a similar failure of neural growth and development.

* * * * * * * * * *

Sociogenic brain damage is a condition produced by impoverished social environments. There is reason to believe that poverty and the ghetto, often associated with both physical and social malnutrition, constitute a combination of conditions capable of producing severe failures in neural development with its attendant failures in learning ability...

Our concept of psychogenic brain damage concerns itself mainly with deleterious effects of the failure of properly programming, during sensitive periods of the child's development, of his frontal lobes which prevents him from behaving in an appropriate social and intellectual manner. While the failure of proper programming may or may not affect the normal growth and development of neural connections it certainly causes the frontal lobes to behave as if they have been incompletely developed, damaged or surgically disconnected from the rest of the brain which it is responsible for regulating so that certain behavioral ends may be achieved.

The Frontal Lobes. We've already indicated that some of the general functions of the frontal lobes include the formation of plans, intentions, of programs of behavior, the regulation of attention and concentration. The frontal regions are chiefly responsible for regulating the rest of the brain and body so that the individual may behave in a way appropriate for completing a planned program of action. They observe and evaluate the behavior as it is being performed and compares the completed behavior with the original plan of action, correcting as much as possible any deviations from the plan. The frontal lobes have the very important responsibility of allocating the appropriate mental and physical energy available to the individual so that set goals may be achieved. They also regulate the individual's attention and concentration so that he may not be easily diverted from his goals by irrelevant stimuli. Thus as Luria (8) concluded..."the frontal lobes of the brain are among the vital structures responsible for the orientation of an animal's behavior **not only to the present, but also to the future,** and are responsible for the most complex forms of active behavior."

The acts of programming, regulating and verifying behavior is accomplished by the frontal lobes with the aid of speech. Though instinctive, elementary forms of behavior take place with the aid of speech, complex and higher mental processes depend heavily on it.

As pointed out some time ago by Vygotsky (19) speech which is utilized by the frontal lobes is social in origin, i.e., it is introduced into the individual as a result of his interactions with others (and as a child, with his relations with adults). It therefore stands to reason that restricted, distorted, negative human relations, (particularly in the early years of development) and the speech engendered by these kinds of relations, when utilized by the frontal lobes as a means of regulating behavior brings about social and intellectual maladjustment.

Development of the Frontal Regions. The frontal lobes as compared to the rest of the human brain are relatively late in completing their development. It is not until the child reaches the age of four to seven years are they ready to function in a manner similar to that of adults. The rate of growth of the frontal regions increases sharply by age 3½ to 4 years. A second period of rapid growth occurs around the ages of 7 to 8 years. These two growth stages are one of crucial importance because prior to the first one the child finds it difficult to follow spoken instruction since he is unable to resist being easily distracted by new or irrelevant events occurring in his vicinity. New stimuli easily diverts him form his original plan of action usually initiated by parental instructions. Only when the first growth stage is reached is the child able to follow through on spoken instructions in a fairly reliable way without being easily distracted by irrelevant stimuli. During the first stage of rapid frontal region growth the child gains the ability to subordinate himself to the verbal demands and instruction of his caretakers. He begins to systemize these parental instructions and use them in regulating his own mental and physical behavior. He now gains the ability to recall earlier parental instructions, to order their fullfillment in terms of his immediate or future behavior.

It is not until the second and final period of rapid frontal region growth (shortly before entering school) that the child acquires an effective and reliable, socially-organized ability to focus his attention and effectively resist the distracting influence of irrelevant elements in his environment. The child by then has reached a higher level of behaving which is subordinated to the spoken demands or demands of adults and his own internalized speech.

Thus, it should now be apparent that the demands, instruction, values, etc., of parents and society begin to have major impact early on the child's behavior and his ability to control his own behavior early in his life. The ability to set goals, to follow instructions, to not be distracted by irrelevant occurences, begins in earnest to develop around age 3, and continues to develop rapidly through the preschool period at about age 7 or 8. This ability which is handled by the frontal regions is aided importantly by the kinds of parental instruction the child receives from other adults and peers in his environment. And language is one of the principal means by which instructions are given to the child.

It would be mistaken to suppose that verbal intercourse with adults merely changes the content of the child's conscious activity without changing its form.

Intercommunication with adults is of decisive significance because the acquisition of a language system involves a reorganization of all the child's basic mental processes; the word thus becomes a tremendous factor which forms mental activity, perfecting the reflection of reality and creating new forms of attention, of memory and imagination, of thought and action. (Luria and Yudovich, 9)

Since the frontal lobes mediate purposeful, goal-oriented and intellectual behavior and does so through the medium of language, the failure to properly instruct the child how to behave in a socially acceptable manner, the failure to instruct him in terms of definite, productive cultural norms, to supply him with an adequate vocabulary, to instruct him in socially acceptable ways of thinking, to teach him how to set goals and follow through on them, to give a positive image of himself and his ethnic group, to expand his views and experiences, all of these things which too often happen to black children, is tantamount to severely damaging the frontal lobes of these children. It behoves the alert black parent who is concerned about the successful social and academic adjustment of her child but cannot wait for the child to enter school so that he may learn to behave in a socially appropriate manner. If the child is not properly oriented by the time he begins school his chances of making a successful social and personal adjustment are significantly reduced and it will be more difficult after that time to normalize his behavior.

We have discussed psychogenic brain damage, particularly damage to the frontal lobes. We have asserted that psychogenic brain damage somewhat parallels actual physical brain damage. What then, we may ask, are the symptoms of frontal lobe brain damage? This is a very complex question and we will therefore not attempt to answer it in detail. However, we will list some of the symptoms of what is referred to as the "prefrontal syndrome" (a syndrome produced by extensive cutting of the nerve fibers running from the lobes to other parts of the brain or produced by lesions in those areas) - the inability in some people to synthesize information, "to maintain an energetic, goal-directed line of thought and behavior(18),"!lack of ability not to become distorted by irrelevant or immediate stimuli while pursuing a goal, blunting of of the mind in general, lack of motivation, indifference, apathy, loss of "some of the very qualities that make them human: sensitivity, imagination, the ability to plan (14)," irresponsibility, social behavior, impaired judgement, reduced creativity, inability to perform tasks which involve delayed gratification under ordinary conditions, difficulty in solving verbal problems. Luria (10) sort of sums these symptoms up in his description of a patient who suffered from frontal lobe injury:

"... the patient begins to lose his stable system of interests and becomes indifferent, and his motives become narrow and primitive. He loses his intentions which he has formed; ideas coming into his head are transitory and put into operation with difficulty, or they easily disappear. This inability to concentrate on an internal intention, and the absence of persistent goal-directness are among the most characteristic features of behaviour in lesions of the frontal lobe.

All-too-often we observe the symptoms which are characteristic of patients who suffer from frontal lobe damage also characteristic of much of the behavior of the inhabitants of the numerous black ghettoes of American towns and cities. When we stop to think about this situation we soon realize that these people not unlike physically brain damaged patients have had their brains damaged by the psychological battering they have received at the hands of slavery, jim crowism, negative racial propaganda, poor schools, ignorance, malnutrition, and a hundred other evils related to white racism, bigotry and colonialism. However, more than these things it is the uncertainty of black life in America, the confusion among black parents as to theirs and their children's future, the marginality of being black in America, the lack of being an intimate and accepted part of a definite culture (blacks not fully having their own culture nor being fully members of the larger culture - they're "betwixt and between") the lack of a true black sense of self and identity, inability of blacks to control their own destiny and that of their children, which damages the brains of black American youths. These factors make it difficult for many black parents to properly program and orient their children and thereby equip the controlling parts of their brain (the frontal regions)-so that their children's present and future behavior can be of positive personal and social value. Under current conditions it is difficult for many black parents to full-heartedly reinforce the aspirations of their children and thereby solidly instill in their children that definite sense of direction and high motivation which is so vital for academic and social success in America. This is the major reason that a strong sense of black identity and culture is so necessary for the mental health of black children and in turn the social health of America.

The "Split Brain." It is common knowledge that the brain consists of two apparently symmetrical parts. These are referred to as the left and right hemispheres. Though both hemispheres possess an apparent anatomical similarity, each being practically the same size and exhibiting the same general appearance to the eyes, recent research (4,13) has shown that there exists some intriguing and vast psychological differences between them.

Some years ago in an effort to alleviate the suffering of some patients who were prone to having severe epileptic seizures, a technique was devised which involved the cutting in half a wide band of nerve fibers connecting the two cerebral hemispheres called the **corpus callosum**. The problems ailing the epileptic patients were significantly relieved and they continued to function in their daily lives as normally as people who had theirs still connected. But it became apparent after careful experimentation and testing of "split brain" patients that the two hemispheres operated according to very different plans and dealt with the world in very different ways. It became dramatically apparent that the two hemispheres were not mirror images of each other. Unfortunately the scope of our present study will not allow us to detail the exciting facts revealed as a result of the testing of "split brain" patients. Therefore, we must satisfy ourselves with only listing some of the functions of each hemisphere.

Generally it has been found that the left hemisphere specializes in functions which underlie the use of mathematics, language, scientific concepts, writing and logic. It deals with the world in a rational, verbal, analytical, well-ordered sequential way. It literally is that part of the mind which analyzes the world into many parts and is concerned with the lawful relationships between those parts. It generates mental concepts, classes and stratas.

The functions of the right hemisphere are generally opposed to those of the left. It specializes in those functions which underlie the appreciation of music, art and dance. It is concerned with perceiving things as a whole, it tends to ignore parts, to concern itself with fantasy, sensuality and utilizes intuition as its chief mode of knowledge. It deals with concrete objects in physical space instead of conceptual objects in mental space as does the left hemisphere. Unlike the left hemisphere it tends to be receptive and is therefore more subject to the influence of suggestion.

Normally we use both hemispheres of the brain in a more or less complementary fashion. However, it appears that early in life individuals begin a continued use of one hemisphere more so than the other. Thus, it seems that people can be generally classified in terms of which hemisphere dominates their behavior hence we have "left-hemisphere types" and "right-hemisphere types." These types are characterized by the functional orientation of their predominnant hemisphere.

What hemispheric type the individual becomes seems to be determined by his personal, social, and cultural experience. At some point early in the life of the individual one hemisphere's functions becomes inhibited, repressed, or suppressed relative to the other. At that point the individual begins to behave as if his hemispheres were surgically disconnected or not in full and equal communication with each other (2). The individual who becomes too one-sided in the use of his hemispheres may develop a narrow personality and point of view. Which hemisphere becomes dominant in the life of the individual seems to depend on which of them has been the most successful in gaining for the individual positive rewards or the one which helps him to avoid negative experiences (3). It is possible and does happen that the two hemispheres with their two different approaches to the world often conflict with each other.

It appears that what applies to individuals here applies equally as well to groups of people. That is to say, just as one can classify individuals as left or right hemispheric types, groups can likewise be classified. The social, cultural and historical experience of a people can apparently cause them to predominantly utilize the functions of one hemisphere in deference to the other. The fact that the history of the black man in American has been one in which he is punished, ignored, or not rewarded by the dominant white society for exhibiting those things which characterize left hemispheric predomination such as assertiveness, intellectuality, independent and analytic thinking, etc., and his rewarding and encouraging those things which characterize the predomination of the right hemisphere such as. passivity, anti-intellectuality. sensuality, dancing, singing, entertaining, etc., might help to explain the following finding (14):

"Most people are dominated by one mode or the other," observes Dr. Ornstein. They either have difficulty in dealing with crafts and body movements, or difficulty with language." Culture apparently has a lot to do with this. Children from poor black neighborhoods generally learn to use their right hemisphere far more than their left and later **do badly on verbal tasks.** Other children, who have learned to verbalize everything, find this approach a hindrance when it comes to copying a tennis serve or learning a dance step. Analyzing these movements verbally just slows them down and interferes with direct learning through the right hemisphere. (Emphasis by author).

While the ideas and implications developed above might be branded as tentative and tenuous it is undeniable that the historical experience of blacks in America has been such that they are literally   forced to function with only "half a brain." Of course, whites in America also function with only half their brain also - the half opposed to that half used by blacks. Only the rewarding of their children by black parents and the black community for intellectual achievement, the sincere encouraging of conceptual thinking from the early years of their lives. can intellectual achievement become an intergal part of their way of life.

REFERENCES

1. Bennett, E., et al, Chemical and Anatomical Plasticity of Brain. Science, October 30, 1964.
2. Galin, D., The Two Modes of Consciousness and the Two Halves of the Brain. In *Symposium on Consciousness.* Ornstein, R., ed. New York: Penguin Press, 1977.
3. Gazzaniga, M., Changing Hemisphere Dominance by Changing Reward Probability in Split-Brain Monkeys. Experimental Neurology, Vol. 33, 1971.
4. Gazzaniga, The Split Brain In Man. Scientific American, August, 1967.
5. Greenough, W. Experiential Modification of the Developing Brain. American Scientist, Vol. 63, Jan. – Feb., 1975.
6. John, E., "Multipotentiality" A Statistical Theory of Brain F nction –Evidence and Implications. Private copy.
7. Luria, A., The Functional Organization of the Brain. Scientific American, March, 1970.
8. Luria, *The Working Brain*- An Introduction To Neuropsychology. Maryland: Penguin Books, INc., 1973.
9. Luria, and Yudovich, F., (Speech and the Development of Mental Processes in The Child. *Maryland: Penguin Books, Inc.,* 1971.
10. Luria, Valenstein, E., *Brain Control*- A Critical Examination of Brain Stilulation and Psychosurgery. New York: John Wiley and Sons, 1973.
11. Montagu, A., *Culture and Human Development- Insights into Growing Human.* New Jersey: Prentice Hall, 1974.
12. Noback, C., *The Human Nervous System.* New York: McGraw-Hill, 1967.
13. Ornstein, R., *The Psychology of Consciousness.(Maryland: PenguinBooks. 1975.*
14. *Pines, M.* The Brain Changers: *Scientists and the New Mind Control. New York- New American Library, 1973.*
15. Rosenzweig, M. et al, Brain Changes in Response to Experience. Scientific American, Vol. 226, Feb. 1972.
16. Rosenzweig, Effects of Evironment on Development of Brain and Behavior. In *Biopsychology of Development. Tobach, E., ed. New York: Academic Press, 1971.*
17. *Shneour, E., (The Malnourished Mind.* New York: Anchor Press/Doubleday, 1974.
18. Valenstein, E., *Brain Control:* A Critical Examination of Brain Stimulation and Psychosurgery. New York: John Wiley and Sons, 1973.
19. Vygotsky, L., *Thought and Language.* Mass.: M.I.T. Press, 1962.

THE BLACK CHILD - THE ROLE OF PLAY IN DEVELOPMENT

Play is such a universal phenomeon among children until one is forced to assume that it stems from some intrinsic, innate need and serves some vital human function in children other than just that of a leisure time activity of little real value to the child or society. It apparently plays a part in the child's future development. Play provides an opportunity for the child to pursue his own inclinations in a relatively self-determined way and also provides the opportunity for the child to express, develop and evaluate his capacities, potentials, etc., not ordinarily expressed or explored. It is a child's way of dealing with reality, learning various ways of perceiving it, discovering its organization, determining his relationship with it and learning to master it and himself in the process. In play the child may freely explore reality, to accept it or reject it, to escape or distort it to suit his own interests, needs; wishes, and desires.

Freud (4) assumed that play was important to the child's emotional and social development and saw it as a means by which the child tests reality, learns mastery of the environment and as a means of developing fantasy and imagination. For Freud, play was principally an outlet for ideas and emotional needs unfettered by social restrictions and punishments. In play the child can assume various roles related to his or her family-community environment or related to his fantasies and creative imagination. By assuming the roles of adults through observation, imitation and practice, the child begins to understand the world of adults and begins to identify with that world. It is through these means that the child begins to understand the role of his parents, group, play in the world and begins to get some vague idea of the role he is expected to play, some idea of the social standing of his family, ethnic group, etc., with which he identifies. In play if he wishes or is encouraged to do so the child can reject those roles and expectations and explore by imaginative means ways of overcoming their limitations. The ways chosen if they become a part of the child's basic personality structure, lead to healthy social adjustment or social maladjustment.

Erikson, expanding Freud's views, sees play as important to the development of the ego, particularly in its efforts to integrate social realities with the child's own intrinsic self (3). Through play the child learns and develops adaptational tools to facilitate his coping with the world. For Erikson, play facilitates the child's developing ability to cope and adapt to the demands of external reality.

For Piaget (6)., play facilitates the child's intellectual and thought development. By means of play the child adapts himself to reality by acting out past and present experiences and thereby changing his perceptions and conceptions of his world.

Altogether the views of Freud, Erickson, and Piaget point to the fact that play provides the child with essential opportunities for learning and for healthy psychosocial development. It makes vital contributions to the child's development that cannot be assumed by other activities. Consequently, play-deprivation, the duration, quality and quantity of it, will significantly influence the cognitive, psychological and social development of the child. In interaction with a rich environment, i. e., an environment which gives the child's imagination ample exercise, range and flexibility, an environment which is relatively psychologically and physically unrestricted and allows the child's imagination to become a principal problem-solving, creative tool, adds significantly to his future characteristic adult personal and cognitive style (e.g., the flexibility of thought approaches, initiative, creativeness, lack of fear of new ideas, willingness to experiment, etc.)

Through participation in group games and sports the child establishes social relationships and learns social norms, rules, expectations and how to get along with others. It is here that the child develops a sense of limits, fair play, self-control, honesty, how to take defeat and how to fight against overwhelming odds and overcome them by using the legitimate rules laid down by himself and others. Thus group play serves a very important function in the child's moral development in that he learns to be responsive to peer group control, to heed instructions and to become one with others in working toward a socially acceptable goal. The child who is severely restricted in his play activity with other children and adults is quite likely to suffer from personal and/or social handicaps as an adult.

There are a number of different forms of child's play which varies according to the child's chronological, physical, social, mental and emotional development. The forms we are concerned with here are the forms which most clearly hinder or facilitate his future personal and social adjustment. In this regard we mention two other forms of preschool play that are important to the child's development - fantasizing and constructive.

Freud (4) saw child's play as an outcome of the child's fantasies, guided by his emotional needs. To a certain extent this is true. Daydreaming and fan-

99

tasizing are forms of thinking and mental play. In fantasy and daydreams the child assumes roles and does things not permitted or that cannot be fitted into other forms of play. They also serve an important adjustment function but can become a serious hindrance to social adjustment if they become the principal means of dealing with problems facing the individual.

At age five or six the child begins to construct objects and things according to preconceived plans and patterns. Provided the right materials are available the child can have optimal opportunity to develop his creative and constructive abilities. Constructive play is important to the child's creative abilities and to the development of achievement motivation. Children who possess the creative potential but who lack the relevant materials may suffer dissatisfaction and stunting of their creative and motivational growth. They may also lose or not properly develop the sense of initiative and feelings of satisfaction that can be derived from engaging in constructive activities and completing challenging tasks.

The child's life is not all playful physical activity. In this society a good deal of the child's time may be spent reading, looking through picture books, playing various sit-down games, playing with various toys and enjoying various spectator events such as t.v., movies, listening to the radio. Besides these activities the child likes to be read to or told stories to. All of these activities influence the child's behavior and development in numerous and complex ways. How much time the child spends in the various types of play activities are a function of socioeconomic, sociocultural factors as well as his own personal inclination and the number of play activities available to him. Social class to a degree determines what games will catch a growing child's fancy as well as to what types of play activities will generally not be available to him. It is well known that social class influences the kind of books the child reads, what he listens to on the radio, looks at on t.v., sees in the movies or theatre, the types of organizations he joins or helps form. Not only the quality of such activities are to a degree socioeconomically and socioculturally determined but so is the quantity of such activities determined by these factors. For instance, lower class children engage in less cultural activities, organized group activities, community supported activities such as music, art, dramatics, boys or girls clubs, scouting, etc., than their middle class counterparts. The lower class child will generally have less space to play in and fewer toys and games to play with.

Toys in many instances serve as the child's bridge to reality. They provide him with replicas of the adult world he will one day be a part of and allow him to be introduced to that world on his own terms, at his own pace, to get to know its interrelations and prepare to take part in it. The absence of toys may reduce the child's imaginative, cognitive, creative possibilities. A lack of basic constructive materials such as blocks, sand, hammer, nails, etc., may reduce the child's chances to engage in constructive play. A well-selected array of various toys will be quite adequate to satisfy the young child's short attention span and his need for variety. This situation is seldom fulfilled in the lower classes. The middle class child is more likely to be exposed to age-graded toys, construct units, toys which are designed to make strong demands on the child's intellect such as puzzles of various types, art and drawing toys, chemistry sets, modeling toys, and toys requiring a certain amount of technical facility, such as telescopes, microscopes, scientific sets, electronic sets. In this class category the child is exposed to more games with which he can share with adults, such as scrabble, monopoly, etc. The middle class child's play activities are therefore more likely to contain more elements of adaptive reality than that of the lower class child.

We do not wish to leave the impression here that the middle class child does not play hop-scotch, tag, roughhouse, stickball, etc., just as does his lower class counterpart. For in our culture all classes of children play many games that fit no class distinction. However, it is the variety of games available, the relative amounts of time allotted to certain games and play activities, the motivations behind such activities that set the classes apart. Many of the childhood activities of the middle class child serve as transitional activities, activities that are continuous with the class lifestyle than is the case with the lower class child. For instance, engaging in certain hobbies, becoming interested in certain activities such as dramatics, spectator sports, etc., can serve as transitional means by which the child can smoothly enter into the adult world of work and leisure time activities that have positive value for the community.

Not only do play activities reflect the child's social status but also his intellectual orientation. What activities are engaged in and to what extent they are engaged in, and what objects are required to meet his needs during his leisure time differs according to the child's mental age. The normal or bright child shows a marked preference for play materials that lead to constructive play (clay, scissors, paint, blocks, with which he makes relatively complex designs, crayons for original drawings (5).

Being read to, particularly from more advanced books which provide information, is one of the main pleasures of the bright child.

Older bright children tend to involve themselves in more solitary and less socially active play activities and to involve themselves less in vigorous physical play activities than children of average intelligence.

The brighter child shows significantly less interest in games and sports than his less gifted counterpart. But they do show more interest in intellectual games and games that place some challenging demands of their intelligence or basic skills.

At every age level, highly intelligent children spend more time reading and show broader reading ranges and interests than children of average intelligence. They also differ in their reading preferences.

Gifted children enjoy reading dictionaries; atlases; encyclopedias; books on science, history, and travel; biographies; folk tales; informational fiction; poetry; and dramatic works. They dislike fairy tales and show relatively little interest in emotional fiction. They prefer detective stories to crude adventure and mystery and show an interest in romance even before the age of ten (Hurlock, (5).

The differences which were listed by Hurlock are also paralleled by similar differences regarding other leisure time activities between the bright child and the average child. For example, bright children show preferences for movies t.v. and radio programs markedly different from those of average intelligence We must not overlook the fact that there is a reciprocal relationship between the influence the child's intellectual orientation has on his leisure time activities and the influence these activities have on the intellectual development and orientation of the child. These types of activities will make the child brighter.

Reading of Comics. Though comics appear to play a less important role in child development today than in the past, we think they are prevalent enough to warrant a brief examination. "Comics are cartoon stories in which the story element is less important than the pictures . . . their appeal is principally emotional . . . The comics present a vivid and realistic picture of contemporary American life. Characters coming from every walk of life reflect the cultural patterns of acceptance and rejection regarding ethnic groups" (5). Comics can serve as a first step to more serious reading. The child usually begins seriously reading the newspaper as a result of his earlier interest in comic strips. His daily reading of the comics establishes a basis for the daily reading of the paper as a whole. Sex and intelligence differences found in other areas also prevail here. For instance, boys and girls show different comic tastes. More comics and fewer books are read by slow learners. Slow learners read different types of comics than do their more advanced counterparts (1).

The child's interest in comics often is coincidental with a common hero-worshipping stage in his development, particularly during late childhood. Boys tend to identify with comic book heroes and are mainly interested in subject, action and plot that elevate masculinity, aggressive mastery of dangerous situations. Those comics which emphasize crime and violence, sports and athletics seem to be most attractive to boys (5). The interest of girls generally appears to be a greater interest in women, animal comics and less interest in adventure, mystery and thrillers than boys. Hurlock (5).while admitting that not all children read comics for the same reason, did identify certain universal trends among childhood comic readers. Quite frequently the child identifies with the characters which may be used as a means to solving emotional problems and the release of frustrations. The emotional nature of comics allow for a bit of catharsis and "comic relief" for the child.

The plot of the comics usually contains a simple moral lesson which the child may accept. The characters in the comics may come to represent certain facets of the child's personality and what he desires to be. "The characters do things that child himself would like to do, and they are brave, strong, and beautiful, with an unfailing ability to master difficulties" (5). Hurlock goes on to list a number of arguments in favor of the positive value of comics:

1. The comics constitute a kind of modern folklore, . . .
2. The comics supply to children of limited reading ability a reading experiences which is thoroughly enjoyable. They may be used to motivate the child in the development of his reading skill.
3. They stimulate the child to read further and may break down his resistance to reading if the material is presented as entertainment.
4. If children actually read the text of the comics, they will be introduced to a wide vocabulary, including words which they repeatedly encounter in other reading.
5. The comics offer an excellent technique for propaganda, especially anti-prejudice propaganda.
6. They serve as effective methods of simplified teaching.
7. They meet children's need for overcoming, in imagination, some of the limitations of their age and ability and for obtaining a sense of adventure denied them in real life.
8. To normal children, the comics offer the mental catharsis which Aristole claimed for the drama. Thus the readers are released from feelings of inadequacy and insecurity and from fear of aggression toward or from others.
9. They give the child pleasure by offering him a chance for identification.
10. Normal aggressive reactions find release in fantasies stimulated by comic books. Through identification with the characters in the comics, the child is able to adjust himself better to life.

More important than the comics themselves is what the child brings to the comic book reading situation and what he takes away from it. The child's personality and sociocultural-family background will interact with the comic material and will determine its ultimate effects. The discriminative child does not allow the comics to dominate or distort his sense of reality or proportions. He is able to cull the negative aspects of the comics and assimilate their positive aspects.

Movies. The effects that we listed concerning the comics on the child's mind are amplified greatly by the movies. In a sense movies are comic strips "come to life." Therefore their effects, though very similar in their essential nature to the comics, are by far more influential. Of crucial importance here, as in the comics, in evaluating the influence movies have on the personality of the child, is whether the child identifies with one or more of the characters on the screen and with what type of character he identifies as well as what needs the character vicariously satisfies in the child. The characters with which the child identifies become the vehicle for the expression of the child's needs, wishes and desires and the child vicariously shares his character's world, his experiences, defeats and triumphs. For the child who closely identifies with his favorite character life may be for him an imitation of the movies. Thus, the child of aggressive temperament or inclination, who closely identifies with an aggressive movie character is more likely to act-out his aggressive feelings as a result of this identification process. The aggressive subjugation of groups and character types with which the child does not identify or does not like will permit cathartic release for repressed aggressive feelings against those groups or character types. The sex, age and race of the character and whether the character's actions are relevant to his needs, aspirations, etc., are of critical importance in determining the child's identification process and its direction.

Similarities of the character's age, sex, race, etc., to the child's own physical and psychological characteristics will more likely positively influence identification with the character on the child's part. However, under special conditions the child may identify with characters who distinctly differ from him in race, age, sex, etc. This situation is more likely to occur when the child's own ethnic, sociocultural background are sources of self-hatred.

The movies serve a knowledge function as do the comics. The child assimilates, acts-out and practices what he sees and learns from the movies through dramatic play with his peer group. Through remembering and rehearsing in his mind the actions of his favorite characters and the unfolding of the filmed events, by acting-out the roles and ideas of his characters, the child learns new modes of thought, perception, and behavior. Or his current modes of behavior, perceptions and thought might be reinforced. This may not be advantageous in that the child's current behavior may be socially dysfunctional. Of course, as with the comics, the child is not passively influenced by what he sees. What he brings out of the movie experience depends largely on what he brings in. The child brings to the movies certain needs and a unique experiential background which functions as "filters" through which certain elements will not influence him in one way or another and other elements will not influence him at all. All-in-all, the child will interpret and react to the movies in terms of what he thinks of himself; what he thinks others think of him and expect of him; what his needs are; how his family and sociocul tural background have stereotyped the various roles displayed on the screen.

Television. Much of what we've said about movies also holds true for t.v. Again, it is what the child brings to the set that largely determines its influence on him, The well-adjusted child will not be harmfully influenced by t.v. Children whose environment and personality orientations predispose them toward social and personal maladjustment are more likely to be adversely influenced by t.v. To a significant extent it is not what is seen on the t.v. screen that adversely affects children but the disproportionate amount of time allotted to t.v. watching that is harmful. Overindulgence in t.v. watching may leave little time for the development of personal and social potentials, the development of good study and work habits, reading skills, and psychosocially realistic, relevant attitudes and beliefs. For the socially and personally predisposed child, " A constant television diet of crime, terror, and cruelty will, in time, blunt the child's sensitivities; he will consider antisocial and destructive behavior almost "normal." Furthermore, repeated exposure to crime and violence will eventually blunt the child's sensitivity to human suffering..."(5). t.v. is not all bad like the movies, and even more so, it can serve as a means by which the child gains knowledge, is introduced to new worlds and ideas, etc. It is not a question of whether the child should not watch t.v. but of balancing t.v. watching with other important activities.

With increasing age the child spends a substantial portion of his time listening to the radio. As a constant source of music it fulfills a function largely unfulfilled by t.v. or movies. However, in its potential to adversely affect good adjustment, study habits, work habits, etc., it can be as effective and in some cases even more so, as t.v. or films. The constant diet of music and messages radio instill in the minds of its young listeners by their repetitive nature can work against the best interest of the child. The hypnotic rhythms and romantic-erotic lyrics of the music broadcasted by "rock" stations if not listened to discriminately by the child, can become sources of addiction and escapism.

Play Activity and The Black Child. The general nature of the child's play acttivities reflect the general nature of the geophysical, psychosocial, and politico-economical environment in which it takes place. This is true for the black child. The three variables which we used to define the character of black psychosocial existence in general can be seen operating in the play activities of the black child.

Schizoid Play. In his dramatic and imitational play, play where he imagines himself the embodiment of some legendary, cultural, folk, comic-book, t.v. or movie hero, play during which the modes of behavior of these heroes and figures are imitated, the child tends to identify with the hero or figure copied. He tends to at times lose his own self-identity and merge totally with the hero he is imitating to such a degree that he becomes one with the figure imitated.

He literally becomes "dressed" in the skin of his hero and takes on his hero's mannerisms, attitudes and values. Temporarily, he *is* the heroes, the persons, he imitates and acts in their world of action. One of the results of such play behavior is that portions of the imitated behavior and the values, attitudes and standards they imply may become a permanent part of the child's personality and may influence his own behavior, values, attitudes and standards in both conscious and unconscious ways.

Since the cultural heroes, figures and their worlds they act in America are virtually all white, it means that when the American black child imitates and identifies with them and introjects the behavior, values, attitudes, etc., they imply, to the degree that such introjected behavior, values, attitudes, etc., do not "fit" within his own psychosocial reality and contains elements which degrade his own physical, cultural, ethnic self, his play activities are "schizoid" in nature. The black child whose imitative play is peopled by white heroes and figures imagines himself white during such play. He becomes a "black-white" personality. Thus, in early childhood the black child begins to identify with and imitate whites. It is the white heroes and figures which populate the black child's mind during imitative play which are "powerful," "invincible," "masterful." "smarter," etc. Commensurate black heroes and figures are absent. In this child's mind the attributes of his white imaginal heroes and figures may become attributes of whites in general and not the attributes of the black "heroes" and "figures" which are absent from his imagination. Under the influence of American racist culture the black child's imaginal and imitative play may surreptitiously lay the foundation for his own growing feelings of inferiority, his own self-hatred and rejection of his people. It may lead to his frustrated attempts to identify himself as white or to deny his blackness. We think figure 1, in chapter 3 attests to this situation. In light of our previous discussions we think that the black middle class child or the black child coming from families operating on "middle class" value-behavioral orientations.

Even if the black child rejects the use of white heroes and figures in his imaginal and imitative play due to the fact that such play is disapproved by peers and adults, the absence of comparable black heroes and figures or the imitation of and identification with socially dysfunctional or low-level black figures in his imitative play may lead to results similar to the ones we listed above. In addition the rejecting black child may suffer a poverty of imagination and imitation and thus may fail to develop in intellectual, creative. personality and social· potentials and fail to introject the positive behaviors, values, attitudes and standards that may come from imaginal and imitative play peopled even by white heroes and figures. When we speak of the "poverty of imagination" we are not implying an imagination poverty-stricken in its quantitative aspects. We are implying an imagination that lacks in its quali-

106

tative aspects, a breadth and depth, a richness and flexibility which will become the foundation of a well-adjusting personality and creative intellect. The "rejecting" type of child's imagination is probably more prevalent in the black lower classes. Overall, one could wager that the "split" in the black personality begins in the play of black children.

Frustrated Play. If the black and white cultures were in effect one, "colorless," or truly integrated the "schizoid" play of the black child would be of no moment. However this is not the case and there is the rub. The black child early begins to realize that the heroic and imitatable images which crowd his imagination are not members of his ethnic group and that such images of his ethnic group are not projected. If he does not wish to imitate white figures and yet no suitable substitutes among his own people are available, his play is likely to be frustrated and from an imaginal point of view, unfulfilling. Black child's play which fully "accepts" white images for identificative and imitative purposes or such play which "rejects" such images in the absence of viable black substitutes, leads to fantasy and imagination which are often dysfunctional for further positive personal growth and development. In the sense that the materialistic and positive imaginational objects necessary to serve as a bridge for the smooth crossing over from his world to that of adults, are absent or sparse, the black child's play is also frustrated, i.e., it is deflected from what should be its natural goals of reality testing, broad environmental mastery, ego strengthening, integrating of the self with social reality, the facilitation of intellectual and thought development.

Restricted Play. Through using his play to master his immediate environment and to adapt to that environment the black child adjusts to a social reality that is very often personally and socially dysfunctional. The restricted black lifestyle, especially of the black urban ghetto, when imitated by and identified with by black children during their play activities lays the basis for later personal and social adjustment problems in a world dominated by white middle class values, standards, etc., and managed by the members of this same class. Restricted black child's play is discontinuous with the broader society and therefore does not adequately prepare him to deal with that society efficiently. The overall pattern of familial and societal relation and organization serves as models during much of the childs imitational and dramatic play. If these models are negative, confused, maladaptive so will be the child's play which is built around them. Family and community confusion and disorganization which is so characteristic of much of black life that children's imitational activities modelled on such confusion and disorganization lead to later maladaptive behavior. When one observes black children's play in the urban ghetto it seems to contain remarkably few elements which one would regard as imitation of family relations. Mother-father relations seem not to be imitated to any great degree. Though this may be due to the absence of space and toys which would allow such behavior to take place un-

107

disturbed, it may also be equally likely that absence of fathers, the emotionally charged nature of the home environment, family role confusion, absence of identifiable mother or father occupational roles, that characterize so much of black family life may discourage black children's imitation of family relations as a means of avoiding the anxiety and confusion such imitation may engender. Consequently, urban black child's play seems to be centered around strictly physical activities such as running, playing ball, cycle riding, skip, etc. While these types of play activities assumes the greater part of the average child's play regardless of race it seems to take up a far greater part of the black child's play than is healthy for his all around development. This almost total involvement with hedonistic physical play leaves little time for the child to practice the assuming of various social roles, to reflect on social-emotional problems, to develop strategies and abilities important for efficient functioning in areas of life other than physical pleasure and exercise, e.g., reasoning skills, reading skills, etc.

In a sense one could say that the play of the black urban ghetto child is escapist in nature, i.e., in the sense that it does not allow the child to "playfully" deal with problems that will confront him in later stages of maturation, particularly during his school years and later adult life. His play takes him away from his "problems." We think the "escapist" tendencies of black children's play is reflected in part in the escapist pursuit of physical pleasure, in the face of family and community problems which needs solving, of a very large segment of the black adult population, especially black adult males.

Play Activities and The Black Child. As we intimated earlier in this chapter the child's toys and games in many instances serve as bridges to adult reality. Logically then, the paucity or absence of facilitating toys and games makes a little more difficult the child's entry into that reality. But this may not be significantly detrimental to the child's development as other compensating means usually are available and whatever "deficit" which may accrue from the absence or paucity of toys and games in childhood can be rather easily overcome in adulthood. Quite often it is not the absence of toys or games which sets the black child apart but his interest or lack of interest in certain toys, games and play activities and his attitude toward them. Playing with certain toys and games, such as tea sets, white dolls, periwinkle, etc., and developing certain leisure time activities and hobbies such as collecting and classifying objects of various types, working with constructo units, building crystal sets, making model toys of varying complexity, etc., may often be viewed by the black child as activities which are "white." Thus certain play and leisure time activities may take on certain sociocultural ethnic flavors and may be rejected or accepted by the child depending on his personal needs and desires and those of his parents and peers. Often games or activities which may involve reading, mathematical operations, sustain concentration, solitariness, are actively discouraged by the child's peer group. They may be tagged as "sissy" games by the boy's age mates. Games that would facilitate parent-child interactions are usually less encouraged in the black community. Thus, this type of interaction which can add measurably to the child's intellectual capacity is not often enough available to the black child. Games which involve parent-child participation also add markedly to the child's emotional stability, feelings of belongingness and security.

Often the black child's leisure time activities do not follow an age-graded developmental sequence as far as would be acceptable. His involvement in strictly physical activities and his relative lack of interest in hobbies, collecting, reading, etc, his relative lack of interest in "cultural" activities such as music, art, theatre-going, etc., and other activities which can continue into adulthood or which can lay the basis for adult leisure time activities and professional life, may bring about discontinuities in his life which may cause adjustive problems in school and adult life. What kind of leisure time activities as does the ghetto black child have to look forward to after he grows too old for stickball, tricycles, junk toys, and the like? All too often he only has to look forward to boredom, restlessness, idleness, the overcoming of which leads to vandalism and various forms of juvenile delinquency, or to an imitation of easily observed adult forms of leisure time activities such as becoming intoxicated, gambling, "running women," or "bullying" on the street corners for endless hours. Thus, the relative lack of "transitional" games, games which can be further elaborated in adult life lay the basis for much of black adult maladjustment or involvement in activities which prove detrimental to black family and community life.

In reviewing the play preferences of the bright child on page 103 , it becomes readily apparent that the sociocultural and economic factors influential in large segments of the black community operate against the black child of average or above-average intelligence. The overall interest and orientations fostered by such communities and which are reflected in the interests and orientations of their children's play work against the intellectual and pro-social development of their children.

Reading of Comics and The Black Child. Generally, the comics are written and designed for the white child in America. They principally concern themselves with the white world and indicate only a tenuous concern with the black world. While they may serve as a bridge to the white world and as a means for the black child to vicariously assimilate the knowledge and values of that world, they may also help to bring about a rejection or create a lack of interest in his own world. The absence of his own cartoon heroes may leave him with the impression that his people are not heroic, that they are "invisible," and not worthy of depiction. Thus, while assimilating the myths of other groups, he alienates himself from his own and thereby begins a process of self-alienation. More often than not the black child has an ambivalent attitude toward comics since he senses that the worlds of fantasy depicted there do not include him and quite often abandons the reading of comics very early. This may become the source of two major problems. His ambivalence or rejection of "white" comics means that he loses a source of learning about the archetypal values of the larger society and he may lose the opportunity to develop a reading habit. While the danger exists that in reading the "white" comics the black child may establish ultimately unhealthy identifications and assimilate attitudes and feelings detrimental to his self-esteem and positive self-image, to not read them may also place him in danger of losing a good source of inspiration, information, of new ideas, and as we just indicated, reduce his motivation to continue to read and develop his reading skills. Comic book reading, like reading in general count for too small a portion of the black child's growing activities. Through selected comics the black child may begin to develop word skills beyond those offered by his restricted urban environment.

However, the black parent must keep in mind the inimical aspects of the comic for her child and that the uncritical acceptance of these books by the child opens him to the propagandistic influence and the "schizmic" influences of these books that we alluded to at the beginning of this chapter. Because these books often do not enhance positive ethnic self-love and often work against it by consciously and unconsciously promulgating "white" values and perceptions, the black child may unwittingly assimilate those values and perceptions which are at odds with his own self-interest. The relative sparsity of black comics, particularly comics which seek to accentuate the positives of black culture, leaves the black child open to unconsciously developing feelings of inferiority. One wonders if the comics with their white heroes do not early begin to help instill a "black dependency syndrome" by implying through their stories and designs that "white will always win," "only whites can be true heroes," "mastery of the universe is whitey's destiny," "white people can solve all problems," "let whitey do it."

Utilizing white characters he has seen in the comics and more so, on t.v., the black child during fantasy and dramatic play may actually see himself as those characters and keep them constantly before his eyes as he plays and imagines. His imagination is not peopled by blacks like himself while he holds sway over all he surveys. It is he as a "white" hero that dominates, rules and conquers all. With this kind of imaginative play taking place in childhood there is little wonder that many blacks find it very difficult to imagine themselves as being active masters and progressive shapers of destiny and at the same time being fully black. A very large segment of blacks believe the world would fall into utter chaos and revert to the "dark ages" if the white man

110

were not present in it. One wonders how much the early fantasy life of black children contribute to such a myth. Under the present circumstances the thrills the black child garners from his imitations of white comic book characters and their t.v. counterparts are counterfeit at best. These imitations make it more and more difficult for him to separate his own reality and destiny from those of whites and simultaneously lay a foundation for a dependency-ambivalent attitude toward whites and a rejective-ambivalent attitude toward himself.

Speaking of reading in general, the child's early reading experiences will markedly influence his later reading behavior, in terms of both quantity and quality of reading. Although a child has learned to read relatively well in early childhood or more precisely, show a meaningful interest in reading, his reading behavior may be adversely affected by what reading materials are provided in his home, his familial-cultural attitudes toward reading, the attitudes of his peers and toward reading, the availability, adequacy and utilization of the public or school library. Of major importance in this regard is the child's socio-cultural and socio-economic background. The black child's reading activities are relatively unsupervised and under-encouraged when compared to the white child as is the lower class child's when compared to the middle class, regardless of race.

Generally, the black child is not exposed to an adequate amount of age-graded reading material. This is especially true for the black lower class child This child may have an adequate amount of story and picture books in early childhood but an inadequate amount of or an absence of books and reading materials appropriate for late childhood and early adolescence.

The black condition and all it implies works against good reading habits in the black child. Moreover, "the oral tradition" existent in black culture in general and in lower class subculture in particular, operates effectively against the acquisition and enjoyment of reading. The use of the written record as a source of communication, cultural transmission, information, learning and enjoyment is of relatively recent origin in much of African culture, especially western African culture from where originated the majority of American blacks (2). The black slave experience, though it did teach a few of the blacks to read did not lay a sound foundation for the establishment of a viable literary tradition among them. In fact, the African oral tradition was essentially continued and encouraged by the white society. Reading by a black was a punishable offense during "slavery time" and continued to be so for many, many years after slavery was abolished. Actually, until the very recent past reading was not encouraged among blacks by the dominant white society and was often punished, albeit not by "legal" means, especially when such reading threatened to undermine the ideology of white supremacy, to encourage black independent thought and action, and to encourage blacks to throw off the yoke of white domination. The development of reading skills among blacks was encouraged by whites for what amounts to basically utilitarian purposes—to serve the white man and his interests. Thus, blacks have been literally "conditioned" to avoid reading except when it is demanded of them, to not see reading as an exemplary source of enjoyment and as the major source of learning, communication and power. As we shall discuss in detail later on in this book, the largest source of information for blacks and the lower classes' information is carried by word of mouth. This oral tradition is passed on to the black child early in life.

A viable black literary tradition was and is also effectively discouraged by employment discrimination and the slowness of the black social mobility. It takes no great insight on the part of the black child to realize that the unskilled and semi-skilled labor which his parents provide and which he will most likely provide in turn, makes masterful reading a superfluous and frustrating activity. Even if the child had high aspirations he more often than not does not realize the relationship between the development of reading skills and the attainment of his aspirations. It goes without saying that in a society centered around a literary tradition a person or group without such will suffer a serious disadvantage and is bound to be maladaptive in such a society. This is the case with blacks in this country. In sum, as a consequence of the "black experience" in America the black parent does not adequately encourage and reward and demand the development of reading skills in their children. They are prone to see the teaching of reading skills as the responsibility of the schools and to underestimate the importance of their own influence in the development of these skills. Consequently, black children suffer from massive reading problems.

Blacks in general, as in the case with large segments of American culture also, are anti-intellectual. This is particularly true of the black lower classes and in a rather peculiar way of the black middle class. However, in the black ghetto culture this anti-intellectualism is often the cause of the ridiculing of the black child who persists in reading and who shows a strong literary interest. Peer group pressure often negates these orientations early in the child's life. Persistent reading may be viewed by the black child's peers as "acting white", strange, a sign of queerness and may create in the ridiculed child an identity problem and a problem of being accepted by his peer group. In opting for acceptance it may be necessary for him to reject reading as a major activity and forego its benefits. These factors along with others such as the fact that historically and currently the white society has been and is unenthusiastic, to say the least, about the development of a literary tradition among blacks, has aided and abetted the oral orientation among blacks and retarded the development of reading skills in the black child.

Movies, T.V., Radio and The Black Child. Essentially the same psycho-

112

dynamics which are apparent during the black child's comic book reading activities and his dramatic-imitational play when these activities and play relate to white images, are apparent during his t.v. and movie-watching activities. Here these psychodynamics are maximally demonstrated due to the overwhelming influence of these media. Therefore we will not belabor the point.

The recent plethora of "black" movies have not been of much benefit to the black child in the sense of creating more positive psychodynamic effects which contribute to healthy personality growth. The same can be said of t.v. programs which feature blacks. This is mainly due to the fact that the same racist-commerical interests which control "white" films and t.v. production also control "black" films and t.v. production. The racist message in both black and white visual entertainment gets through. However, the "black" film is more insidious than its white counterpart due to the fact that the black child in viewing such becomes even more uncritical and accepting of the racist "hidden agendas." The vast majority of "black" films seek to exploit the sensationalism of negative ghetto existence and black bourgeois fantasies that soar far beyond reality. Thus hustlers, pimps, drug pushers. criminals, and other sordid characterizations crowd the screen that is presented to the mind of the black child. These characters are in a way glorified and the general dsyfunctionality of black ghetto existence elevated to a major art form. Seldom is the black child exposed to films which are concerned with a serious and realistic exploration of the black world and which critically exposes the negative factors of black existence. He is virtually not exposed to black films which positively educates him, which teaches him how to cope with his problems in creative, realistic and legitimate ways.

A very substantial amount of the black child's time is spent listening to or overhearing radio whose constant fare is music. This radio listening is suplemented by the constant stereo playing of records, albums and tapes by many parents. The music is usually played at deafening levels and may continue from early morning to late night. The romantic-erotic and rhythmic-hypnotic nature of much of the music listened to by black children almost without notice reinforces attitudes and developing lifestyles centered around sensuality, mawkish sentimentalism, escapist dancing and partying. Black rhythmic music which served the positive functions of cartharsis, inspiration, enter-tainment, etc. during the dark days of slavery and during the heydays of jim-crowism have now virtually become an opiate of a large segment of the black community. This music along with the ever-present dancing which accom-panies it serve as a means of diverting attention away from personal and community problems, as a means of escaping ugly reality, as a social accepted form of fantasy life, as ends in themselves. The chronic playing of such music reduces the ability to concentrate and along with chronic t.v.

watching reduces interest in reading and study. We wish to make it clear here that it is not the nature of the music itself that is at fault but the inability to control the listening to of music in the interest of more wholesome personality development that is the problem. The major problem with black child play and leisure time activities as a whole, including t.v. and radio watching and listening, is the black child's inability to inhibit such activities so that other parts of his personality may be developed. The time allotted to such activities is so great that little if any time is left over for the development of reading, intellectual, creative and problem-solving skills. Such activities become the end and be-all of the child's and adults existence. This turns out to be the case because the child is not taught how to delay pleasure in the interest of cognitive, personal and pro-social development. The black child's continuous concern with hedonistic play is reflected in the large percentage of black adult's continuous concern with physical pleasures and "partying." They are parallel and continuous activities. The greater part of the black adult's day consists of the following (1) Work (though a large segment do not engage in this activity for various reasons); (2) Passing-Time (in activities usually not of positive personal, familial, communal or educational value, activities not geared to solution of personal, familial or communal problems or to self-improvement) and; (3) Sleep. This is paralleled by the black child's day which consists of the following: (1) School (for the school age child); (2) Passing-Time (which is not wrong in itself but is principally made up of activities which contain few elements of rehearsal for future reality, which lay the basis for future intellectual, personal and prosocial growth, time almost fully spent playing along purely hedonistic lines) and (3) Sleep. Of course, these day activities vary according to class orientation but are prevalent enough on all class levels to help maintain the personal, familial and communal disorganization which characterizes the larger segment of the black community.

Implications and Recommendations. In this chapter we have seen that play plays a very important part in the child's development. Child's play is a serious activity in that the form it takes gives shape to the child's more mature intellectual, personality, and social orientation. When continuous and congruent with the broader social context in which it takes place, play adds greatly to the child's future adjustment, both near and far. When discontinuous and incongruent with the broader social context, i.e., when it establishes cognitive-behavioral style which serve as mechanisms of escape from reality, then future adjustment will be marginal or outright dysfunctional.

The parent must take her child's play seriously. This does not mean that the heavy hand of adult supervision and purposefulness should direct the child's play activity. It means that the parent should be given an "opportunity to play in a way that will meet his personal needs and thus eliminate his having

114

to find substitute forms which will give him less satisfaction or which will be socially disapproved" (5), or lead to hedonistic play which becomes an end in itself and which ultimately stifles the child's intellectual, personal and social maturation. To avoid this we recommend the following:

(1)   Enrich your childs play environment through making available a variety of toys, basic play material and games.

(2)   Buy or invent games that you and other family members can play with him.

(3)   Present the child with games and toys that are interesting yet demand just slightly more of his intellect than he currently exhibits.

(4)   See what kinds of adult roles your child likes to imitate and if positive, provide play materials, books, support, etc, related to that role.

(5)   Take walks with your child in the park, the beach, or other interesting areas and help him collect and classify materials he finds interesting if he feels so inclined.

(6)   Discuss your child's fantasy characters with him if he initiates such discussion. Listen to his stories—they can give important clues to the direction of his personality development. The stories you tell can also have therapeutic and developmental value for your child.

(7)   Look through picture books with your child. Read stories to him. Show sincere interest in the picture books, stories, and activities he brings to your attention.

(8)   Teach your child how to inhibit play activities when told to do so or as a means of controlling impulsive behavior and of delaying gratification.

(9)   Do not let your child become addicted to purely physical hedonistic play. Place enough restrictions on such play so he can explore other areas of functioning such as reading, writing, creative thinking, etc.

(10)   Involve your child in group and community activities and projects. Interest him in a broad variety of cultural activities especially those of his own culture.

(11)   Use your child's desire to read as a chance to teach him. Teaching of reading can begin as early as the child's second year (see appendix).

(12)   Note the possible dangers of your child's "schizmic" play. However, do not restrict your child's reading of "white" comics, seeing "white" movies and t.v. and movies or his imitation of white just because they happen to be white. He will live in a "white" world and must finally adjust to it. If you follow our recommendations of the last two chapters and have helped to establish a sense of ethnic pride, self-love, self-confidence, and a strong ego in your child, then you need have little fear of him becoming "white" or developing feeling of inferiority or self-hatred.

REFERENCES

1. Butterworth, R., & Thompson, G. Factors related to age-grade trends and sex differences in children's preferences for comic books. *Journal of Genetic Psychology, 78,* 1951.
2. Davidson, B. *A history of West Africa: To the nineteenth century.* New York: Doubleday, 1966.
3. Erikson, E. *Childhood and Society.* New York: Norton, 1950.
4. Freud, S. In Papalia, D., & Wendkos, S., *A child's world: Infancy through adolescence.* New York: McGraw-Hill, 1975.
5. Hurlock, E. *Child development.* (4th ed.) New York: McGraw-Hill, 1964.
6. Piaget, J. *Play, dreams, and imitation.* New York: Norton 1951.

116

THE BLACK CHILD–INTELLECTUAL DEVELOPMENT AS
REVEALED BY STANDARDIZED TESTS

There exists a sizeable number of tests designed to measure the so-called intelligence of children and adults. One of the best known and utilized tests is the Stanford-Binet test which yields a single Mental Age (MA) score, from which an Intelligence Quotient (IQ) can be derived. The three most popular infant intelligence tests are The Gesell Developmental Schedules, The Cattell Infant Intelligence Scale and The Bayley Scales. Other childhood tests which are often utilized are the Merrill-Palmer and the Wechsler Intelligence Scales for Children (WISC). The scope of our study does not allow for a fuller explanation and review of these and other tests used to measure the intellectual development of children. We therefore refer the interested reader to a suitable book about psychological testing.

Mental Age (MA), a concept developed by Binet, is attained by comparing the individual's (in terms of our interest here, the child's) test performance with the average performance of a large number of other individuals (children). The essential procedure for constructing and standardizing intelligence tests of scales involves giving the proposed test to a large population of children and/or adults and finding the ages at which a determined majority of these individuals have passed each item included in the test and arranging these items in order of difficulty. To calculate the MA of a particular child, he is tested and his results are compared to the average test performance of other children his age. For example, if the child passes the test items passed by the average 7-year-old, but not those passed by 8-year-olds, his MA would be 7. If his chronological age (CA) is also 7, then he may be said to be of average intelligence. If his CA is 6, it may be said that he is above average intelligence. But if his CA happens to be 10, it may be said that he is below average intelligence.

The German psychologist Wilhelm Stern developed the concept of the Intelligence Quotient (IQ) which can be computed directly by using the formula, $100 MA/CA = IQ$.

117

It has been found that the IQ is *relatively* constant for each individual (all other things held constant). This should not be taken to mean that IQ is an absolute, intrinsic, immutable quality of the individual and not subject to influence by a number of other factors and circumstances. As we shall see later in this chapter IQ is more a measure of cognitive style as related to social class, motivational state and cultural background than it is to any innate biological capacity. Many variables affect the score of an individual in an intelligence test. However, preschool and school-age intelligence tests can be said, with a fair degree of accuracy, to predict later intelligence test performance, the duration of time between tests being of prime importance. By age 6 the predictive value of tests is signficantly reliable though even at this point the predictions have to be made within large ranges due to considerable individual variations. The measured I.Q. of children does give a fairly good indication of the child's academic possibilities.

Up to this point we have written of intelligence as if a universally accepted definition of this concept existed. This is by no means the case. Guilford (7), a highly-regarded psychometrist, spoke to the issue of definition:

After tests had been invented to measure intelligence, quite a number of thinkers felt the urge to define it. Symposia were held on the problem, and numerous voices were heard. The outcomes were far from agreement. As Spearman (1927) put it, intelligence became a "mere vocal sound, a word with so many meanings that it finally had none." He further quoted J.S. Mill in a statement that described the situation well and that should serve as a warning: "The tendency has always been strong to believe that whatever receives a name must be an entity of being, having an independent existence of its own. And if no real entity answering to the name could be found, men did not for that reason suppose that none existed, but imagined that it was something peculiarly abstruse and mysterious."

Despite E.G. Boring's (2) somewhat facetious definition of intelligence as "a measurable capacity (that) must at the start be detined as the capacity to do well in an intelligence test", there are serious questions as to what IQ tests test and what is the "structure of intelligence." Binet saw intelligence as a single, unitary factor: Spearman (22) as a general factor plus several independent factors: Thurstone (24), as a composite of simpler processes combining in complex ways to deal with the problems confronting the individual: Guilford (7) posited a model for the "structure" of intelligence that consists of some 120 factors. From just these few examples one can surmise that psychologists are far from agreement as to what intelligence really is and what is it that intelligence tests are therefore really measuring. The reader should keep this in mind when discussing "intelligence" or uses the terms to characterize some individual or group. It seems that the prime concern of psychologists in this area—i.e., dealing with the problem of finding a universally and scientifically acceptable definition of intelligence, has been misplaced toward the dubious area of trying to establish individual and ethnic group intellectual superiority or inferiority. Such exercises are patently ridiculous in light of the fact that the standard of comparison is undefined. We shall examine briefly why psychologists have moved in this direction at the end of this chapter.

In the lay mind, and in the minds of unknowing professionals such as school administrators and biased psychologists, the IQ tests have been greatly overrated. As Joanna Ryan (17) stated:

It is important to clarify the meaning of IQ scores before considering, . . . the differences that are found between groups of people. IQ scores are very complex in the sense that many assumptions and operations are involved in their calculation, and it is only when the complexities are fully understood that it is legitimate to try to explain the origin of differences in score between people.

The fact that most IQ tests are "standardized" and involve the use of a large amount of statistical-mathematical formulae and work and that the IQ score is a number, leaves the impression on both lay and professional persons that these tests are "objective." In other words, psychological "sleight-of-hand" such as "scientific" methods of test construction and standardization, and the representation of an individual's performance by some neutral number, creates in the mind of the uninitiated an "illusion of objectivity." The objectivity of intelligence tests is largely mythological, Ginsburg (5) listed "four myths concerning the IQ test":

This first myth is that the IQ test measures an intelligence which is a unitary mental ability . . . There is not one intelligence, but many; and because of this it is not clear what the IQ score reflects.

The second myth is that differences in IQ scores reflect fundamental differences in intellect. The usual assumption is that differences in IQ reflect those abilities which are at the heart of the intellectual life; in addition, it is assumed that what the test fails to measure is not very important . . . Again, the proposition is in error. . . .

The third myth is that the IQ test measures intellectual competence. The common view is that an individuals IQ reflects the best he can do in the intellectual sphere.The IQ represents the upper limit on his mental capabilities. While this may be true for some people, it is not for all. In the case of poor children especially, the IQ test may not measure intellectual competence; it may not give a true picture of what poor children are capable of . . .

The fourth myth is that the IQ test measures an innate ability which is relatively unaffected by experience. In this view, the child's level of intelligence is set at birth and later experiences have relatively little effect on the IQ . . . This view is incorrect. The level of IQ is not determined at birth; it can fluctuate and change. . . .

We must terminate our discussion of the general nature of IQ tests at this point due to the fact that such a discussion will go beyond the intended scope of this work. For those interested in what factors affect the "capacity to do well in an intelligence test," we shall address three of those factors, race, class and adaptational demands, for the duration of the chapter.

The Differing Responses of Classes and Ethnic Groups to IQ tests. Generally, *as a group,* lower class children of any ethnic extraction score lower on IQ and other standardized tests than do higher class children and black children *as a group* score lower on these tests than do white children. Terman and Merrill (23), in classic studies of intelligence, found a 22-point difference between the mean score of white children between the ages of 2½ and 5½ belonging to the lowest and highest socioeconomic groups. The difference was in favor of the highest income group. McNemar (13) found that between the ages of 2 - 5½ the score for children of professional parents (doctors, lawyers, etc) was 114.8 compared to 93.8 for children of day laborers—a difference of 21 points. A 30-point difference between advantaged and disadvantaged children between the ages of 4 and 6 was found by Mumbauer and Miller (15).

On the average as indicated in the table below blacks score lower at every class level than whites on IQ tests. . . .

RACE AND CLASS DIFFERENCES IN IQ SCORES

	Group	Mean IQ
SES	I	
	White	97.24
	Negro	91.24
SES	II	
	White	105.59
	Negro	94.87
SES	III	
	White	114.92
	Negro	102.57

Deutsch and Brown, 1964. (SES = socioeconomic status. I = lowest, II = middle, III = highest class)

When one correlates the average scores attained on IQ tests by whites and blacks one finds an overall 12 - 15 point difference in favor of the whites. The difference between these two ethnic groups on IQ test performance has motivated professional psychologists and lay persons to offer various explanations for their occurrence.

120

However, we should note again (as was first noted in chapter 2) that ethnic and social class differences in measured IQ are usually not apparent until around age three and after, the exact time being not yet fully established. Bayley (1) who we mentioned in chapter 2, in an extensive and carefully controlled study of child intelligence found that significant social class differences in IQ clearly emerged between the ages of 2½ and 5½. Golden, et al (6), in a longitudinal study of social class differences and intellectual development among preschool black children, found no differences in IQ at ages 18 and 24 months between children of the highest and lowest socioeconomic classes. But at age 3 the difference was 19 points. Not unexpectedly, the middle class black children attained the highest scores, the black children from poor but intact and stable families attained the next highest scores. The lowest scores of all were attained by black children from fatherless welfare families.

Thus, in terms of social class and ethnic origin, measured differences in IQ are usually not found prior to ages 1½ - 3 years. It is between ages 3 - 4 that differences become apparent, i.e., by kindergarten age, "socially disadvantaged" children as a group will score lower on tests of "general intelligence, language, fine motor development and most other cognitive tests (8, 18)." As we noted in chapter two the differences in measured IQ between black and white children occurs at the age when race awareness, sociocultural-linguistic factors begin to influence the child's further intellectual and personality development. Thus, as Ginsburg said, "As black children grow older, . . . their average IQ decreases (5)." Stikei and Meyers (20) made a comparative cross race-class study of 4-year-olds from black and white, middle and lower class groups and noted how these groups differed on seven factors included in the IQ tests. The largest difference between the black and white children was in the area of verbal comprehension. The white middle class children scored highest, the black middle class and white lower class next and the black lower class lowest. No differences were found in the area of ideational fluency and the free use of language. The verbal comprehensive difference between the two groups as a whole seemed to center around the efficient use of standard English not the lack of ideational ability. We should add that the white group was not superior in all of the areas tested.

Let us enter an important note of caution here. Not *all* lower class or black children score lower on IQ tests. There are many black and/or lower class children (as high as 40% in one study) who score as high or higher than white and/or upper class children. The scores we have been discussing are *average* group scores and must be carefully interpreted.

"Intelligence" As a Function of Environmental Adaptation. Earlier in this study we quoted from Ginsburg's listing of four myths concerning IQ tests. Of particular interest to us here is his fourth statement of that series: "The fourth myth is that the IQ test measures an innate ability which is relatively unaffected by experience." It is this belief in the genetic and social immutability of "intelligence," in spite of the ample evidence that proves such a belief untenable, that has caused great difficulties in psychological thinking and which has brought on brutally detrimental social consequences. This view of a rigidified, structured, constant, totally genetically determined "intelligence" works against the concept of evolution and the evidence of Man's incredible ability to adapt to all types of circumstances and environments. Man's behavior takes place within various psychological, sociological, geophysical contexts and his behavior reflect his interactions with those contexts. His behavior only "makes sense" when defined in terms of his interactions with a particular set of psychosocial and geophysical circumstances. This behavior includes "intelligence" as well as any other you would care to name. "Intelligence" not defined by or rooted into a particular set of psychosocial, geophysical circumstances, like all other forms of behavior "makes no sense." The overall characteristic of Man's interaction with a particular psychosocial, geophysical environment is its reciprocal nature, i.e., the environment influences him and he adapts to its influence and he influences the environment and it adapts to his influence. In order for this to happen, particularly in order for Man to adapt appropriately to the many environmental circumstances which may confront him, he must not be behaviorally rigidified, structured, inflexible and immutable, his behavior must not be "fixed" or "fixated". This includes behavior called "intelligence". "Fixed" or unchanging "intelligence" is maladaptive in an unfixed and changing world. "Intelligent" behavior, like all behavior, in order to be adaptive must be malleable, i.e.. capable of being molded according to varying environmental demands and as such it is but a reflection of the environmental molding it has endured.

Let us look for the moment at verbal behavior, language if you will, the principal means by which "intelligence" is revealed and measured. The flexibility and adaptability of language behavior is obvious to even the most casual observer. He sees that there is no fixed, constant or immutable language behavior unaffected by or unreflective of psychosocial, geophysical circumstance. An individual or group innately capable of learning only one language of a fixed range and vocabulary, would be highly maladaptive if they moved about in a world of many languages and a world that was in flux and which provided many new experiences which needed assimilating, interpreting, classifying and transmitted to posterity. Thus, man is born with a capacity for language behavior, not a language, and this capacity is filled with the linguistic contents of the particular environmental surround into which he *happens* to be immersed.

All men, as far as we know are equally endowed with the capacity to develop and use language appropriate to their particular circumstances and as their circumstances change so does their language. Equally endowed with the capacity to develop and use language, men develop and use differing linguistic styles befitting the demands of their particular environment. Thus linguistic style whether written, spoken or otherwise demonstrates its adaptive qualities whenever it is expressed; it does not express the *limits* of linguistic capacity, only the means by which that capacity is expressed. Therefore, a particular language is neither "superior" or "inferior" to another, Italian is neither superior or inferior to English, the language of commerce is neither superior or inferior to that of science, they are *different;* different linguistic adaptations to different life styles, life styles which make different demands on a common linguistic capacity.

Similarly, we will venture to say that all men are equally endowed with the capacity for "intelligent" behavior and that they develop and use "intelligence" appropriate to their particular circumstances and as their circumstances change so does their "intelligence." "Intelligence" is as much, if not more so, an adaptive process as is language and as with language, is deeply embedded in an individual's or group's psychosocial and geophysical experiences and also as with language, reflective of their attempts to meet a set of psychosocial, geophysical environmental demands. A language bereft of its cultural roots soon dies and has little meaning. The same is true of "intelligence." As with language "intelligence" however it is expressed does not express the *limits* of intellectual capacity, only the *means* by which that capacity is expressed. Consequently, the "lower class" individual is not necessarily less "intelligent" than his "middleclass" counterpart, but his cognitive style (the means by which he expresses his "intelligence") which reflects his adaptation to his lower class status is different. This difference may handicap him in a middleclass dominated world that sees its adaptive cognitive style or traits as "superior." A similar situation exists when an individual's language or linguistic style differs radically from the language of those around him.

We have cited studies in chapter two and in this chapter which indicate with certainty that there are no significant differences in the tested IQ of black and white children before age 3 — implying that these two groups have an equal intellectual capacity. As we have repeatedly pointed out the difference that develops after age 3 is due to the difference in the demands placed on their intellectual capacities by their differing psychosocial, geophysical environments. Further evidence of this will be shown presently. Thus, intelligence is an adaptive dimension of an individual's personality and measured "intelligence" reflects more the circumstances to which the individual has adapted than his innate capacity for "intelligent behavior."

Piaget, the foremost student of intellectual development, places adaptation at the very center of his cognitive developmental theory of He posits that human intellectual growth and development springs from and is shaped by two innately basic tendencies: *organization* (the tendency or predispostion to integrate, coordinate and combine geophysical structures and psychosocial experiences and perceptions into more complex and coherent systems) and adaptation *(the tendency or predispostion to adjust consonantly to the environment). Adaptation involves two related processes* which interact to transform the individual's experiences into knowledge and cognitive schemes: *assimilation* (the tendency or predisposition to 'take in' or incorporate new objects or experiences, or concepts into an already existing cognitive system or to form new systems from the old) and *accomodation* (the tendency or predisposition to adjust to environmental demands, to or modify one's concept of the world and response to things as a result of new experiences). For Piaget the intellectual processes seek to maintain a balance with their environmental surround through the process of equilibration (the process by which the individual is stimulated to bring harmony and stability into his perceptions of things and to reduce inconsistencies and dissonance created by environmental changes and demands).

One can readily see that for Piaget "intelligent behavior" is a result of adaptive interaction between assimilation and accomodation, that adaptation is the very core of "intelligent behavior." Adaptation, the very essence of "intelligent behavior," takes place in and is shaped by the relevant environment. Cognitive development and cognitive style result from the changes wrought in intellectual systems by the individual's assimilative and accomodative drives to organize and adapt to experiences provided by interactions with the environment. Thus, "intelligence" is not something which floats beyond and unattached to its environmental ground.

The tendency of individuals to intellectually adapt to a particular environment (such adaptation may show an increase or decrease depending on the type of environment) and the ability of IQ tests to reveal the effects of that environmental adaptation on intellectual functioning has been demonstrated by studies of identical twins reared apart. It has been assumed that since identical twins come from the same egg and share the same set of genes what differences they exhibit in intellectual functioning must be principally the result of environmental influences. One report shown that 19 identical twins who were separated at ages ranging from six years and reared apart demonstrated IQ differences as large as from 10 to 24 points (16). The average point spread (8.2) would have been larger if the age range was not so broad and if the homes in which the twins were raised were more dissimilar in socioeconomic background. For we shall see later that the earlier a child is adopted into a new environment the more influence that environment will have on his intellectual functioning.

A dramatic study which demonstrates the substantial effects of adaptation to a particular environment and the effects of that environment on intellectual functioning was done by Skeels (21). We will quote from Hetherington's and Parke's (9) description of that study:

In the late 1930s, Skeels set out to determine whether the debilitating impact of early institutionalization could be overcome by exposure to a more enriched environment. Two groups of children were involved in this investigation: Due to crowding, one group of children was transferred from the orphanage to a mental retardation institution; children in the comparison group remained in the orphanage.

... The institution for the mentally retarded to which the "subjects" of this study were transferred could easily be described as "enriched" in comparison to the orphanage. It was not simply a more varied and stimulating environment, but one that provided abundant opportunities for social and emotional development as well.

The thirteen children who were sent to this setting at an average age of nineteen months of age were considered mentally retarded, with an average IQ of 64.3. The twelve children in the control group who stayed in the orphanage were close to normal in terms of intelligence, with a mean IQ of 86.7. To assess the impact of living under these contrasting conditions, the children's intellectual status was reassessed about one and one-half years after the transfer had taken place. The experimental subjects showed a marked increase in mental growth, with the average gain being a dramatic 28.5 IQ points. These "mental retardates" now had an average IQ of 91.8. The losses of the children who stayed in the orphanage were just as spectacular; the average loss was 26.2 IQ points, resulting in a mean IQ of 60.5 for the control group. The two groups had reversed positions over the two-year period.* Skeels was interested in determining whether the gains achieved by the experimental subjects would last. His first follow-up study was conducted two and one-half years after the termination of the initial study. Of the original thirteen children, eleven were adopted while two remained institutionalized until adulthood. The adopted children maintained their intellectual status: the mean IQ for these children was 101.4, but the institutionalized children dropped in IQ. The unfortunates in the control group, of course, remained wards of the state and in spite of slight gains were still classified as mentally retarded, the mean IQ for this group was 66.1.

Twenty-one years elapsed between the first follow-up study and this final assessment; by this time the "children" were between twenty-five and thirty-five years of age. Did the groups maintain their divergent patterns of competence into adulthood? Clearly they did.

*   *   *

*This resembles the trend between black and white children noted earlier.

The implication of this study is clear: the deleterious effects of early environmental restriction can be effectively reversed. Similarly, these findings suggest that continued deprivation has obviously harmful effects. In general, prediction of the adult's status is affected by all periods of life and later age points in childhood, adolescence, or adulthood can only be understood by a close examination of the intervening environmental factors that are present at any developmental period. In short, it is not just "early" experience but experience at all age points that needs to be continuously considered in attempting to understand the child's development.

Other studies of a similar nature have been performed and similar results were found. It should be noted that though IQ gains may be substantial as a result of adapting to an "enriched" environment the gains may only be temporary or reversed if the individual's stay in such an environment is relatively brief and/or if the individual is returned to his old environment or the effects of the old environment are allowed to simultaneously negate the enriched one. This type of situation is principally responsible for the IQ reversals suffered by children in "head-start" and other enrichment programs.

The effects of environmental adaptation were revealed by a study done by Scarr-Salaptek and Weinberg (20) who found that black children adopted by white parents scored higher than black children reared by black parents and higher than the national average IQ. 101 white families in the Minneapolis, Minnesota area who adopted black children were studied. These white families tended to be professionals and most were college graduates and personally committed to racial equality. They generally lived in areas where their adopted children rarely saw other blacks. These adoptive households often contained adopted children of other nationalities — whites, Asians or American Indian. The authors of the study arrived at the following conclusions:

The typical adopted child in these families — of any race — scored above the national average on standard IQ tests. But the child's age at adoption and his or her experiences before moving to the new family were strongly related to later IQ. The earlier a child was placed, the fewer disruptions in his life, and the better his care in the first few years, the higher his later IQ score was likely to be. The white adopted children, who found families earlier than any other group, scored 111 on the average; the black adopted children got IQ scores averaging 106; and the Asian and Indian children who were adopted later than any other group, and more of whom had lived longer in impersonal institutions, scored at the national average, 100.

If the black adopted children had been reared by their natural parents, we would expect their IQ scores to average about 90. The black adopted children, however, scored well above the national averages of both blacks and whites, especially if they were adopted early in life. In fact, the lowest score of an early-adopted black child, 86, was close to the average for all black children in the nation. (emphasis by author).

The fact that the earlier the black child is adopted the higher his IQ gain is likely to be attests to our premise that in terms of the black child's intellectual functioning as compared to that of the white child's, the psychosocial environment in which the average black child is reared very early begins to negate his intellectual potential. The adoptive white family "rescues" the black child from such a fate if the child is adopted before the negative effect of the child's normal environment sets in. Of course, the same could be done by a black family of appropriate educational, economic and psychosocial background. The chart below summarizes the findings of the study:

All adopted children	IQ Scores		
	Number	Average	Range
Black	130	106	68 - 144
White	25	111	62 - 143
Other	21	100	66 - 129
Early adopted children			
Black	99	110	86 - 136
White	9	117	99 - 138
Other		only three cases	
Natural children	144	117	81 - 150

After Scarr-Salapatek and Weingberg

The reader will note that the highest score made by "all adopted" black children (144) is 6 points below the highest score made by the "natural children" (150). In both the "all adopted" and "early adopted" categories the highest black scores virtually equals the highest white scores. All things considered, eventhough the average IQ score of blacks is lower in this study there are blacks who score just as high as do the highest scoring whites. This situation is repeated in other comparative studies. The authors of this study indicate that average IQ score obtained by black and white adoptees are subject to the following qualifications:

When we compare black and white adoptees, it seems that the white children still have an IQ advantage, 111 to 106. However, the black children had lived with their adoptive families for fewer years than the white children and were younger when we tested them. Adoption at an early age increased the scores of black children an average of 110. There was a trend for early adoption to increase the IQ scores of white children too, but we have only nine cases in that category.

Thus, this study plainly indicates the directional influence psychosocial environment can and does have on intellectual functioning beginning early in the child's life. That environment can have the effect of "increasing" the child's IQ, holding it steady or "decreasing" it. Black children adopted into middle and upper class white families show an increase in IQ from early childhood onward as do white children raised naturally in these families and black children reared in their "normal" environment show a decrease in IQ from early childhood onward. These trends have nothing to do with the "whiteness" or "blackness" of the families concerned but with the educational, socioeconomic status, psychosocial, psychoemotional background of the family-community in which the child is reared. The various social classes and ethnic group place different demands on the intellectual capacity if their children and the latter's cognitive style reflect these demands. The IQ tests measures their effects on the child's intellectual capacity and orientation. With this in mind let us study the chart below:

ETHNIC GROUP AND SOCIAL CLASS MENTAL ABILITY SCORES

	Chinese	Jewish	Negro	Puerto Rican
Verbal				
Middle Class	76.8	96.7	85.7	69.6
Lower Class	65.3	84.0	62.9	54.3
Reasoning				
Middle Class	27.7	28.8	26.0	21.8
Lower Class	24.2	21.6	14.8	16.0
Numerical				
Middle Class	30.0	33.4	24.7	22.6
Lower Class	26.2	23.5	12.1	15.7
Spatial				
Middle Class	44.9	44.6	41.8	37.4
Lower Class	40.4	35.1	27.1	32.8

Adapted from Lesser, Fifer, and Clark (1965)

A close look at the chart indicates that though the middle class of each ethnic group scores higher in all the areas listed, the pattern of scores of the lower class of each ethnic group are quite similar to their middle class counterparts. The apparent difference between classes then is quantitative, not qualitative. Here we find a difference in degree, not kind. This works against the "species specific" class orientation of psychologists which sees the middle class child as a "different kind of animal" from his lower class brother. The major difference is one of a difference in values, attitudes and standards and a dif-

128

ference in material, financial, social, legal resources which places different adaptive (accomodative, assimilative, organizational and equilibrational) demands on their children's intellectual-behavioral capacities. The same is true for ethnic groups when these two groups differ in social status and psychohistorically. As a result of extensive studies, Harvard University researcher, Jerome Kagan came to the conclusion that "all humans eventually master a basic set of cognitive capacities, but they do so at different rates. ... (He) believes these differing rates of development are not due to racial differences but to the varying demands each... culture(s) makes on its children. ... "(as reported by HUMAN BEHAVIOR' Sept., 1974; emphasis by the author).

Intelligence as a function of environmental demands. A number of studies have indicated that when blacks from the South, whose IQ scores are generally lower than blacks in the North, migrate from South to North their IQ scores show a corresponding increase. Their IQ scores tend to increase until they equal the average IQ scores of their northern counterparts. The chart below illustrates this point:

INTELLIGENCE AS A FUNCTION OF LENGTH OF RESIDENCE IN NEW YORK CITY

Years of Residence	Number of Cases	Mean IQ
Less than 1	42	81.4
1 – 2	40	84.2
2 – 3	40	84.5
3 – 4	46	85.5
Over 4	47	87.4
New York Born	99	87.3

Adapted from Klineberg (1935)

It should be apparent that New York City and its native black residents was quite a different society from that of the essentially rural South that existed especially at the time that this study was performed. This being the case New York City society made different demands on its southern migrants, provided them with all types of material and psychological resources, instigated changes in cognitive, attitudinal amd motivational structures which was reflected by corresponding changes in IQ scores. Of special interest here is the tendency for the IQ increments to stop at or near the average IQ of the community of residence. This would appear to support Piaget's concept of equilibration where the individual attains a new balance and reduces to a minimum differences and incosistencies between himself and his environment. It seems that the intellect tends to rise (or lower) itself to meet the demands of its environment and as soon as it equals the demands of that environment it tends to remain static unless the environment is one that stimulates and rewards advancement beyond present levels. In situations where advancement is not encouraged or rewarded or perhaps, punished, being a "smart guy" can be just as distressing and painful as be the "class dummy." Being too far ahead of the crowd or "of your time" generally leads to alienation and to avoid such a state most people hover around the average "intelligence" of their peer group though they may be capable of far better. Thus, the southern migrant attains equality with his northern counterpart and becomes a part of the "in-crowd."

Middle Class Cognitive Style. The middle-class (which includes most academic types and other professions - including psychologists) tends to see a cognitive style which contains a relatively high amount of "abstract," "symbolic," or "conceptual" thought, as indicative of "high intelligence." The psychologists who represent this class point of view see such a style as innately "superior" to a cognitive style that is essentially "concrete." Drucker (4) in his paper titled: Cognitive Styles and Class Stereotypes makes relevant observation:

In their zealous search for the bases of differences between the children of middle- and lower-class background, many researchers and educators have asserted that the thought and language of the lower-class child is relatively "concrete", while that of the middle class child is "abstract" and of a higher developmental order. By "abstract" is usually meant a type of thought characterized as more "logical" and "symbolic" while "concrete" thought is seen as dominated by personal reference, sensory-motor qualities and a functional organization of events.

Our guiding hypothesis here is in line with those social scientists who see the relationship between "concrete" thought and "abstract" thought as continuous, as essentially different manifestations of the same thing, not as dichotomous, separate and unrelated things. We see the individual moving up and down the "concrete-abstract" continuum in accordance with his life circumstances. Thus, whether a person tends to think primarily in abstract or concrete terms is a function of his life style conditions, his adapting of a a relatively flexible "intelligence" to a particular environment which may demand that he deal with it in a predominately "concrete" or "abstract" fashion. The studies we have cited thus far have indicated that cognitive style ("intelligence") assumes the principal "concrete" or "abstract" thought forms required by different class levels (i.e., different environments). Drucker (4) goes on to indicate the following:

Specifically, I would like to argue that tests and data of the sort presented above*do reflect differences but not differences in **level** (author's emphasis) of **conceptualizing** and **abstracting ability** or the **capacity** (author's emphasis) for the **adaptive use of thought.** Instead, I think they reflect an **arbitrary dichotomy** (author's emphasis) which has been imposed on a mass of data which lends itself to many interpretations and differentiations.

In line with Drucker's statement we do not deny that one does not find differences in the degree to which conceptualization and abstraction is utilized by certain individuals and groups but we do deny that the differences found do not indicate differences in the **capacity** for conceptualization and abstraction.

That the middle class child and the lower class child are different in the concreteness of their thought patterns is an illusion. The middle class child's thought is as "concretely" tied to his middle class world as is the lower class child's thought is "concretely" tied to his. Not only does the lower class child's "concrete" thought make him maladaptive in a middle class world:the middle class child's"concrete" thought makes him equally maladaptive in a lower class world. The lower class child abstracts, conceptualizes and symbolizes his universe just as the middle class child abstracts, conceptualizes and symbolizes his universe. The differences then, do not lay in the ability to abstract, conceptualize and symbolize but in differences in the objects and purposes and context of these activities. It also depends on who is evaluating the differences. We shall have occasion to return to this important topic when we discuss differences in linguistic style in our next chapter.

*Drucker is referring to test data which purports to have established differences between children from a "culture of poverty" and those not so, in their ability to abstract and conceptualize.

The Black Family and "Intelligence." It is not class membership which plays the primary role in the mental development of the child but the parent-child, family-child relationship which does so.

In America, the family is responsible for the acculturation and intellectual stimulation of the child. The process of family interaction is vital to the child's growth and to his ability to benefit later from the educational experiences offered in school. The family is the first and most basic institution in our society for developing the child's potential in all its many aspects; emotional, intellectual, moral and spiritual, as well as physical and social. Other influences do not even enter the child's life until after the highly formative years. (Hurley, 1969)

Hurley goes on to say that ". . . the household is the complete world of the child for a long period of time, and the quality of life in that world is crucial. If the child is not stimulated adequately in all his senses from birth, his intellectual potential will wither."

The parent-child relationship, interfamilial relations in many black homes are often seriously handicapped by poverty, fatherlessness, unemployment or employment of the single parent or both parents and the relatively large size of the family. Such problems coupled with lack of knowledge and inadequacy of parental socialization detract from a family's ability to stimulate the child's mental growth and may actually do much to retard it. It should by now be obvious that the child's cognitive-behavioral potentialities are to a large extent shaped by the nature of the psycho-social forces which act upon him. One of the most important of these forces is the mother's socialization of her child.

In a practical sense, in order to succeed according to the standards of the dominant white society, to achieve a high score on culturally biased IQ tests, the black child has to be virtually "white", at least in the cognitive -behavior sense if not in the full cutlural sense. Many a black mother is not prepared or so inclined to bring such a transformation about either due to her not wanting to, her "ignorance", her outsider racial status or possibly her fear that by doing so, she may succeed in alienating her child from his family ethnic roots. We do not wish to imply here that blacks cannot be and are not as cognitively capable and creative as whites unless they are "white" - we are implying that the current social situation is such that it tends toward that end-of demanding that blacks become "white" before their talents and cognitive functions are permitted full and free expression.

The chronic uncertainty of black life, the tenuous nature of its future possibilities has the effect of forcing many black parents to practice a certain defensive apathy and to concern themselves with the immediates of their 's and their family's lives. This is especially true of a large segment of lower income parents but also cuts deeply into the ranks of middle class parents which is still heavily influenced by its recent segregated, poverty stricken, "deprived" past. The racial climate in America in its economic and educa-tional sense as well as in its social sense, forces many a black parent to rear her child in a relatively constricted manner and does not allow her to be as future-oriented as her white counterpart. The black mother's relatively low expectations for her child is in part due to her own disappointing experiences and in part due to what she perceives as his realistic chances of succeeding in a white dominated world. Added to this is her confusion of values brought on by black and white cultural differences, her ambivalence toward herself and her child, which prevents her from systematically meeting her child's cognitive needs, training him in self-control and discipline, persistence, rational thinking that goes beyond his immediate world of experience and from planning realistically for her child's future.

We intimated in an earlier chapter that the black parent's way of relating to their world, especially to the dominant white world, has very definite effects on the way she socializes her child and subtly shapes the black individual's cognitive approach to problem solving. We also stated that the dependent relationship of black adults to white adults has the effect of stunting fully actualized cognitive-behavioral development in both black parents and their children. Black children are literally taught to be as mentally dependent as their parents, to not have confidence in their own rational abili-ties, not be mentally assertive where such assertion may come in conflict with white authority. This type of situation leads the black adult as well as the black child to await answers to his problems from others instead of solving them himself, to substitute the congealed thoughts of others for his own, to confuse the ability to parrot information with actual thinking, i.e., to confuse recalling with productive or creative thinking.

132

The dependent black parent, the educationally deprived or psychologically insecure black parent (all of these traits are usually combined in the same parent) may feel threatened or shamed by her child's growing intellectual power and consciously or unconsciously ignore, not reward or punish the child's efforts to learn (usually marked by a great deal of questioning on the child's part). Thus, she may quash her child's intellectual curiosity, discourage mental growth or encourage "mental recklessness".

In a middle class home the child's curiosity is encouraged and rewarded. Just the opposite occurs in the disadvantaged home. Early in life when the infant begins to crawl, his explorations are curtailed, for there are too many people and not enough room; his growth must be subjugated to the needs of others. As the child grows older and begins to question his parents, this activity is also suppressed because, as has been suggested, the adult does not have the information that the child desires.

The poor child thus suffers not only from a paucity of information about the world of words and labels, but the very spirit of intellectual curiosity is significantly stunted, and the child does not learn how to use questions, an all important intellectual tool. In the child's formulation of concepts of the world, the ability to formulate questions is an essential step in data gathering. If questions are not encouraged or if they are not responded to, this is a function which does not mature. (Hurley 10)

The absence of the father in the home, which is prevalent in almost half of black homes, generally tends to depress the intellectual development of the child and to significantly increase the chances of "pseudo-mental" retardation in poor families. There is ample evidence to support the assertion that the presence of the father in the home is measurably helpful to the normal intellectual development of the child. Deutsch and Brown (3) found that ". . . children from homes where fathers are present have significantly higher IQ scores than children in homes without fathers." The number of fatherless black families is twice that for whites. Moynihan (14) estimated that ". . . only a minority of Negro children reach the age of 18 having lived all their lives with both parents."

Cognitive development is an extremely complex phenomena and is influenced by many interacting factors. A concentration on these many factors and other minutae tends to obscure the major variable of which these two things are but byproducts - American racism. Peter Watson (25), after a review of the relevant literature and in reviewing his own work in the field, concluded the following:

. . . there is at least a double handicap to your intellectual performance when you are black: (1) the white environment, particularly in America, is threatening and stressful, evoking reactions that drain on your

133

performance; (2) your expectancy of success is low (realistically, usually) and this only makes matters worse.

After making the interesting observation that somehow "race" and "ability" get tied up in the mind of the youngster and ". . . this, in turn, can both improve and impair his performance," Watson goes on to say:

. . there is enough evidence to enable one to say this: till now, psychologists, whatever their views on the origins of differences in IQ, have recognized only two kinds of environmental influence - those related to childrearing and those related to cultural differences. It is time a third was added - differences in motivation due to chronically poor race relations . . . this could be one of the strongest drains of all on ability.

Motivation is at the center of all types of human behavior, including intellectual. As we shall see in a later chapter (7) where we will discuss this matter in detail that motivation is a familial-culturally based phenomena. An ability without the appropriately energizing motive forces compelling it is an ability that is basically inoperative. Blacks in America suffer from serious motivation problems and these in turn cause serious problems in cognitive-behavioral functioning. We attempt to describe these in chapter 7.

"Intelligence" Testing, The Hidden Agenda. Throughout this chapter we have always enclosed the term "intelligence" in quotations marks to keep ourselves mindful of the fact that this concept is essentially undefined, that it is a very tenuous, illusory concept.   It essentially has no meaning in and of itself. We also wanted to keep ourselves mindful of the fact that IQ and "intelligence" are not synonymous. IQ tests do not, repeat, do not, reveal or demarcate in any reliable way intellectual capacity or "intelligence." No test, IQ or otherwise, has been found or created that determines the true intellectual capacity of an individual. **The "intelligence" determined by IQ tests is the "intelligence" which may be defined as the degree to which an individual has assimilated and accomodated, i.e., adapted, himself to a certain set of values, standards, attitudes, ways of verbalizing, ways of thinking, ways of perceiving and other ways of behaving that a particular culture, subculture or individual evaluates as important to the maintenance and advancement of its way of life.**

Thus, "intelligence" is always culturally or individually defined. The concept of "intelligence", the concern with testing it arises from cultural roots. Western culture is basically the only culture which sees the testing of "intelligence" as of overwhelming importance. The very fact that one engages in the testing of "intelligence" is a cultural phenomenon. No test is free of its cultural roots. This includes "culture-fair" tests   for they still test cognitive-behavioral-perceptual patterns that are deemed important by a culture or test-maker. The fact that one would try to devise such a test is indicative of a subjective cultural or individual concern. The very way one tests his subject, whether it be with paper and pencil, by oral means or by observing the subjects behavior, etc., is determined by culture. "Culture-fair" tests themselves are cultural products and their attempt to wash themselves clean of their cultural contamination by depending principally on the subject's nonverbal perceptual and manipulative behavior is an illusion due to the well established fact that these two forms of behavior are themselves "culture-bound" and are significantly influenced by the individual's motivational state and developmental history.

This brings us to the important question: If IQ tests do not reveal intellectual capacity then what purpose do they serve, why are they utilized with such great frequency and deemed so important by their users? This is a very broad and complex question and we can only deal with it in a very general fernal here. The principal function and purpose of IQ tests is to "objectively" justify, maintain and advance the white middle class life and cognitive style. It is a means by which this class seeks to protect its prerogative, privileges, status, dominance, and a means by which this class excludes and isolates those persons whose life and cognitive styles do not serve these ends. These tests determine who will have access to certain privileges. resources, etc., the white middle class and the white man in general have the power to give or take. Drucker's (4) thoughts on this matter are of particular relevance here:

> The use of intelligence evaluation procedures as a basis of differentiating individuals is a sort of cultural litmus test which serves the simple social function of screening and sorting for individuals who may adequately respond to a particular educational system. Thus the predominant middle-class definition of intellectual style is fostered and preserved through systemic selection to fit a certain model. . . A technique whose primary and intended function is to make a social discrimination is viewed as objectively measuring quantitative differences in basic dimensions of intellectual competence. The cycle of mystification becomes complete when this gatekeeper is called in as a witness to attest to the validity and superiority of the system it served. Observations of failures (e.g., in school) are then attributed to "deprivation" in the life or cultural experience of those affected. Conversely. "success" is due to the enriched content and superior lifeways of the dominant group. There is therefore, a strong tendency to develop simple, idealized stereotypes of class life styles which are then juggled about in an attempt to explain phenomena of school performance. . . .

The history of the conceptual framework on which it and most other current intelligence measures rests is the history of attempts to justify the superior or inferior position of a particular group by looking within that group for causal factors. . . . While this and other, elaborate systems of rationalization may assuage guilt, they cannot forever delay confrontation with reality. (emphasis by the author)

In a word "intelligence tests" are a white middle class and white racist conceit. Why is the testing of "intelligence" so diligently pursued by whites? Because it provides a rationale by which the white man may justify his racist behavior and attitudes. A deeply ingrained Western cultural fiction is that Man is above Nature, that it is Man's inherent right to dominate, rule over and manipulate Nature in accordance with his Will and to serve whatever ends he deems important. This right is his due to his "God-likeness" and primarily because he is the "most intelligent" of Nature's (or God's) creation. The general unspoken assumption is "that he who is the more intelligent than the rest has the inherent right to do as he wills with them." Since Man, according to Western thought is "more intelligent" than the rest of Nature he is free to guiltlessly exploit, experiment with, destroy, plunder, drastically change, whatever, he wishes to the "less intelligent" elements of Nature. This includes other races of men who are "less intelligent" than some particular race, the white race in this instance. Thus, herculean efforts of the white man to "prove" his "intellectual superiority" is a first step toward carrying out his "hidden agenda" whose major purpose is to exploit, plunder, and ultimately "eugenically" destroy the nonwhite races, especially the black race. This is brought out by a fact that is readily observable, the IQ tests are used principally to **deny** a person the opportunity to enjoy certain privileges, prerogatives, etc., enjoyed by others. This can be easily stretched to include the opportunity to enjoy just being alive.

A Note On Human Differences. American white "liberal" and black scholars are intimidated by almost any emphasis on racial differences. It is not considered fashionable to discuss racial differences in "intelligence", especially if this implies black intellectual inferiority. These scholars approach the subject of black-white intellectual differences with fear, anxiety, guilt, and apologetically. The reaction to Schockley, Jensen, Eysenck, and others of their orientation attests to the immensely volatile and inflammatorily mixed emotions the discussion of black-white intellectual differences can and do arouse.

There seems to be an unconscious-preconscious reason for this peculiar situation. When black-white racial differences are discussed the assumption is that the most important of those differences would automatically point to white superiority and black inferiority. This unexamined assumption provokes feelings of guilt and fear in "liberal" whites and shame and anxiety in "liberal" blacks. It never seems to occur to the vast majority of blacks that the differences between the two groups could just as well point to black superiority and white inferiority, or at the very least black equality. Thus, the differences that are found to exist between the two groups are either overlooked, hastily and shabbily treated, trepeditiously dismissed or explained embarrassingly out of existence. Neither group shall benefit in the long run from this process. It is the honest and courageous study of differences and their underlying causes that must become the foundation of any true push for equality between the two groups.

Paradoxically, it is the very ditferences that we observe between human cultures and behaviors that point to their ultimate alikeness, sameness and equality. The innumerable variety of human cultures and individual configurations points to the final commonality of all men. We believe that by properly emphasizing the differences between men and digging at the common roots of these differences we will be able to establish at what point all men are equal, to establish to their basic equality, oneness and commonality. For we feel that it is the commonality of men that is the foundation of their differentness. What then, is this commonality?

The thing that makes for the differentness and variety found among peoples and individuals is the commonality and plasticity of the uniquely human Central Nervous System - the human brain and spinal cord. It is the remarkable flexibility and adaptability of this system and its interactions with varying geophysical, psychosocial, politicoeconomical situations that accounts for the great variety of differences between cultures and individuals. This system which is common to all men is the ultimate entity that makes all men equal, yet unequal, makes them the same, yet different. Even though it is modifiable and flexible, which accounts for Man's extreme adaptability, it also has a strong tendency under various conditioning contingencies to stabilize, retain the imprint of experience and to become stereotypical in its response inclinations, which accounts broadly for Man's remarkable memory and learning capacity, and incidentally, for his resistance to change. Thus, this extremely finely tuned system which is responsible for the plasticity and malleability of human behavior is simultaneously responsible for the inflexibility and refractoriness of human behavior. In sum, men are equal and the same in that they possess a common central nervous system and are unequal and not the same in that this system is exposed, conditioned and therefore ultimately shaped by the various, differing, and dissimilar environments and circumstances which happen to impress themselves on peoples and individuals.

This central fact, this commonality is too often overlooked by scholars who tend to be culture- and stimulus-bound to superficial differences between peoples and individuals and who act as if these differences were the end and be-all of the study of Man. It is as if one would study the immense variety of waves forms of the oceans and ignore the water which is common to all the forms.

Implications and Recommendations. Since the implications of this chapter have already been discussed in some detail we will go directly into our recommendations.

1. Remember the "four myths" about IQ tests mentioned in this chapter. Remember that IQ tests do not determine "intelligence."

2. Remember that the 12 – 15 point difference between the *average* score of whites and blacks on IQ tests does not indicate a difference in the "intelligence" of the two groups. It merely indicates the degree to which the cultures of these two groups represent are different. IQ tests are "culture tests", not "intelligence tests."

3. Do not permit yourself or your children to be ashamed by performance on an IQ test anymore than you would permit yourself to be ashamed by any other test.

4. The fact that IQ tests do not measure intellectual capacity does not mean that they are not useful, but know what they are useful for. For example, IQ tests fairly well predict academic success in schools which are based on white middle class educational approaches and values.

5. If you want your child to succeed in schools based on white middle class educational methods and values, which includes virtually all public schools to score high on IQ tests, then you must thoroughly familiarize yourself with the factors that are conducive to such ends. Prepare yourself and your child through your interactions with him and arrange his environment in such a way that he may move toward these ends (in the appendix you will find a list of books which will give you detailed instructions on how to increase the "intelligence" of your child).

6. It is very important to keep in mind that in your efforts to increase your child's IQ test and academic performance, the success of which to a large degree calls for him to assimilate cultural values and attitudes not his own, you stand in danger of imposing standards incompatible with your child's personality, innate inclinations and/or alienating him from himself, his culture and yourself. Though your child may be smart, he may also be "sick."

7. Remember, your ethnic or social class origin do not determine or limit your child's IQ. The major determinants of this will be, besides his own congenital potential, the quality of his relations with you, his family, and other important persons, events and experiences in his life. Do not swallow the "cultural deprivation" pill.

8. Don't get emotional or involved in racial-class polemics based on tests which are questionable in nearly all aspects of what *they're supposed to test. Don't forget that "intelligence" has not been defined. So, why fight over an*

138

undefined issue or over someone else's arbitrary definition?

9. Beware of political, educational, economic and racist "hidden agendas," justifications and implications lurking behind the "illusion of objectivity" of so-called "intelligence" tests.

10. Always be mindful of the fact the key to developing the full and healthy cognitive and personal potential of your child if first and foremost the fostering of self-love in him. This is inextricably tied to ethnic self-love — teach him to love his own black self and to make that the basis for unbigoted relations to other ethnics and the world in general.

11. The black church can play an important role in this area by using its influence and facilities to convene and educate black parents in methods of child-rearing which will effectively increase the intellectual functionality of their children.

12. We recommend that a new type of social worker be trained whose major job it will be to visit, observe, educate, and support black parents of very young children so as to aid them in their efforts to rear their children to be fully functional, both personally and cognitively. Perhaps the worker herself could be trained as a teacher of early childhood education and pass her knowlege on to the relevant black parents and also aid in training their children.

REFERENCES

1. Bayley, N. Comparisons of mental and motor test scores for age 1–15 months by sex, birth order, race, geographic location, and education of parents. *Child Development, 36,* 1965.
2. Boring, E. G. Intelligence as the tests test it. *New Republic, 34, 1923.*
3. Deutsch, M., & Brown, B. *Social influences in negro-white intelligence differences.* Journal of Social Issues, 20, 1964.
4. Drucker, E. Cognitive styles and class stereotypes. In *The Culture of Poverty: A critique,* E. Leacock (ed.), New York: Simon & Schuster, 1971.
5. Ginsburg, H. *The Myth of the Deprived Child: Poor Children's intellect and Education.* New Jersey: Prentice-Hall 1972.
6. Golden, M., Birns, B., Bridges, W., & Moss, A. Social class differentiation in cognitive development among black preschool children. *Child Development 42,* 1971.
7. Guilford, J. P. *The Nature of Human intelligence.* New York: McGraw-Hill, 1967.
8. Hertiz, M., Birch, H., Thomas, A., Mendez, O. Class and ethnic differences in the responsiveness of preschool children to cognitive demands. Monographs of the Society for Research in Child Development, 33:1, 1968.
9. Hetherington, M., & Parke, R. *Child Psychology: A Contemporary Viewpoint.* New York: McGraw-Hill.
10. Hurley, *Poverty and Mental Retardation.* New York: 1969.
11. Klineberg, O. *Negro Intelligence and Selective Migration.* New York: Columbia University Press, 1935.
12. Lesser, G., Fifer, G., & Clark, D. Mental abilities of children from different social class and cultural groups. Monographs of the Society for Research in Child Development, 30, 1965.
13. McNemar, Q. *The Revision of the Stanford-Binet Scale. Massachusetts:*
14. Moynihan, D. The Negro Family: The Case for National Action.Office Policy Planning and Research, United States Department of Labor, March 1965.
15. Mumbauer, C., & Miller, J. Socioeconomic background and cognitive functioning in preschool children. *Child Development, 41,* 1970.
16. Newman, H., Freeman, F., & Holzinger, K. Twins: A Study of Heredity and Environment. *Illinois: University of Chicago Press, 1937.*
17. Ryan, Joanna. IQ – the illusion of objectivity. In *Race and Intelligence: The Fallacies Behind the Race–IQ Controversy.* K. Richardson & D. Spears (eds.). Maryland: Penguin, 1972.
18. Ryckman, D. A comparison of information processing abilities of middle and lower class negro kindergarten boys. *Exceptional Children, 33,* 1967.
19. Scarr-Salapatek, S., & Weinberg,R. The war over race and IQ: When black children grow up in white homes. *Psychology Today,* December 1975.

20. Sitkei , G., & Meyers, E. Comparative structure of intellect in middle, and lower-class four year olds of two ethnic groups. Developmental Psychology, 1, *1969.*
21. Skills, H. Adult status of children with contrasting early life experiences. Monographs of the Society for Research in Child Development, 31, 1966.
22. Spearman, C. *The Abilities of Man.* New York: MacMillan, 1927.
23. Terman, L., & Merrill, M. (Mearsuring Intelligence. *Massachusetts:* Houghton Mifflin, 1939.
24. Thurstone, L. I., & Thurstone, T. G. Factorial studies of intelligence. *Psychometric Monographs,* No. 2, 1941.
25. Watson, P. Can racial discrimination affect IQ? *In Race and Intelligence.* Maryland: Penguin, 1972.

THE BLACK CHILD – LANGUAGE AND COMMUNICATION

The ability to understand and produce speech, i.e., to generate language, is a universal genetic endowment of all normal human beings. This inherent linguistic capacity permits the child of any race, color or creed to learn within about four years the largest percentage of "probably the most complex systems of rules a person ever learns (9)." The innate linguistic capacity of humans, like their intellectual capacity we referred to earlier, is extremely flexible, allowing the child to adaptively respond to and learn any language it is exposed to regardless of its racial origin. The human linguistic capacity is stimulated and developed in the growing child by his exposure to the speech of its caretakers, family and culture. These innately specialized human linguistic capacities naturally predisposes the infant to respond to human voice and speech of adults around him in a selective manner from the very first month of life. From the first weeks and ensuing months of life before it can clearly utter its first single word the infant can and does (1) "vibrate" synchronously with the rhythmic and syncopated speaking patterns of its caretakers, parents and others who may be conversing within his hearing range, (2) distinguish the human voice from the nonhuman voices and other sounds (24), (3) distinguish its mother's voice from that of other females (13), (4) modulate their own cooing, babbling, etc, in systematically responsive ways to the tone quality and pitch of the speech they hear around them and to speech directed at them (7), (5) modulate and intonate their babbling in a way that resembles the tonal and pitch qualities of their "native" language, (22), (6) respond in a differentiated manner to the "intonation patterns of both individual syllables and sentences (23)," (7) respond in a differentiated manner in the pitch of its babbling responses to its mother and father (14).

All infants regardless of cultural or environmental background, in their acquisition of spoken language follow basically the same rate, sequence or order of prelinguistic oral behavior, e.g., undifferentiated crying, differentiated crying, cooing, babbling, lallation, echolalia, expressive jargon (18). Even in their early linguistic speech they all follow the same basic pattern, the one-word sentence or "holophrase," then the multiword sentence and finally, grammatically correct verbal utterances (18). There is also substantial evidence that all children acquire language by use of the same basic rules:

> Despite the fact that during acquistion each child hears a different set of language utterances, the same basic rules for understanding and speaking are acquired by all children exposed to a given language or dialect (9).

Let us "recap" in a more conventional and very cursory way the sequencing and timing of the child's "linguistic" accomplishment up to age two. In the early weeks and months all infants make essentially the same sounds, some of which are not found in their native language and which are very difficult for adults to pronounce. After passing through the prebabbling phase children all over the world begin making babbling sounds at about six months and this babbling soon begins to exhibit the systematic qualities we mentioned above. Through a series of successive approximations the child's babbling takes on the shape of its "mother tongue." As the babbling stage ends near the end of the first year the child moves on to use his first word in his communicative utterances. From approximately the age of eighteen months to two years he begins to use two-word combinations. At around this age he also is maturationally ready to begin in earnest to master the basic syntax of his "mother tongue" and this mastery will basically complete by four or five (9). The use of spoken language expands the child's world tremendously. The world is decoded and differentiated through the child's phenomenally growing use of language. Language comes to signify things, actions and psychological states in terms of the past, present and future. The acquistion of language presages remarkable personality and cognitive changes.

The Biological Basis of Language Behavior. The "universal" features which marks the acquistion of language by children regardless of culture or environmental background that we have just finished describing seems to indicate that a basic biological mechanism or set of mechanisms that are common to all human beings must be at work here. The evidence for such a position is substantial enough for us to say with confidence that the basis for language development rests on the anatomical, physiological, biochemical nature of the human central nervous system — the system which distinguishes the human species from the nonhuman species and the system that is common to all human beings (14, 6, 16,). The anatomical and physiological features which are the foundation of uniquely human language include:

> . . . differences in oropharyngeal morphology, cerebral dominance, specialization of cerebrocortical typography, special coordination centers for motor speech, specialized temporal pattern perception, special respiratory adjustment, and tolerance for prolonged speech activities. All of the special features together permit speech reception and the precise and very rapid movements of the articulators that are necessary for speech production (17).

We accept as fact the view which is well-supported by evidence, that prelinguistic and early linguistic behavior such as differentiated crying, cooing, chuckling, prebabbling and babbling, time of onset of using one word meanings, two word and later multi-word sentences, etc., that are apparent in children the world over, develop under the influence of an inherently human biological-maturational process. This biological-maturational process in its early phases of development is relatively uninfluenced by social or environmental-experiential factors.

Lenneberg (14), in a classic study of language development set the tone and direction the "biolinguistic" point of view we have alluded to above. It was he who argued most pursuasively and supported with substantial evidence that the human language learning capability is a correlate or result of maturational processes; that certain stages in language development are interlocked with certain relevant stages of motor development —themselves related to other physical-maturational factors; that the onset of language behavior is biologically determined and not sociologically determined; that specifically, human language behavior is related to uniquely human anatomical and physiological features and that language development follows a definite fixed sequence at a relatively constant chronological age. He demonstrated that individual differences in time-of-speech onset are related to differences in rate of motor development which are basically biologically determined (if the reader will recall black children as a group up to about the second year are psychomotorically more advanced than are white children as a group. This may in part account for the fact that black children on the average have been found to be more advanced in their language development during this period also). Lenneberg also suggests that individual differences may also be due to complex biological-social interactions. But the basic process is biological. Unfortunately, we cannot pursue the interesting linguistic and psycho-linguistic viewpoints as represented mainly by Chomsky (6) and McNeill (16) who see certain innate capacities, endowments and unlearned abilities in the maturing child for analyzing speech input, and hypothesis testing.

The Sociocultural Basis of Language Behavior. It is obvious to even the most casual observer that different races and nationalities speak different, that within races and nations language and dialect differ according to region, cultural, class and educational background. Yet as we have documented in the foregoing section no one is born speaking or born with a special predisposition to speak exclusively one particular language or only his "mother tongue. For apparent adaptive reasons the human neonate is born only with the *capacity* for learning to speak *any* language it is exposed to for a certain period of time. Consequently, regardless of race the infant is capable of learning with equal ease any language he is exposed to for the first four or five years of his life. Thus, a black infant if reared in China from the first days of his life by Chinese caretakers and surrounded by Chinese speaking people, would grow up to speak Chinese as fluently as his Chinese caretakers and neighbors.

In the previous chapter we saw that all races are born with an equal learning or intellectual *capacity* but the ways in which this capacity is transformed or how it manifests itself is socioculturally, geophysically and situationally determined. Language capacity shares these same properties and is transformed and made manifest by the same determinants. It is the influence of these determinants on the innate human language capacity that is the essential concern of a group of linguists referred to as sociolinguists (or more accurately, environmentalist/sociolinguists). The environmentalists and the sociolinguists emphasize the part played by environmental and/or social factors in language acquisition and production e.g., the role of imitation and reinforcement in the acquisition of certain speech patterns and habits and the role of social class membership, regional habitation, etc., in language behavior.

One of the articles of faith to the sociolinguist is that a considerable diversity exists in the way in which language can be used to meet needs demanded by individual social structures. . .Many of the central problems in developmental sociolinguistics have been summarized in the statement that in addition to the child's acquisition of the structural rules of his language, he also must learn another set of rules which refer to when he should speak, when he should remain silent, which linguistic code he should use, and to whom (17).

The sociolinguists recognize as did Haskins and Butts (10) that:

In learning language, the baby is not only learning to communicate verbally, but he is also assimilating the culture's system of meanings and its ways of thinking and reasoning.

It is from the sociolinguistic orientation that we derive most of our evidence relevant to the black child and his use or non-use of "black English" and/or "standard English." We shall now briefly review the history and usage of "black English" in this country and in later sections study its relations to cognition and education.

A Brief History of the Black Dialect. Black Americans dialects are probably the result of a creolized form of English, at one time spoken on southern plantations by black slaves (20, 21, 1, 8). This creolized plantation English appears to be related to the creolized English spoken by some blacks in Jamaica and other Carribean islands. Through the interaction with white speech, the black dialect can no longer be considered true creole dialects, but still they maintain many creole features and structural characteristics (8).

Africans who were captured as slaves and brought to the New World were forced to learn to use some type of English. Dillard, a student of black English states:

African languages survived in the New World for a time. . .Although many of the slaves may not have had to relinquish their African languages immediately, they all found themselves in a situation in which they had to learn an auxillary language in a hurry in order to establish communication in the heterogeneous groups into which they were thrown. This mixing of speakers of a large number of languages, with no one language predominant, is the perfect condition for the spread of pidgin language, which is in a sense the ultimate in auxillary languages. In the colonies which became the early United States, Pidgin English served the purpose of a *lingua Franca*... in a very complicated language contact situation... When the African slaves produced children, there was no one African language which those children could use with their peer group. Even though the mothers (or fathers) spoke African languages and may in some cases have taught them to their offspring, the children would have found little use for these languages. With their playmates they would have used the common language — in some cases Pidgin English, which is classified as an English creole as soon as it has such native speakers... In view of the general conditions of the West African slave trade, it seems reasonable to believe that Pidgin English was in use in the slave trade by the beginning of the seventeenth century, if not slightly earlier... Slaves coming to the New World by 1620 must have had some means of communicating with their masters and among themselves. A little reflection will show that the latter is probably the more important consideration (8).

Thus, for many blacks pidginized English became their native language. Stewart (20), in an effort to explain the widespread use of a number of varieties of pidginized English in the New World (Americas and the Carribean) offered the posibility that pidginized English "originated as a *lingua franca* in the trade centers and slave factories on the West African coast."

As time passed during the course of the 18th century the character of pidgin English changed in response to changes in the black population and other social pressures. Among blacks during this time language behavior differed according to their social-occupational status. The more privileged domestic servants, educated, wealthy and free blacks spoke a more standardized form of English than did the "field hands" who used a more creolized English.

This situation existed up to the time of the Civil War and until after the war when the dissolution of slavery and the plantation system and the increasing access to education to blacks of all social ranks, the older creolized, field-hand English began to lose many of its unique characteristics and to assume those of the white oral and written English dialects. Both whites and blacks influenced the language behavior of the other as they continued to interact.

Since the abolishment of slavery the number of blacks who speak standard English has increased greatly. However, it has been estimated that a large majority of blacks still speak a "radically nonstandard" English (18). In fact, it has been estimated that some 80% of blacks speak some form of black English which has maintained identifiable characteristics of their ancestral pidgin English.

The term "pidgin" is not well understood, and many people feel—without cause—insulted when told that their ancestors depended upon such a language. From the point of view of the linguist, such a feeling is irrational. A pidgin language has rules (regular principles of sentence construction) like any other language. Syntactic rules of a high order of regularity can be written for any pidgin, and those rules will generate an infinite number of new sentences . . . In short, pidgins are not formed by distortions of the syntactic patterns of the "standard" language, even if the prejudice of Europeans has usually led them to conclude that this is true . . . It (pidgin) is designed to be used by diverse linguistic groups. It tends to "lose" or "rid itself of" . . . the more finicky, trivial features of language . . . . Pidgin English doesn't have all those irksome irregular verbs (18)–Dillard.

Thus, present-day black English still features the linguitic remmants of its Creole past in addition to the fact that it reflects the current black sociocultural situation. This demands that we conceive it as a dialect in its own right, not as just a distortion of standard English.

. . . . this means that such negro patterns as the zero copula, the zero possessive, or undifferentiated pronouns should not be ascribed to greater carelessness, laziness, or stupidity on the part of the negroes, but rather should be treated as what they really are – language patterns which have been in existence for generations and which their present users have acquired, from parent and peer, through a perfectly normal kind of language-learning process (21).–Stewart

Some Structural Differences Between Standard and Black English. Baratz (2) listed a number of basic assumptions made by linguists concerning different languages:

1. The linguist takes as basic that all humans develop language.
2. Subsumed under this is that the language is a well-ordered system with a predictable sound pattern, grammatical structure, and vocabulary (in this sense, there are no "primitive" languages).
3. The linguist assumes that any verbal system used by a community that fulfills the above requirements is a language and that *no language is structurally better than any other language.*
4. The second assumption of the linguist is that *children learn language in the context of their environment.*
5. The third assumption of the linguist works with is that *by the time a child is five he has developed language; he has learned the rules of his linguistic environment.*

(emphasis by the author)

In terms of the above quotation what is called black English or the black dialect qualifies without reservation as a language. Particularly, in terms of statements 2 and 3, black English must be approached as a *bona fide* language. The evaluation of the competence and academic performance of the black child must be considered in this light.

What are some of the structural characteristics of black English? How does it differ from standard English?

Firstly, it is obvious that black and standard English contain many more similarities than differences. The major differences seem to occur in the area of the sound system, grammar, and vocabulary. Let us interject something here which we will discuss in detail later: The differences between black English and standard ("white") English is not due to any "deficiencies" or "deprivations" of black people or children. The following examples will give us some idea of the differences between black and standard English (taken from Baratz (2):

Variable	Standard English	Negro Nonstandard
Linking verb	He *is* going	He . . . goin'
Possessive marker	John's cousin	John . . . cousin
Plural marker	I have five cents	I got five cent . . .
Subject expression	John . . . lives in New York	John *he* live in New York
Verb form	I *drank* the milk	I *drunk* the milk
Past marker	Yesterday he walk*ed* home	Yesterday he walk . . . home
Verb agreement	He runs home	He run . . . home
	She *has* a bicycle	She *have* a bicycle
Future form	I *will* go home	I'*ma* go home
"If" construction	I asked *if he did it*	I ask *did he do it*
Negation	I *don't* have *any*	I *don't* got *none*
Indefinite article	I want *an* apple	I want *a* apple
Pronoun form	We *have* to do it	*Us* got to do it
	His book	*He* book
Preposition	He is over *at* his friend's house	He over *to* his friend house
	He teaches *at* Francis Pool	He teach . . . Francis Pool
Be	Statement: He *is here all the time*	Statement: He be *here*
Do	Contradiction: No, *he isn't*	Contradiction: No, *he don't*

The above schema indicates only a few of the systematic differences between standard and black English. The important thing to remember here is that the differences are *systematic,* that black English has a definite grammatical structure and structured rules for producing understandable sentences for conversants within the black subculture and for those who use the black vernacular.

Baratz reported an experiment in which the subjects were third–and fifth-grade students from two schools in the Washington, D.C. area. "One was an inner-city, impact-aid school; all the children in this school were negroes. The other was a school in Maryland, located in an integrated low-middle-income community; all the children from that school were white." A sen-

148

tence repetition test was constructed that contained thirty sentences, fifteen in standard English and fifteen in black nonstandard. The sentences were presented on tape to each child, who was asked to repeat the sentence after hearing them once. Examples of some of the sentences presented are:

Standard English:	Does Deborah like to play with the girl that sits next to her in school?
Nonstandard English:	Do Deborah like to play wid da girl that sit nex' ta her at school?
Standard English:	I asked Tom if he wanted to go to the picture that was at the Howard.
Nonstandard English:	I ask Tom do he wanna go to the picture that be playin' at the Howard.
Standard English:	She was the girl who didn't go to school because she had no clothes to wear.
Nonstandard English:	Dat girl, she ain' go ta school 'cause she ain' got no clothes to wear.

Each child was asked to repeat exactly what he heard as best he could. After the child had repeated all the sentences he was asked to listen to the sentences and to identify who was speaking by choosing from a set of pictures which contained images of black and white men, women and children. The data was analyzed to ascertain what had happened to the following constructions:

Standard Construction	Nonstandard Construction
Third person singular	Non-addition of third person-**s**
Presence of Copula	Zero copula
Negation	Double negation; and **ain't**
If + subject + verb	Zero "if" + verb + subject
Past markers	Zero past morpheme
Possessive marker	Zero possessive morpheme
Plural	Use of **be**

Here are the results of the experiment:

(1) Although the speaker of both the standard and the Negro non-standard sentences was white, third-graders identified the standard sentence 73.3 percent of the time as being spoken by a white man, and the nonstandard sentences 73.3 percent of the time as being spoken by a Negro.

(2) Of the fifth-graders, 83.3 percent judged the standard sentence as being spoken by a white man, while 93.3 percent judged the nonstandard sentence as being spoken by a Negro. Eighty percent of the white children and 76.6 percent of the Negro children identified standard sentences as being spoken by a white man. Nonstandard sentences were

149

judged to be spoken by a Negro by 83.3 percent of the time by both Negro and white children.

(3) ... results of this sentence-repetition experiment indicated that whites were superior to Negroes in repeating standard English sentences, but on the other hand, Negroes were far superior to whites in repeating Negro nonstandard English sentences ...

(4) Although white speakers did significantly better than black speakers in responding to standard English sentences, it is clear that the black child's responses to standard English were consistent. An examination of the black child's errors revealed that he did not fail utterly to complete the sentence; he did not jumble his response; nor did he use a "word salad." His error responses were consistent ...

(5) This same behavior was evident in the white children when asked to repeat Negro nonstandard sentences. Black children were superior to white children in repeating these stimuli. Here again the error responses followed a definite pattern ....

(6) ... The results of this research clearly indicate that 1- there are two dialects involved in the education complex of black children (especially in schools with a white middle-class curriculum orientation); 2- black children are generally not bidialectal; and 3- there is evidence of interference from their dialect when black children attempt to use standard English.

(7) The fact that standard and nonstandard speakers exhibited similar translation behaviors when confronted with sentences that were outside of their primary code indicates quite clearly that the language deficiency that has so often been attributed to the low-income Negro child is not a language deficit so much as a difficulty in code switching when the second code (standard English) is not as well learned as the first (nonstandard English).

(8) ... The disadvantaged black child must not only decode the written words, he must also "translate" them into his own language. This presents him with an almost insurmountable obstacle since the written words frequently do not go together in any pattern that is familiar or meaningful to him. He is baffled by this confrontation with 1- a new language with its new syntax; 2- a necessity to learn the meaning of graphic symbols, and 3- a vague, or not so vague (depending upon the cultural and linguistic sophistication of the teacher) sense that there is something terribly wrong with his language.

We have quoted Baratz's work at length because it elucidates so excellently the central problem of the speaker of black English in confrontation with a dominant standard English-speaking society. It should be obvious from this study that the white child is as **linguistically "deficient"** when it comes to dealing with black English as is the black child when it comes to dealing with standard (white) English, and for the same reason, as each child is imprinted with the language of his own environment he becomes less capable of dealing competently with the language used in another. His "deficiency" has nothing to do with an inherent or learned "deficiency" in cognitive ability. Standard English for the speaker who uses black English exclusively, is for all practical purposes a foreign or second language. His difficulties with standard English is very similar to the difficulties that any non-English-speaking immigrant would have. If the black child speaks "bad" standard English then the white child speaks "bad" black English and if the black child does this because he is supposed to be disadvantaged or "deficient" then the white child must also be disadvantaged or "deficient."

Black English and Linguistic Conflicts of the Black Child. What are some of the difficulties faced by the speaker of black English when dealing with standard English? The work of Labov and his co-workers (Cohen, Robins and Lewis) (12), seems to provide most of the relevant answers to this question.

In Labov's view the use of nonstandard English adversely affects the acquisition of reading skills and the acquisition of other skills requiring the use of standard English in at least two ways. First, there may exist a **structural conflict** between black English and standard English so that a written or spoken standard English sentence is almost rendered or translated in its nonstandard equivalent. Thus the sentence **"Does** Deborah like to play with ..." becomes for the speaker of black English **"Do** Deborah like to play wif ..." Parenthetically, all too often teachers tend to over-react to this tendency of the black child to translate standard English into his own vernacular or they tend to see this translative behavior as an indication of ignorance, or of "cultural deprivation." In approaching standard English the black child, as is the case with any non-standard English-speaking child, does not simply throw away his previous language experience. That prior linguistic experience "interferes" with his efforts to read, write and speak standard English just as French born and reared child's French-speaking experience would "interfere" with his efforts to learn English. As Baratz demonstrated, the situation is reversed in the case of the white child who "translates" nonstandard English into his own standard English vernacular. The white child's standard English experience "interferes" with his competency in dealing with black English.

Secondly, Labov sees a **functional conflict** as being a source of difficulty confronting the users of nonstandard English in attempting to acquire standard English sentences. One's language serves, in addition to its communicative function, an identity function. The black child, like any other child or individual identifies with his primary groups and culture through a shared

151

language. Standard English may appear to be strange, effeminate or generally "white" or alien or as unimportant and for him to learn it and speak it exclusively may imply to the child that he has to repudiate one of the most important things, his language, which identifies him with his family, race, culture, peer group and with himself. The learning of a new language often is a first step toward cultural alienation. Therefore, when confronted with learning to speak or read standard English, the black child is placed in the midst of a conflict which involves learning that English and possibly by doing so breaking a strong connection which ties him to his peers and his ethnic-family background. At bottom, the functional conflict boils down to a question of not whether the black child **can** learn to fully use standard English, but whether he **wants** to learn to use it.

Labov, and we agree, sees the conflict between the different structures and functions of black English and standard English as one of the major sources of the failure of many black children in school. This is especially true since these schools usually demand that standard English be used exclusively and these schools are also a source of conflict between black values and white middle-class school ideology. Labov is also correct when he says that in order to understand the function of black English one has to know something about the value system and social structure which are the foundation of that language.

Some writers see the use of black English as indicative of "inferior" speech behavior, which, in turn, is the basis for deficient thought processes and academic failure (3). These writers seem to have been influenced by the early work of Bernstein (4), a British sociologist, who promulgated what may be referred to as the "verbal deficit" model of lower class (often interchangeable with "black") language behavior. (We must note here that Bernstein's later work (5) takes on a significantly different orientation) Bernstein's work was based on the child rearing practices of the British middle and lower classes. However, his American disciples have sought to transplant his theoretical (and largely speculative) ideas to the American class situation and specifically to the "culturally deprived" black children of the urban ghettos.

According to Bernstein, middle class life is characterized by a value system which emphasizes stability, rationality, order and emotional self-control. The middle class is future oriented, i.e., it values delayed gratification as necessary for achieving long-term goals as contrasted with the present orientation of the lower class which seeks immediate gratification and concentrates on short-term goals. Instead of using direct physical punishment in disciplining their children, which Bernstein sees as a characteristic of the lower class, the middle class in disciplining its children uses verbal methods, explanations, reasoning and justifies in rational terms to the child why he is being punished. Because the middle class child is often rewarded or punished in verbal terms, terms which are often subtle and complex in their meanings and implications

152

and because the child is also called upon to explain, justify and logically set forth reasons for his behavior he is forced to develop the ability to decode relatively elaborate and complex sentences and concepts and he is also forced to code his verbal explanations and expressions using similar types of sentences and concepts. This type of linguistic behavior as expressed by middle class speech in general and which is typical of middle class mother-child interactions is seen by Bernstein as "elaborated" because of its supposedly subtle, rational, complex, differentiated grammatically precise nature. The "elaborated linguistic code" used by the middle class apparently allows for a broader range, abstract and conceptual thought. The middle class child exposure to this **elaborated code** causes him to learn this linguistic code and the cognitive style it represents and is also the means by which the child learns to accept certain class and cultural values such as delay of gratification, the striving for order, stability, rationality, self-control, "social competence and moral behavior (9)."

Bernstein sees the conceptual, abstract and rational skills acquired by the middle class child as a result of his exposure to his class's elaborated code as prime factors necessary for flexible, complex cognition which is essential for academic success, intellectual advancement and for successfully coping with the demands of a middle class society.

According to Bernstein the lower class (in this country read black) socialization process produces almost the complete opposite results of the middle class. The lower class world is relatively unstable, less orderly and rational as compared to the middle class. Lower class parental discipline is less rational and more arbitrary and the demands placed on the child are not rationally or conceptually justified. Neither is the child demanded to rationalize his behavior, attitudes or intentions in a logical, abstract or conceptual terms. The linguistic code used by lower class and in lower class mother-child interactions is referred to by Bernstein as a **restricted code.** This simple, direct, emotion-laden code does not contain the subtlety, complexity and various shades of meanings that supposedly characterizes the elaborated code of the middle class. As a result of his exposure to the restricted code the lower class child does not develop the ability to understand or produce complex verbal expressions, particularly those involving conceptual, abstract and complex relational categories. The restricted code is also seen as at least partly responsible for the inculcation of certain lower class values in the child such as overconcern with immediate gratification, lack of concern for order, stability, self-control, "social competence and moral behavior." The restricted code ill prepares the lower class child for academic success, for advanced intellectual thought, etc.

The zero copula and the zero "if+verb+subject" expressions which characterize black English, in terms of Bernstein's theory, implies that the "deficient" restricted code (black English) cannot adequately deal with logical implication, that future-oriented concepts are not well handled. The restricted code confuses ready-made conclusions and cliches with reasoning. Self-reference and personal and interpersonal experiences are the core of decision making by lower class youth, not logical, objective rationality. The restricted black English code with its idiomatic, culture-bound, concrete-functional and simple characteristics supposedly cannot serve as a vehicle for universal, conceptual-analytic, complex thought. The restricted black English code then leads the child or individual to confuse description with analysis, personal experience with generality. It also restricts his understanding of causal and conceptual relations. In summary, the user of the restricted code, according to Bernstein, has (1) a low level of conceptualization, (2) a disinterest in processes, (3) a concern with the immediately given, (4) "a tendency to accept and respond to an authority that inheres in the form of social relationships, rather than in reasoned or logical principles."

A comment by Hetherington and Parke (9) regarding Bernstein's superficially attractive theory very adequately sums up our own attitude in this matter:

The influence of Bernstein's work has had, especially in the United States, is both surprising and dismaying for several reasons. For one thing, although his claims are often cited as if they were established fact, they are actually highly speculative. . . . Bernstein makes value judgements that can be called "classist." He clearly judges the linguistic style as well as many other values and characteristics of the middle class to be more desirable than those of the lower class. Social class stereotyping is certainly involved in his very broad descriptions. . . Bernstein's work is often applied in the United States to black-white language differences, which involve other issues in addition to social class . . . Perhaps Bernstein's work has been so widely accepted and cited, despite it inadequacies, **because it feeds into preconceived notions of the "inferiority" of lower class speech, and especially lower class black speech.**

Bernstein, like many psychologists, when analyzing lower class behavior and especially black behavior makes the fatal mistake of not beginning at the beginning. They confuse the symptoms of a disease with its causes. They see the symptoms as the disease. This is the main reason studies based on Bernstein's theory have been generally nonsupportive of his theory or inconclusive (9).

While we agree with Bernstein that lower class (viz, black) socialization processes lead to linguistic styles different from those of the middle class (viz, white) and that the lower class linguistic style and its concomitants make adjustment to middle class society difficult for its users, we cannot support the idea that the black or lower class linguistic style represents a "deficit" in their language or "deficits" in their cognitive-intellectual abilities. Bernstein, as do many psychologists, confuses performance and ability or performance and competence. The fact that black English may have zero copulas, "If-then" categories, possessives, etc., does not mean that blacks cannot think as elaborately as whites or that they do not possess the logical capacity the same as whites. For much of what is left unverbalized by the users of black English is fully implied, and is understood by its users. Many people, psychologists included, make the unwarranted assumption that "a well-turned phrase" is inherently more logical than one considered not so. "Correct" language usage is not intrinsically correlated in a one-to-one fashion with "correct" or logical thinking. There is often a confusion of the content of speech with its vehicular characteristics.

Robinson (18) tested the hypothesis that the "restricted code" may be descriptive of poor children's linguistic performance but not their cognitive functioning or competence. The implication of this hypothesis is that the lower class child has the competence to use effectively the "elaborated code" but for various reasons may not develop it or use it. Robinson found that children who normally used the restricted code could use the elaborated code effectively when the situation demanded, thereby indicating that the necessary competence existed. When the children did not need the elaborated code they used their usual mode of speech. This supports our contention that the manifest character of speech, like the manifest character of "intelligence," is socioculturally, geophysically and situationally determined; that speech like "intelligence" is an adaptive dimension of the human personality. For instance, one study showed that poor black children aged 11 years used two linguistic "registers" - a "school register" which they used with persons of authority and a "non-school register" which they used with peers and in their neighborhoods. The first "register" was characterized by simplistic syntax, a lack of fluency and expressiveness, and shortened sentences. The second, was characterized by the fluency, expressiveness, syntactic complexity and sentence length one would expect of an 11-year-old (11). When black children verbalize about things of interest to themselves and their peers and when this verbalization takes place in its natural setting it becomes obvious that the black child is as narratively and creatively gifted as his white counterpart. However, white middle class conceit which sees the interests of black children as inferior and white middle class oriented schools which do not allow for the expression of black creativity conceives black verbal behavior as being inferior and as something to be extinguished.

Bernstein and similar thinkers confuse cause and effect when it comes to dealing with black linguistic behavior and black behavior in general. Linguistically speaking their assumptions if followed to their logical conclusions would have the individual hopelessly a prisoner of his own language. For Bernstein: "Different speech systems or codes create for their speakers different orders of relevance and relation " (4). Which comes first, orders of relevance and relation or different speech systems? Isn't it more likely that spoken language reflects a social-psychological-physical reality than the other way around and that language changes as that reality changes? In an adaptive sense, isn't that the way it should be? Language is an outgrowth of social and physical reality. This does not deny that there may exist a reciprocal relationship between reality and language wherein language may effectively influence one's perception of reality. There is no argument here. However, this is not the same as saying that language *creates* "relevance and relation" and reality.

The so-called restricted code that black English may represent faithfully reflects the restricted world or social-physical reality of black existence. (let us note at this point that strictly speaking, black English is no more "restricted" than standard (white) English in the sense that they are both bound and restricted to their cultural roots in equal ways. In the sense that white English was evolved for functional adaptation to the concrete social-physical world of white existence, it is as "functional" and "concrete" as black English is accused of being though black English serves exactly the same purpose as does its white counterpart. Similarly, white English which has evolved to symbolize a comparatively broader white universe of action is in essence no more "universal" than is black English which was evolved for exactly the same purpose. The reason black English appears to be less "universal" in its meanings is because that English is designed to define the lesser universal sphere of action of blacks as compared to whites. As we have stated before the white individual is as "concretely" tied to his cultural world as is the black individual, linguistically speaking and otherwise.

The "particularistic" nature of lower class and black English then reflects the restricted, particularistic role played by these groups in their communities and in the world as well as the narrow demands made on them by the society and culture. Bernstein himself implies this when he indicates that the lower class child is not faced with the problems of understanding complex reasoning, enduring relations and abstract-conceptual categories demanded of the middle class child. He is not expected to play the same role in the society and the world as his middle class brother. The relatively "simple," direct, "concrete," realities of the ghetto is reflected in the "simple," "direct," "concrete," language of black English adaptively designed to fit the inhabitants for survival and functioning in such an environment. Black English, as is the case with any other language, is designed to be spoken within a particular community of people. Italian is meant to be used principally by Italians and therefore is not "inferior" because it is not English. One must be careful and not take a simplistic view of black English such as its "incapacity" to communicate complex ideas. Even standard, everyday English cannot handle many complex ideas and relationships in many areas. These must be handled by other "particularistic," "restricted" languages such as the languages of many professions — the sciences, philosophies, mathematics, etc.

The implication should by now be clear, that language, like "intelligence," is an adaptive instrument, necessary for meeting environmental demands. As environmental demands change so will the language which reflects those changing demands. Bernstein in a later work (5) could have had this in mind when he stated:

How do different forms of communications arise? *The particular form of social relation acts selectively upon what is said, when it is said, and how it is said; the form of social relation regulates the options that speakers take up at both syntactic and lexical levels.* . . . To put it another way, the consequences of the form the social relation takes are transmitted in terms of certain syntatic and lexical selections. . . . *Thus different forms of social relation can generate very different speech systems or linguistic codes. . . . Children who have access to different speech systems or codes – that is, children who learn different roles by virtue of their families' class positions in a society – may adopt quite different social and intellectual orientations and procedures despite a common developmental potential.* (Emphasis by author).

Implications and Recommendations:

1. Black English is a language like any other. Therefore, it is not "bad" English and does not represent mental inferiority.

2. Do not permit your child to be made to feel bad because he does not speak standard English and do not allow him to be degraded because of his dialect.

3. However, you must recognize that in order for your child to fully function in a white middle class dominated world he must learn to handle standard English as competently as any white middle class child.

4. Consequently, you must teach your black child to become truly bilingual. You must teach him to speak fluently standard English while at the same time not denying him the use of his black English under the appropriate circumstances.

5. Tell your child that in order to attain his career goals which more than likely lies within the realm of white middle class functioning he must learn to speak standard English, build his vocabulary, read and write well, but that there is nothing "wrong" with the language spoken by his people.

6. You as a parent must be your child's major teacher of standard English because by the time he begins school his language patterns would have already been set and are difficult to change. Your language training must be rigorous and intensive to offset the influence of peers and other influential persons in your child's life whose language behavior may not be what you desire for your child.

7. Watch your own language behavior when around your children. Read often to your children and encourage good reading habits in them.

8. Check the appendix of this book for books which will aid you in linguistically training your child.

REFERENCES

1. Bailey, B. *Jamaican Creole syntax.* London: Cambridge University Press, 1966.

2. Baratz, J. Teaching reading in an urban negro school system. In F. Williams (ed.), *Language and poverty.* Illinois: Markham, 1973.

3. Bereiter, C., & Engelmann, S. *Teaching disadvantaged children in the preschool.* New Jersey: Prentice-Hall, 1966.

4. Bernstein, B. Social class and linguistic development: A theory of social learning. In A. H. Hakey, J. Fland, & C. A. Anderson (eds.), *Education, economy and society.* New York: Free Press, 1951.

5. Bernstein, B. A sociolinguistic approach to socialization: With some reference to educability. In F. Williams (ed.), *Language and poverty.* Illinois: Markham, 1970.

6. Chomsky N. *Language and mind.* New York: Harcourt, Brace & World, 1968.

7. Condon, W., & Sander, L. Neonate movement synchronized with adult speech: Interactional participation and language acquisition. *Science, 183,* 1974.

8. Dillard, J. *Black English: Its history and usage in the U.S.* New York: Random House, 1972.

9. Hetherington, E., & Parke, R. *Child psychology: A contemporary viewpoint.* New York: McGraw-Hill, 1975.

10. Haskins, J., & Butts, H. *The psychology of black language.* New York: Barnes & Noble, 1973.

11. Houston, S. An examination of some assumptions about the language of the disadvantaged child. *Child Development, 41,* 1970.

12. Labov, W., et al. A study of the non-standard English of Negro and Puerto Rican speakers in New York City. Final report, U.S. Office of Education Cooperative Research Project No. 3288. New York: Columbia University, 1968.

13. Laroche, J., & Tcheng, F. *Le sourire du nourisson.* Lorrain: Publications Universitaires, 1963.

14. Lenneberg, E. *Biological foundations of language.* New York: Wiley, 1967.

15. Lieberman, P. *Intonation, perception, and language.* Massachusetts: Massachusetts Institute of Technology, 1967.

16. McNeill, D. *The acquisition of language, the study of developmental psycholinguistics.* New York: Harper & Row, 1970.

17. Osser, H. Biological and social factors in language development. In F. Williams (ed.), *Language and poverty.* Illinois: Markham.

18. Papalia, E., & Olds, S. *A child's world: Infancy through adolescence.* New York: McGraw-Hill, 1925.
19. Robinson, W. The elaborated code in working class language. *Language and Speech, 8,* 1965.
20. Stewart, W. Sociolinguist factors in the history of American Negro dialects. *Florida Foreign Language Reporter* Spring 1967.
21. Stewart, W. Continuity and change in American Negro dialects. *Florida Foreign Language Reporter,* Spring 1968.
22. Stewart, W. Toward a history of American negro dialect. In F. Williams (ed.), *Language and Poverty.* Illinois: Markham, 1973.
23. Weir, R. Some questions on the child's learning of phonology. In F. Smith and G. Miller (eds.), *The genesis of language.* Massachusetts: Massachusetts Institute of Technology, 1966.
24. Wolff, P. The Natural history of crying and other vocalizations in early infancy. In B. M. Foss (ed.), *Determinants of infant behavior.* Vol. 4. London: Methuen, 1966.

SOCIALIZATION AND THE BLACK CHILD

From essentially a biological organism whose main concern is with maintaining its physical comfort, the human infant develops into a full-fleged individual with a unique set of values, attitudes, aspirations, tendencies, and characteristic ways of perceiving and responding to the world and to himself. This metamorphosis is accomplished through the interaction of many forces — some accidental and some not so accidental. The process by which the infant develops from its relatively undifferentiated state to that of a fully individuated human being is called socialization. Just as physical maturation is the result of the interaction of biological forces and mechanisms over a period of time so is social maturation the result of the interaction of psychosociological forces and mechanisms over a period of time. Socialization involves an acommodation to and the assimilation of group expectations, values, and norms. The socialized individual is expected to behave in accordance with these group expectations, values and norms. Socialization represents a sort of sculpturing process whereby the exceptionally pliable human infant, with all its potentialities and possibilities, is chiseled, shaped and molded by the hands of its culture, class, family and political environment.

Socialization, while an adaptive-functional process, is also a restrictive process in that it confines the individual to a relatively narrow range of what is considered acceptable and nonpunishable forms of actions, beliefs and values. The socialization process involves the shaping of the individual to fit a socially engraved perceptive, cognitive and behavioral mold, thereby determining how the individual perceives, thinks and behaves in the world. The individual is expected to play a socially defined role in his group by means of which he is to contribute to the preservation and advancement of his group. The group ascribes particular roles and sets of behavior to sex gender, occupational status, kinship relations, etc. The group rewards those individual attitudes and behavior tendencies that are congruent with its expectations. The person whose attitudes and behavior are congruent with his group expectations tends to develop and maintain a feeling of oneness and belongingness with his group and shares with the other group members a "group consciousness." The person then identifies himself and the group as one and the same and thus any unfair attack against the group is seen as an attack upon the person himself. Any degradation of the group is felt as a degradation of the self.

Prosocial, unsocial or antisocial behavior are not innate. The person develops his characteristic social behavior as a result of learning, especially as the result of early childhood learning experiences. These early childhood

160

learning experiences and their formative effects on the personality of the mature individual are themselves in part determined by the opportunities provided by his parents, peers, teachers and significant others in interaction with his own innate gifts and orientations. Obviously the prosocial individual is usually the outcome of a favorable concomitance of these factors. The unsocial or antisocial individual usually represents an unfavorable mix of these factors.

Unsocial or antisocial attitudes and tendencies often mark the behavior of persons who as children have been deprived of opportunities for favorable social interaction due to prejudice, unfavorable socioeconomic circumstances or restrictive practices of a religious or politico-social nature. Obviously, these same attitudes and tendencies may develop as a result of too much social interaction with a highly unstable, disorderly and confused social environment. What behavior is considered social or antisocial depends on the particular group norms which are used as a standard. What is socially acceptable in one group may be considered socially unacceptable in another. The characteristic behavior of a person which may be considered as adaptive in one group or culture may be considered maladaptive in another group or culture. A chief cause of black and white conflict in America is the differing attitudes of these two subcultures as to what behavior should be considered social or antisocial. Since cultural and group membership are so important to individual and group adjustment we will briefly examine the functions of these institutions —along with family and social class.

Culture is a product of human behavior and individual human behavior is in turn, a product of culture.

From their life experiences, a group develops a set of rules and procedures for meeting their needs. The set of rules and procedures, together with a supporting set of ideas and values, is called a culture... culture is everything which is socially learned and shared by the members of a society. The individual receives culture as a part of his social heritage, and in turn, he may reshape the culture and introduce changes which then become a part of the heritage of succeeding generations. (Horton and Hunt, 1968).

Only when the individual imaginatively steps outside his body and objectively observes himself does he begin to realize how much his entire personality is suffused by his culture, his society and its belief and customs. He then realizes that under the vast majority of circumstances he obeys these beliefs and customs to such a degree that he thinks that they are "naturally right" and that all others to the contrary are perversely wrong or unnatural. Assimilation and integration into a particular society leads to the tendency of all the members of that society to develop what may be called a social character, i. e., a character structure shared by all the members of a particular society in addition to their own uniquely personal character. Culture is a purposive system of behavior norms, values, attitudes, etc., which its members follow unthinkingly and by force of habit.

In the culture of his own society a man lives and dreams, shapes his ideals, formulates his questions, stages his rebellions, trains his body, and disciplines his mind. He dreams the dreams his culture suggests, wishes the wishes his culture develops, and fears the fears his culture inspires... Each person is, far more than he will ever know, *the product of his culture.* If we would understand people, we must study culture. (Horton and Hunt).

According to Horton and Hunt (10), culture has several important functions:

(1) **Culture defines situations.** Culture determines how any specific event or situation is to be interpreted by the individual. He will react to that event in terms of his cultural frame of reference.

(2) **Culture defines attitudes, values and goals.** What the person perceives as important, worth sacrificing for, "what is good, true, and beautiful" is determined by his culture. The culture controls certain individual goals and ambitions through a system of punishments and rewards. "Each society excels in those activities which the culture rewards and encourages."

(3) **Culture defines myths, legends, and the supernatural.** "Culture also provides the individual with a ready-made view of the universe... gives answers for the major imponderables of life, and fortifies the individual to meet life's crises."

(4) **Culture provides behavior patterns.** The culture provides ready-made patterns of coping with events and situations and of decoding the environment.

Social Class: Rarely is a culture monolithic and homogenized throughout its structure. This is especially true of modern complex cultures where there exist many subcultures of differing social status and power and many more primary groups which leaves their imprint on the individual character. The imprinting process of these subcultures and groups may or may not prepare their members to adjust positively to the larger society.

A social class can be viewed as a subculture. Each social class is a system of dynamically structured and related behavior patterns, values and lifestyles which differs distinctly from that of another collection of persons who also may be defined as a class. Social class differences can be radically different and the behavior and outlook of their members will differ accordingly.

The Family. The family is a subcultural unit which prepares the child to function efficiently in its class environment and in the larger culture. In many ways the family is a "mini" version of the culture to which it belongs. It translates the customs, values, ideals, beliefs and goals of its class and culture for its children through its childrearing or socialization practices. Of course, due to many factors the family may fail to measure up fully to class or cultural expectations (it may measure up to the expectations of one without doing so for the other) and produce children who are considered unsocial or antisocial or who may contribute little or nothing to the maintenance of

162

the culture though they may not behave antisocially. The emotional climate of the family, its size, socioeconomic background, the type of interfamily relations which inhere between the parents and the parents and children and the childrearing methods used by the parents are important factors which determine whether the family produces a favorable or unfavorable outcome resulting from its socialization efforts (11).

The child's relationship with its mother is crucial. It is she who determines to a great extent what happens to the child and the type of world the child experiences. Her personal characteristics will bring about various consequences for the child's development. If the mother is competent, accepts and enjoys her role and non-neurotically loves her child she will reinforce and help to develop social and cognitive competence in her child. The mother who cannot "vibrate" with her child, who is overwhelmed by family and personal problems, who is overly rigid and controlling or overly permissive and smothering, is apt to produce an incompetent child (22). The egocentric, disorganized, emotionally labile, impatient mother does not see her child as a unique human being with its own special needs and feelings. The child for her may be an extention of her own vanity and may be used to represent what she wants in the world or to make up for what she lacks in her own life. She is self-centered and not child-centered.

There is scarcely any solid research relating to the father's characteristics and their relationship to the personality development of the child. The general consensus seems to be that the father is important to the sex role orientation and identification of the male child and to the psychosexual development of the children of both sexes. The father's contribution to the strength and cohesiveness of the family bodes very well for the production of physically and emotionally healthy children. The disorganized family which may result from the father's absence portends ill for the full development of the children (though there are important exceptions to this generalization as we shall see later). The child from the disorganized family is more likely to suffer from a lack of a well integrated, flexible and competent personality and is also more likely to express hostility, alienation from the society and himself and to engage in outright antisocial behavior. Bowlby (2) itemized some of the reasons parents fail to properly care for and socialize their offspring:

CAUSES OF THE NATURAL HOME GROUP FAILING TO CARE FOR A CHILD

(1) Natural home group never established: Illegitimacy.
(2) Natural home group intact, but not functioning effectively: Economic conditions leading to unemployment of breadwinner with consequent poverty.
Chronic illness or incapacity of parent.
Instability or mental unfitness of parent.

163

(3) Natural home group broken up and therefore not functioning:
  Social calamity — war, famine.
Death of a parent.
Illness requiring hospitalization of a parent.
Imprisonment of a parent.
Desertion of one or both parents.
Separation or divorce.
Employment of father elsewhere.
Full-time employment of mother.

Any family suffering from one or more of these conditions must be regarded as a possible source of deprived children. Whether or not these children actually become deprived will depend on (a) whether both or only one parent is affected; (b) whether, if only one parent is affected, help is given to the other; and (c) whether relatives or neighbors are able and willing to act as substitutes.

There is ample evidence that a very sizeable proportion of American families meet a number of the above listed criteria. For instance, 45% of American mothers work outside the home (one in every there with children under six); there has been a substantial rise toward a 50% growth rate during the last 20 years; 10% of all children under six were living in fatherless homes in 1970; 45% of all children under six in families in poverty were living in single-parent households, the figure for non-poverty families is 3.5% (3).

The above figures are for the general population. However, if we look at black families in terms of these statistics the picture is far more pessimistic: 53% of all black children live in families below the poverty line (white families — 11%); 44% of black children have working mothers (white children — 26%); more than 30% of all black children live in single-parent families (white children —7%) (3). These figures represent national averages. In many urban areas the percentages and contrasts are much larger.

Parental Functionality of the Lower Class Black Mother as Contrasted with the Middle Class Mother. We stated earlier that one of the major functions of the family was to prepare the child to function efficiently in its class and larger culture, to translate the class and cultural expectations into socialization practices used in rearing the child. This requires that the parent's view of the expectations of the larger culture fit the social realities and that they have knowledge of the proper socialization techniques and their purpose. It also requires that a minimal geophysical, economical and psychosocial environment exist to supplement, guide and support the socialization efforts of the parents. If such environmental supports do not exist or are not utilized by the parents the socialization process will be crippled, distorted or fail and the child will grow up to be dysfunctional. The family as a unit or "parental functionality" in the sense of . . . what the family actually *does* for the child in terms of behaviors and values that will help him in later life, is affected by the

164

geophysical, economic and psychosocial resources of the family and community. It is principally the scarcity of these resources that reduces the black ghetto family's functionality to such a degree that their children are socialized to become socially dysfunctional.

The point here is that the lower-class black parent lacks the resources (economic, in particular) to bring about in his children the goals he desires. Inadvertently, ; . . the lower-class parent does serve as a role model for survival in the ghetto. But development of and facility in the ways of a peculiarly lower-class lifestyle are almost always inimical to attainments in the larger society.

The evidence. . . suggests that "difficulties" encountered by lower-class parents are chiefly the result about the resources necessary to bring about desired outcomes in their children's behavior. To the degree that the lower-class black family may be less functional for children in the sense just described, this would be due to its being systematically excluded from dominant society. If a subsystem is to socialize new members to fit the expectations of the larger system of which it is a part, the linkage of the part of the whole should be as intimate as possible. Yet at every level, particularly the economic, the larger society has effectively excluded blacks from participation in its ongoing processes. It follows, therefore, that certain black adults (especially in the lower-class) may be less able to prepare their children to "fit" the expectations of the dominant society (Scanzoni, 20).

Thus, a distinction has to be made between the goals toward which parents seek to steer their children and the means, resources and support systems by which they will aid their children in reaching the desired goals. Therefore, though the goals of two sets of parents for their children may be the same or similar, if one of that set does not have or utilize the appropriate resources, the children of that set of parents will more likely fail to reach the goals set for them or the goals they may set for themselves.

What are some of the differences between black lower class and black middle class socialization practices? Kamii and Radin (18) found the following:

(1) Lower-lower-class mothers are less responsive than middle-class mothers to **explicit** socio-emotional needs children express. . . . The mean frequency of children's attempts at eliciting a reaction (from their mother) was 11.65 for the middle-class or 5.05 for the disadvantaged class . . . It can thus be said that middle-class children not only **receive** gratifying responses significantly more frequently when they attempt to receive such responses but also **seek** gratifying responses significantly more often than do lower-lower-class children. The difference in a frequency of gratifying responses per unit time yielded a ratio of almost 4:1

(2) The mean for **"mother-initiated** interactions related to children's **implicit** need for companionship and affection. . . " was significantly higher for the middle-class mothers . . . statistically significant differences were obtained in "mother initiated interaction", "verbal communication of affection," and "non-verbal communication of affection." "Lower-lower class mothers initiate fewer interactions with children than do middle-class mothers in ways that meet children's implicit need for companionship and affection" can thus be said to be confirmed by the data."

(3) . . . various techniques used by mothers attempt to influence children's behavior. Statistically significant differences were obtained both in 'commanding' and in 'consulting.' . . . it can be said that middle-class mothers were found to use more bilateral techniques and that disadvantaged mothers tended to use more unilateral techniques.

. . . the techniques most frequently used by lower-lower-class mothers were, in descending order of frequency, commanding without explanation (35 percent), requesting gently without explanation (25 percent), coaxing (ten percent), and warning or threatening (6 percent). Middle-class mothers were found most frequently to use gentle requests without explanation (22 percent), consulting (14 percent) gentle requests with explanation (12 percent), and commanding with explanation (12 percent). *The limited repertoire of the disadvantaged mothers become evident when it is seen that 60 percent of all their attempts to influence children consisted of only two categories, i.e., commanding and gently requesting without explanation* (underlining by author).

(4) . . . middle-class mothers reward children considerably more frequently than disadvantaged mothers for behaving in desirable ways; and . . . middle-class mothers gratify children's socio-emotional needs considerably more often than disadvantaged mothers."

Though there may exist significant differences in the childrearing practices of lower class and middle class mothers the childrearing goals of both types of parents are essentially the same (1, 21, 20). In other words, lower-class black parents want their children to share in the "American dream" as much as their middle class counter-parts, but do not have the necessary resources and information to implement their desires for their children.

The lower class parent's childrearing behavior does not merely exist in a vacuum, it is intimately connected with the parents own social status and experience in the larger society. Generally what is demanded of the parents in the larger social context is what the parents demand of their children within the family context. More often than not, whether the poor black adult obeys the society's laws or not, he remains poor and unrewarded. He remains "invisible" to the ruling middle class (unless he erupts into noticeable, boisterous, destructive, riotous behavior) and does not receive equalitarian expressions of affection or rewards from the middle class managers who are too involved in maintaining their own status. For the low-income black it's "damned if you do and damned if you don't." Though the lower classes have little input into or little understanding of the rationale of the laws which middle class uses to control their behavior they are surely punished (many times out of proportion to their "crimes") if they do not obey the laws. Thus, the middle class laws are obeyed not because they are "right" or reasonable, or because they are the result of a contract between the classes or because the lower classes have "internalized" meaning and intent of the laws, but mainly to avoid punishment. The relationship of the lower class child to his parents and their "laws" parallels the relationship his parents has with the middle class managers and their laws. The lower class child does not internalize his parents values and therefore his conformity to his parent's values when they occur are mainly the result of bowing to authority and fear of punishment.

As we stated earlier the poor black parent has little to gain by obeying the laws of his middle class managers - he often remains poor. So why should he obey the laws? The poor black child is in a similar situation when, though he obeys the dictates of his parents he gains little - so why bother - except to avoid punishment. This is mainly due to the fact that the poor black parent has little to reward her child with for meeting her expectations. Consequently the child's obedient behavior responses tend to be extinguished under such conditions and alternative responses encouraged.

What we have been discussing here may be summed up under the concept of **locus of control**. This concept refers to the position or location from which the individual believes his behavior is controlled. Those who believe that their behavior and life are controlled by extrapsychic, external forces are referred to as **externalizers** (19). Those who believe that their behavior and life are controlled by internal, intrapsychic forces are referred to as **internalizers**. The internalizer believes that through his own choices and determination he can manipulate what happens to him, that he is the cause of events, that he can control events through his own abilities and resources. The externalizers believe that outside forces are responsible for what happens to them, that they are controlled by events and that their own initiative, choice and determination count for little in the ordering of things happening in their lives.

The **locus of control** is established early in childhood (6). The largest number of internalizers are found in the middle class and the smaller number in the lower class (5). White children believe more in internal controls than black children. In light of our previous discussion this should not be surprising. The greater power possessed by the middle class in general and whites in particular, their greater control over the circumstances which afffect their behavior and lives, are passed on to their children via their socialization practices and other advantages enjoyed by these groups. Conversely, the relative powerlessness of the lower class in general and blacks in particular, their

167

lesser control over the circumstances which affect their behavior and lives, are also passed on to their children via their socialization practices and the lack of advantages enjoyed by these groups.

From the vantage point of **locus of control** many behavioral and attitudinal differences between the middle and lower classes can be explained. The fabled fatalistic, apathetic attitudes of the lower class members, including parents and children, are in part due to their externalized locus of control. Since it is predominantly the middle class managers that determine what happens to the lower class and blacks, what actually happens to them seems more the result of luck or fate or the maliciousness of others than the result of their own actions or the lack of actions on their part. The externalization of locus of control in the lower class and many blacks tend to make their thinking take on a sort of magical quality,i.e., since they are seldom intimately familiar with the mechanism which bring certain events and things to pass, these events and things being "laid" on them without warning or fore-knowlege, they make their appearances and disappearances as a result of "magic" or by chance.

In summary, the attitude that things and events are occasioned by fate. luck, whites, etc. , are socialized into black children by their parents. The powerlessness, resourcelessness and the generally poor living conditions of the lower class and black parent adversely affect their parental functionality and consequently these parents tend to maintain only tenuous control over their children's behavior (and what behavior is controlled is often accomplished through physical threats and means), to lose control of their children earlier than middle-class parents, to be unsuccessful in getting their children to internalize positive values and behavior habits and in helping their children to develop the ability to delay gratification.

Fatherlessness and the Black Child. As we indicated previously, the percentage of female-headed families among blacks in general is quite large and this percentage increases dramatically in the large urban ghettoes. While there is some evidence (17, 9) that fatherless families may have a greater tendency to produce children who have difficulty in delaying gratification, who exhibit more sex-role confusion, who have more problems developing a sex-role self-image, more externalized loci of control, are more mistrustful of others, have a greater sense of victimization, etc., that such a direct linkage between these factors and fatherlessness cannot be taken for granted or has not been definitively established.

The absence of the father takes place within a geophysical, ecconomical and psychosocial context. In fact, the absence of the father can be listed within limits as symptomatic of the existence of certain socioeconomic conditions. This is supported by the fact economically stable, above average educationally, working and middle class socioeconomic family environments have the greater percentage of intact two-parent homes. Many poor fathers desert or leave home because of severe economic pressures. Many would-be legitimate fathers refuse to marry or are refused marriage due to their economic instability or very poor economic prospects. It appears then that the problems of fatherlessness or broken homes and the mal-socialization of children in these homes are a part of and more directly linked with the larger problems of economics. We do not wish to imply here that the fatherless family does not significantly affect the socialization of children. What we are trying to correct here is the tendency to lay too heavy a burden on this variable which is more a dependent one than otherwise-where the black family is concerned. That there are adverse psychological effects resulting from a fatherless home which exists in a culture very much two-parent centered psychologically, socially, legally, etc., cannot be denied. However, there seems to be more important factors which aggravate or mitigate the effects of fatherlessness. Some of these factors include communal acceptance or non-acceptance of such a family structure, the presence or absence of stigmatization of such a family structure, the availability or nonavailability of kinship or nonkinship father substitutes, and the commonality of such structures within the community. Bernard (1) makes an important point concerning this matter when she stated: "The adverse effects reported for children socialized in fatherless families presupposes that the father would have been a suitable model. In some cases, however, the departure of the father results in little loss. A Philadelphia study of low-income families found that the fathers took very little responsibility for child-rearing duties - such as feeding, bathing, and changing the children, or playing with them - and that the mothers expected little help in the process." In fact Bernard conclued "it is possible that in the Negro lower-class the one-parent family may in reality be the most efficient and functional family type, because the presence of the husband-father may in the long run more negatively than positively affect the mother and child." She goes on to say: "The evidence that fatherless families are handicapped in the socialization of children, especially of sons, should not, however, be overemphasized. Only a minority of Negro children are socialized in such families, and not all of them suffer irreparable damage. Some of the damage associated with fatherlessness undoubtedly arises from deprivation - both of money and of maternal care as the mother struggles to perform both parental roles."

Thus, it appears that what effects the absence of a father will have on the socialization of the children is related to his suitability as a role model and the socio-economic status of the family. Scanzoni (20), in studying fatherlessness or stepfatherlessness in black working and middle class families made the following statement concerning the absence of the father from the family or the presence of a father substitute:

169

In the working class, either the father was not there, or if a father substitute was used by the child, he participated only minimally in these particular phases of the child's socialization, as compared to fathers in whole families. In short, when thinking of resource-provision solely from black fathers, household composition makes little difference in the working class... it is the child from the less advantaged, 'broken' home who 'suffers' more than the one-parent child from 'better' circumstances. Not having the father present is likely to be less detrimental, in terms of later attainments, when the home is relatively well-off than when it is not.

We may infer from this that in the lower class ghetto family the "broken home" does have considerable adverse effects, however, these effects seem due to the presence of economic deprivation. Thus, rather than fatherlessness, the major problem of the black family is "blocked access to the opportunity structure — rather than family wholeness — is clearly more critical with regard to family functionality." (20).

The major result of fatherlessness in black families seems not to be a confusion of sex identity but a critically reduced ability of the children from these families when adults to successfully fulfill their roles as husbands, fathers, wives and mothers. The lack of good role models which serve to show the children wholesome husband-wife, father-child relationships deprives the children of workable models that can be used to maintain their own family relations as adult marrieds.

Socialization, Achievement and The Black Child. The term "achievement motive or achievement need" should be used where many people use the single term "achievement." *Achievement* mean *Accomplishment* on a test ...of knowledge or skill (15). "*Achievement motive or need* refers to the *need* to succeed... and to strive against standards of excellence; it serves to motivate an inducement to do well "(15)."*Achievement motivation* is defined in terms of concern for excellence in doing a task, as reflected in competition with standards set by others or oneself; unique accomplishment; or long-term involvement in a task (16). The standards used to measure the achievement motive or drive include: (1) need or concern for excellence; (2) actions that identify such a need; (3) calculation of risk involved in undertaking a task, anticipation of success and failure; (4) gauging chances of success or failure through conscious consideration of personal weaknesses, limitations or strengths, and environmental factors; (5) active seeking of help to compensate for or overcome personal limitations and environmental factors, and (6) psychological responses to success or failure, such as elation, depression or indifference (16).

170

Persons with a high level of achievement motivation have been studied in detail and have been found to have characteristics important for entrepreneurs: seeking help from experts, moderate risk taking, eagerness to have feedback of results of work being done, taking personal responsibility, interest in activities which they can influence rather than those which depend on chance, etc. (McClelland, 1961).

Genetically speaking, the source of achievement motivation is almost purely of cultural-familial origin. It develops out of the particular social structure of the society which in turn influences the independence training and expectance levels set by parents, especially mothers. Cross-cultural studies as well as studies of individuals with high and low needs to achieve have strongly indicated that *early* demands by mothers on their children to act independently — standing up for rights, knowing the way around town, etc. — prepare their children to meet challenges (23) The demanding and expectation of success from the child by the society, parents, teachers, and significant others early in the child's life (particularly preschool life) have been consistently shown to provide the basis for high achievement motivation.

F.I. Harrison (8), who explored certain attitudes in over one thousand 10th grade students, found that successful students from both advantaged and disadvantaged backgrounds shared three conditions in which they differed from unsuccessful students from both backgrounds: (1) a belief in an internal locus of control; (2) the position that it is worthwhile to associate with formal and informal school groups; (3) the belief that their peer group valued education. This and other evidence point to a cultural-familial foundation and determination of achievement drive. Achievement drive does not exist in a vacuum and has no meaning except in reference to a cultural or other social institutions. It is socially determined.

It is a well known fact that children from middle-class, well-educated families are generally more highly motivated and perform better in many areas of functioning, including school, than children from lower class, poorly educated families (This is principally true because the middle class "measures" both motivation and performance). This is not difficult to explain. The maintenance of social class membership for the middle class child makes high achievement motivation a necessity. The maintaining and furthering of class standards of living and prerogatives, which are so important in American society, depends heavily upon the acquisition of social, academic, occupational skills for the middle-class child. Another reason for the middle class child's higher achievement drive is the encouragement received from parents and the community for the child to succeed in the society. The parents and other adults and peers provide identification models for the middle class child and also openly reward intellectual mastery. Many of these parents and other

171

adults are themselves involved in intellectual pursuits or in professions, vocations, etc., that require intellectual accomplishment. Thus, directly or indirectly, intellectual mastery, skills training, and valued goals are communicated to the child.

The standards, intellectual and otherwise, set by mothers are the most important determinants of academic success in their children. Janis, et al, (12) speaking of the behavioral and cognitive changes in early school years, stated:

> A major transformation... occuring during the *preschool* and early school years is the decreasing importance of motives or speific external goals and the increasing importance of standards...
> The establishment of standards during the *pre-school* years gives rise to a special motive, the desire to think, feel, and behave in ways that are maximally similar to the standard.

An oft-overlooked factor which helps to account for the social class difference in achievement drive and performance is the important part played by the peer group. Generally, the individual values those things valued by his peer group, particularly if the group is important to him and his self-image. The child's or adolescent's peer group approaches and often exceeds the influence of the parent's over the child's or adolescent's behavior and orientation. In many middle class peer groups high achievement motivation to succeed in socially acceptable areas of functioning is encouraged and rewarded by the members of that group. For the lower class groups high achievement motivation ("measured" according to white middle class terms) tend to be punished by the members.

We do not wish to create the impression here that the black family is totally responsible for the low achievement motivation of black children. This would be equivalent to blaming the victim for the crime. The low achievement motivation of black children springs from the same roots as do many other problems of black children — poverty, powerlessness, ignorance and most important of all, racism. To speak of black achievement motivation without dealing with these factors is not to deal with the problem at all.

Achievement Drive and Black Powerlessness.   Udai Pareek (16) developed a very useful paradigm of social behavior which he used to analyze the problems of poverty and the resulting motivational behavior of poverty-stricken people. The major variables of his paradigm indicate that social behavior (B) is a product of the interaction of motives (M) and values (V). The latter two variables are caused and determined by the social system (SS) in which the individual resides. Thus, (SS) = (M,V)=(B). In other words, the demands, expectational, geophysical, economical and psychosocial characteristics of the social system determines the motivational and value patterns of the individuals who operate in that system and these interacting motives and values in turn, determine the behavior of these same individuals. The motiva-

172

tional, value and behavioral patterns characteristic of individuals and classes in a broad societal sense are functionally important in helping maintain the social system, the status quo, of which they are a part. To put it bluntly, one of the functions of the lower income class and its members is to maintain the wealth and prerogatives of the middle and upper classes.

The American capitalistic-exploitative, oligarchically dominated, middle class managed, white racist social system has produced and through certain punishment and reward systems, maintained a large poverty-stricken underclass which is to a large extent black. The result of such a situation has been and is that a disproportionately large segment of the black community exhibits physically and socially dysfunctional behavior. However, this behavior is "functional" for white dominated society as a whole since it helps to maintain white power. Pareek aptly states that "The poor are deprived not only of the minimum adequate provision for physical life, but also of adequate sensory, social, and emotional stimuli necessary for the development of a normal individual." One of the major casualties of societally maintained black poverty is the strong drive to achieve.

...we can start by considering poverty as a structural component of a society, and observe motivations produced by such a structure and the kind of behavior generated by such motivations by certain processes...

The conditions of poverty produce a specific pattern of motivation and, through the relevant processes of socialization, the expectancy of powerlessness. The specific motivational patterns and the expectancy of powerlessness produce behavior seen among the culturally deprived people (the culture of poverty). ....

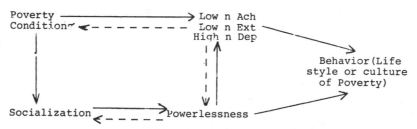

. . . Paradigm of Culture of Poverty.
Low n Ach = low achievement need Low n Ext = low extension need
High n Dep = high dependency need (adapted from Pareek)

173

...According to the paradigm..., poverty as a structural component produces a three-fold motivational pattern characterized by low need for achievement, low need for extension, and high need for

...The process of socialization through childrearing practices and family life plays an important part.

A little further explanation of the concept of "extension need" would seem appropriate here. This need refers to the desire for the individual to go beyond his ego or extend his ego concerns to include the group or society, the tendency to identify one's own good with the common good of the group or society. It refers to active regard for others, joining and working with others to achieve common goals, implicit and explicit trust and faith in group members. *"This motivation is particularly low in poor countries and in poor communities in which persons are so conditioned by control from outside that they not only hesitate in taking initiative, but have little faith in other people, including members of their own groups. Lack of faith leads to suspicion, inability to cooperate, and overconcern with self."* (emphasis by author).

The dependency need refers to the need to have one's wishes, desires, and lackings gratified by another, the need "to be nursed, supported, sustained, surrounded, protected, loved, advised, guided, indulged, forgiven, consoled; to remain close to a devoted protector; to always have a supporter."(7). Dependent behavior can be characterized by lack of initiative, avoidance syndromes (shifting responsibility to others, exaggerating obstacles), excessive fear of failure, seeking favors of superiors, overconformity, and aggressive rejection of authority. Some of the effects of poverty on achievement, extension and dependency drives according to Pareek are:

Low Need Achievement

Disproportionate Risk Taking. The individual with a low need for achievement demonstrates this need by expressing extreme risk-taking attitudes — either taking no risk at all, thereby avoiding the possibility of failure or taking immoderate noncalculated, highly speculative risks, gambling with fate and depending on luck.

Interest in Chance and Not in Control. Because he has not had much opportunity to control things in his life and/or has not been socialized or has no internalization of control, the individual tends to be more interested in activities that revolve around chance and fate.

Lack of Interest in Feedback. Because he has little or no control over circumstances, the individual tends not to be interested in the results of his actions.

Seeking Company of Friends Instead of Experts. In contrast to the individual who has a high need for achievement who tends to seek the aid and company of experts when their help is needed, the individual who has a low need for achievement tends to seek the aid and company of friends who most likely cannot provide him with needed information and help and can only share his frustrations and feelings of helplessness.

Lack of Activity and Initiative. Unlike the individual with a high need for achievement who takes moderate risks, is self-initiating, and exhibits a high level of activity, the individual with a low need for achievement takes extreme risks, is not self-initiating and therefore exhibits a relatively low level of activity.

Low Need Extension

Lack of Regard For Others. The individual with a low need for extension suffers from relative ego restriction; he therefore tends to be self-centered and unmindful of others to the extent that he has little or no respect for others.

Lack of Faith or Trust. The individual with a low need for extension with his relatively restricted ego and self-centeredness tends not to have much faith and trust in others. Because of the instability of circumstances in poverty stricken environments the individual learns that he cannot depend on consistent incomes and outcomes, therefore he loses faith in himself and others.

Lack of Cooperation. The lack of regard for others, the lack of faith or trust in others, leads the low extension individual to be non-cooperative with members of his own group. His self-centeredness and suspiciousness of others contributes to a great extent to his lack of cooperativeness.

High Need Dependency

Lack of Initiative. A high need for dependence in the individual leads him to await actions by others even to solve his own problems. He is apathetic and waits to be led, to be told what to do (usually if it does not demand that he works hard); waits until someone else takes the first steps before acting himself — even when it comes to protecting his own interests.

Avoidance Behavior. This individual has little self-confidence, feels secure only when he can be supported by authority and tends to have an exaggerated fear of failure.

Seeking Favor of Superiors. The gaining of favor or the beneficence of the powerful is a strong tendency in the highly dependent individual. Gaining the affection and attention of superiors are for him more important than actually solving his own problems.

Overconformity. The dependent individual tends to over-identify with his superiors. He tends to over conform to norms established by his superiors even though he has little or no input in their original establishment and also has little or no knowledge of the true reasons for their establishment.

175

Counterdependence. The highly dependent individual quite often has an ambivalent attitude toward authority. While overtly conforming to the demands of authority he may covertly resent their power over him and may express this resentment in several ways. He may use what little freedom and strength he has to aggressively reject authority. In an effort to deny his dependence, which he finds degrading to his self-image, he seeks to deceive himself and others into thinking he is independent by rejecting authority.

Thus, the study of the three motives — achievement, extension, and dependency — and the variables which determine their high or low prevalence — socio-economic conditions, socialization processes and power — can be used to explain much of class behavior, outlook and physical habitation. For instance, the black lower class is caught in the most vicious cycle of all.. Due to racism, economic, social, political, educational discrimination, it has been pushed into a position of powerlessness which lowers its achievement motivation, which ultimately results in an almost total lack of upward mobility or exceedingly slow upward mobility. The lack of knowledge and resources that are necessary for achievement has the effect of maintaining generations of the underclass in a low status position and welfarism. The refusal of the larger society to effectively invest money and resources in the black low income communities (actually, there is a tendency to disinvest in these communities), coupled with overcrowdedness and low extension motivation of the black underclass, produces what are aptly called slums. The low extension need motivation characteristic of the lower income group means that the members of this group have little regard for the property of others (thus he may destroy buildings), does not see the building in which he lives or the sidewalks and streets which he uses or the city in which he resides as an extension of himself. Therefore, he may litter wherever he happens to be with no compunction.. His lack of regard for others, due to his inability to empathize, his self-centeredness, leads him to make noise, play music loudly and late into the night without regard for the fact that others may be trying to sleep. Because the underclasser has a low need for extension, projects which call for his cooperation with others are doomed to failure when there are many others like himself in the community. Thus, among the poor black community, community projects which involve social, political, economic, educational, physical, improvement that will be beneficial to all are more likely than not to be unsuccessful. Therefore, the community continues to deteriorate and the tendency to deteriorate communities spreads with the movement of the under-class.

The children of this class are socialized under its living conditions and are socialized by these conditions and therefore, are inculcated with values and motives which maintain these conditions. Thus, the vicious circle. Through its

176

socialization practices the under-class and blacks forge their own chains of enslavement.. In a larger sense, the larger society rejects the members of the lower class and blacks because of these very same factors and because of the dysfunctional behavior these groups display which is the result of distorted values and motivations for which the larger society is principally responsible in the first place. The adaptation of the underclass and blacks to this situation leads these groups to socialize their children in terms of their socio-economic-political position and their children are in turn rejected by the larger society and therefore the vicious circle grows and is perpetuated. In a sense it becomes self-perpetuating.

This should not be construed to mean that the positions of the underclass and blacks are hopeless and will not change until the larger society (whites) decide they will change. This is not true.

Through a conscious, knowledgeable socialization of their children, blacks can extricate themselves from the vicious cycle which binds them and at the same time change the social system for the better or destroy it in its present form. If the reader returns to the last figure, he will see that to a great extent it is the socialization process that leads to the values and motivations that leads to the dysfunctional behavior of a very large segment of the black community and that keeps them locked in the vicious cycle of poverty. Since socialization is, to a large extent, the responsibility of black parents, conscious and judicious socialization of black children by these parents of their children would do much to change black low achievement, low extension and high dependency drives. If the black mother can be educated to socialize her child for mastery instead of dependence, for internalized control instead of externalized control, for group consciousness instead of individualistic self-centeredness, the cycle of poverty and all of its attendant evils would be broken asunder.

Socialization and Cognitive Style. We have already indicated that cognitive style reflects a certain way of living under certain geophysical, economical and psychosocial conditions. The relative powerlessness of blacks in American society is reflected in the relative powerlessness of their cognitive behavior. We have emphasized that cognitive ability is not an isolate unrelated to physical and nutritional deprivation, self-concept and socialization practices. We shall demonstrate in this section that cognitive style and power are intimately related to motivation, an extremely important variable whenever cognition is to be considered, but which many theorists are prone to forget when they wish to make pronouncements about individual and group cognitive abilities.

The sense of powerlessness which is characteristic of low-income groups and blacks not only imply a paucity of material resources such as money, clothing, food, adequate housing, and the like, but also a paucity of mental resources and drive. The apathy and lack of social organization so character-

177

istic of poverty-stricken people's social, political and economic life is essentially the same apathy and lack of organization which manifests themselves as powerless and poorly motivated cognition. Generations of black maternal socialization of their children under the influence of poverty and American racist propaganda has had a severely negative effect on black cognitive power.

We have seen that powerlessness breeds at least three characteristic types of motivational structures − low need for achievement, low need for extension and a high need for dependency. We have also seen the social effects of these motivational structures. At this juncture we shall look at their cognitive effects, in particular, the cognitive effects of a low need for achievement.

Low Need Achievement

Disproportionate Risk Taking. Cognitively this means that the individual will either not try to solve problems, will attack problems which provide almost no challenge to his abilities or he will go to the opposite extreme and try to solve problems for which he has not prepared himself mentally. This often is the result of the fact that the individual lacks the knowledge and patience to prepare himself to deal with the problem and to correctly gauge his mental prowess and has not calculated his chances of solving the problem.

This approach to problem-solving develops out of a lifestyle where a people (re: blacks) have been told *what* to think and have been punished or rejected for thinking independently and who have not been taught, rewarded or encouraged in terms of *how* to think. Blacks have been made to feel safe and secure only when they cognitively express low-level, nonthreatening, routinized, "approved," cliched thought. Thus, blacks chronically practice this type of cognition which involves little gamble and a wide margin of safety from white critical reaction. The black working and lower classes use three to four times as many imperative responses (responses which indicate *what* is to be done without any accompanying explanation of *why* or *how* it is to be done), commands and requests without explanation as the black middle-class (18, 9).. This means that the largest percentage of black children are being socialized in such a way that they are learning unthinking obeisance to authority, *what* to think or *not* to think at all, and not *how* to think, by their own parents. Strict conformity to the parent's way of thinking is often viewed by the working and lower class to indicate a "good" child. There is evidence to indicate that children of mothers who use a relatively high amount of imperative responses tended to score lower on IQ and concept formation tasks, to be less verbal when dealing with test materials. This tendency is reversed by children of mothers who use a relatively low level of imperative responses.

Interest in Chance and Not Control. Black life in general and lower class black life in particualr are "chancy" affairs. Blacks control over their lives is severely restricted and their continued existence is more a combination of caution and luck than anything else when compared to their white counterparts. Thus, chance and fate, luck and fatalism, are salient factors in the black world and invade black cognitive processes to a remarkable degree. Consequently, black cognition is not oriented toward mastery and control which circumstances have "taught" are not their prerogatives – such prerogatives being seen by them to belong to whites. Therefore, few blacks sharpen their abilities to assume mastery and control of "white people's" problems such as the problems of science, mathematics, literature, etc. They leave their fate to chance and to whites and their problems are left to be solved by these same factors while efforts at controlling and mastering their fate and problems through their own work are lagging or non-existent. "Why put a lot of time and effort into development of mastery and control and into the development of knowledge when the white man will take care of that and us too?", seems to be the guiding fiction of blacks. This myth is even operative in the black school child who figures that learning the "three R's is for white folks."

Lack of Interest in Feedback. Since blacks are given relatively little control over their lives and have little influence over white power and since white favor or disfavor carry a strongly arbitrary flavor, close attention to feedback from their own behavior and the use of such feedback to correct or modify their behavior is not as important as it would be under different circumstances. Since their efforts, whether good or bad, turn out to be almost always considered inferior, bad or worthless when compared to whites or "measured" by white standards, interest in the results of their own cognitive behavior or performance by blacks is bound to suffer. The black in such a situation asks himself – "Why should I knock myself out thinking, learning and working when what results from it will be judged inferior, if noticed at all?" "Why should I give a damn about the results of my behavior if no one else does?"These questions plague the black adult as well as the black preschool and school child and interfere significantly with their cognition. Thus, behavioral and cognitive processes are not informed or controlled by feedback information and therefore productive cognition is not readily distinguished from unproductive cognition. As a consequence, much of the black child's as well as the black adult's cognition is characterized by massive repetitive, unproductive, illogical processes, disorganization and low-level, stereotyped thought processes. Many black school children simply refuse to think and just guess at solutions instead of working at them. The conditions of black life lead to a spirited anti-intellectualism. Hess (9) recognized this when he wrote of the anti-intellectualism of the poor:

> Associated with this stance is a rejection of intellectuality..., following in part from a mistrust of the unfamiliar – a sense of being unable to compete in modes of reasoning not familiar to them – and in

part from a reluctance to accept standards of evaluation which would be to their disadvantage if applied to them. Also, life circumstances of the poor orient them to practical action. Their participation at work has not typically been that of policy making; their gratification is not that of evaluating means and of developing ideas to guide action...

Seeking the Company of Friends Instead of Experts. This characteristic is almost self-explanatory. The anti-intellectualism of blacks which we have just discussed means that they tend to reject the very sources of problem-solving information. Consequently, libraries may go relatively unused, books unread and seldom consulted for problem-solving purposes or for the purposes of increasing knowledge and cognitive power. Research methods, resource development, information retrieval are not utilized competently and the development of knowledge and cognitive power are stagnated or retarded. Academically speaking, it has been observed that what the black student cannot get from his assigned text or is not told to him by his teacher or friends, he does not diligently seek elsewhere. His cognitive supports tend to take on a personal, affiliative tone rather than an objective, factually verifiable one, one that uses the work of experts in the relevant area. Thus, his cognitive processes and outcomes are guided and supported by subjective and personal reference.

Lack of Activity and Initiative. The relatively low level of social, political, economic, educational activity among blacks in general is paralleled by an equally low level of cognitive, creative, activity and initiative. Intellectual and creative activity is not demanded of blacks in America and blacks have been and are being taught that they do not have a major intellectual and creative role to play in America. Their children are socialized with these things in mind. Even when top-notch equipment and resources are available to the black child (we shall see later that many black urban schools are comparable to their white suburban schools do not improve significantly in their academic performances) he may not take full advantage of them to improve himself and activate his cognitive processes. The negative self-concepts inculcated in the black child by American social conditions and by parental and communal socialization practices operate to discourage markedly cognitive activity and development in the child.

The Low Need For Extension And Cognitive Style. We will not deal at length with the low need for extension and its relationship with cognitive style here except to say that the relatively restricted ego characteristic of this need reduces markedly the ability of the individual to perceive the connectedness of things and ideas. Broad conceptualization is inhibited. Concern is shown only for the immediate results of cognition and activity. The power to generalize is reduced and so is the ability to solve problems which involve the consideration of a set of simultaneously interlocking factors as well as a

180

long and complex series of logical steps. The self-centeredness engendered by the low need for extension reduces the individual's consciousness of other factors entering into a problematic situation but which are not at the center of immediate focus. These crucial factors are not held in the preconscious where they may be called up when needed because of the individual's total immersion in the immediately given. In other words, the self-centered, ego-restricted individual suffers from "tunnel vision" even while trying to cope with a multi-factored situation or problem. This leads to failure to solve complex problems. Almost all types of problem-solving behavior take on a personal-subjective flavor, not an impersonal-objective flavor which is often demanded in academic work.

The High Need For Dependency and Cognitive Style. The relative powerlessness of blacks leads to the development of the motive referred to as high need dependency — the strong need to depend on superiors and others who are perceived as having more power. Because of their powerlessness, black parents inadvertently socialize their children to perceive the white group as having the ultimate solution to virtually all their problems. To solve problems of any marked significance, blacks have to beseech the white power structure. The white power structure either punishes or at most gives its stamp of approval or disapproval to black-originated, problem-solving behavior. The white power structure has almost absolute control of resources necessary for problem solving by blacks (the way the blacks conceive it, at least). Consequently, the black social structure is basically parasitic and dependent. It must await white power movement, approval or disapproval before it makes any radical or strongly independent changes under its own volition.

This condition has paralyzed the black community's ability, desire and will to become independent, self-supporting, self-motivating, original and creative. Under this structure blacks are not trained for autonomy — in fact, black autonomy is feared and resisted by the white power structure. Black children are socialized under such a regime. These children are therefore socialized to be dependent, to await solutions by outside (white) superpowerful sources, are not socialized for mastery, but for submissiveness. The black child, then, is not socialized to seek and make solutions to their own problems but to await solutions from others. Therefore, their cognitive processes are characterized by lack of self-confidence, "a sense of inefficacy and passivity... magical thought... a tendency to look to superhuman sources for support and assistance (9)." This dependent orientation leads to a fear of failure which in turn may lead to a refusal to do academic work to solve problems, the seeking of favors from superiors, i. e., the attempt to "brown-nose," cajole or seduce those in power (white) or to "get over" rather than work by legitimate means or through their own efforts to solve their problems, overconformity, i. e., sticking to well-worn, "approved"methods of thinking which may be outmoded, inappropriate and inadequate. These processes lead to a staid repetition of *what* the white establishment has taught them to think in a dependent fashion instead of involving an expression of *how* they learned to think independently through their own efforts at mastery. Finally, the dependency orientation may lead to cognitive counter dependency i.e., the blatant, unreasoned rejection of all cognitive styles wrongly identified with the white structure or an outright undiscriminated anti-intellectualism which rejects profitable and useful thought patterns. This may be done in an exaggerated effort to appear free of white domination or not to "become white."

Thus, we can see that cognitive behavior, style, orientation and power are intimately related to sociocultural, socioeconomic, psychosocial circumstances and cannot be profitably understood without studying the relationship of these circumstances to cognitive behavior. We must also keep in mind that the socialization process is of key importance to the fullness and direction of cognitive and behavioral development and expression.

Achievement Motivation And The Black Child's Academic Performance in Integrated Schools. Twelve years after the 1954 decision, Johns Hopkins University sociologist, James Coleman, was commissioned by the U.S. Office of Education to conduct a survey concerning educational opportunities for all races at various levels of the educational establishment in the U.S. "The Coleman Report" (5)concluded the following:

1. As compared to white students, black students performed poorly. This was found to be true for all areas and grade levels studied.

2. Black students evince a lower aspirational level, a lower level of self-esteem about their ability to succeed academically.

3. Black students tended to be more fatalistic about their ability to change factors which affect their lives.

4. When compared to his white counterpart in terms of academic performance the black students lagged almost as far behind the white student in the first year of school as they did in later school years.

5. Differences in black and white schools were not significantly large in terms of the facilities and services they offered and what differences could be shown to exist could not account for the differences between black and white scholastic achievement.

6. That **"Schools bring little to bear on a child's achievement that is independent of his background and general social context: and this very fact of an independent effect means that the inequalities imposed on children by their home, neighborhood, and peer environment are carried along to become the inequalities of their adult life."**

7. . . . . "within each racial group, the strong relation of family, economic and educational background to achievement does not diminish over the period

182

of school, and even may increase over the elementary years... **most of the variation in student achievement lies within the same school, very little of it between schools.** (Coleman's emphasis) *The implication of these last two results is clear: family background differences account for much more variation in achievement than do school differences."* (Authors' emphasis).

8. In another place (5) Coleman stated: ... **"the task of increasing achievement of lower-class children cannot be fully implemented by school integration, even if integration were wholly achieved. . .(emphasis by author).**
In 1971, the Rand Corporation reviewed and synthesized research findings on the effectiveness of education for the President's Commission on School Finance. One of the conclusions reached by the report was that no —

> "... variant of the existing system... is consistently related to students' educational outcomes... research has found nothing that consistently and unambiguously makes a difference in student outcome... **There is good reason to ask whether our educational problems are, in fact, school problems.'** (Authors' emphasis).

After a ten-year study of the effects of school integration in Riverside, California, Miller and Gerard (14) concluded:

> Overall, the minority children did not gain in achievement, either absolutely or relative to national norms. **After five years of desegregation they were about where they would have been if they had not been desegregated....** (Authors' emphasis).

* * * * * *

> Contact with white children, in short, not only failed to change the minority students' personalities and motivational systems, which we had assumed had major influence on academic performance, but it also failed to change their academic performance.

As we have clearly tried to demonstrate, school performance is determined by the child's preschool personality which are, in turn, heavily influenced by his home and community environment. It seems a bit ridiculous to expect school attendance to change so basic a factor. If the child *enters* school believing that mastery of academic subject matter will increase the likelihood of gratifying one or more of his motives for gaining praise and affection, for becoming like a desirable adult model, for believing that he is competent or superior in some area of academic functioning, for gaining power over others, for completing his sex role identity, he will work hard at learning the required academic skills. The major forces influencing the child's academic performance are:

1. The degree to which the child's parents value academic skills and the degree to which the parents seek to motivate the child to do well.
2. The degree to which the models the child has chosen to identify with display an active interest in intellectual mastery, and

183

3. The child's expectation of success in intellectual work.

We have demonstrated that achievement motivation is a product of the cultural-familial complex. This complex influences measurably the individual's performance and behavior throughout his life whether in school or out.

The Functions of School and Achievement. Schools, whether primary, secondary, collegiate, vocational, etc., are cultural product and are established to maintain and advance a cultural way of life. Schools exist for the culture, not the other way around. Culture comes before schools. Schools reflect culture and change as a result of cultural change. It is the cultural desire to maintain and to go beyond itself that creates the need for schools; consequently, achievement motivation must exist in the culture before there are schools which serve principally means by which certain achievement motives attain their ends. Hence, schools, including performance in them, reflect their cultural roots. With these facts in mind, it should not be surprising to find that black student's academic performance "lags behind" that of whites in a school system designed for the purpose of maintaining white dominance, for the advancement of white culture and in school system based almost purely on white cultural needs, values, and orientations. The different cultural milieus which separate black and white students and yet which loom so large in achievement motivation and academic performance will obviously produce different results even under similar school conditions.

Those educationists who expect the academic achievement of black children to increase due to the mere physical and equipment changes in black schools or due to the busing of black children to predominantly white schools, obviously forget the cultural base for achievement or incorrectly assume that the schools provide the base for achievement motivation. Basically, the schools as presently constituted, can only perpetuate and support culturally based achievement motives — not create them. The child basically gets out of school what he brings to it. Plainly, the black community ill prepares its children to achieve in the white middle class dominated academic world.

Schools in general are much more continuous with the culture of the white middle-class than with that of blacks, especially ghetto blacks. Schools were developed to perpetuate that culture (white middle-class) and its members' control. . . the schools. **The schools are therefore an integral part of the white, middle-class everyday life-style —economically, socially, culturally.** Going to school and remaining in school for long years is not essentially different for the middle-class white individual reared on the principle of delayed gratification. (Janis, 1974) ((Emphasis by author).

The skills and habits necessary for success in school, such as punctuality, orderliness, obedience to authority, cooperation, responsibility, nonaggressiveness, delay of gratification, verbal facility and conceptual thinking (along white middle class lines), are already part of the middle class white student's way of everyday life. Since the school is essentially a white middle class institution, the white student more readily succeeds in it.

For the black ghetto student and also the black middle class student but to a lesser extent, school, particularly beyond the earliest grades, is a discontinuous experience. Disconnectedness and discontinuities are major causes of psychological distress and upheaval in life in general, let alone in school life. Schools as presently established do not form a continuous link with ghetto and black culture and are esentially foreign establishments as far as black students are concerned. They require, without intermediate preparations, that the black child think, feel, and behave in ways quite different from his everyday life. They require the use of language and verbal skills that are also essentially foreign and alien. Unlike the middle class white student, it is not readily apparent to the ghetto student that academic success is necessary to the maintenance and advancement of his way of life. An unskilled, unprofessional culture demands things other than long years of schooling and delayed gratification. To the children of such a culture middle class demands may seem unreasonable, unjust and unnecessary. The verbal skills these children develop and the ways of thinking they use are intimately related to surviving and dealing with their cultural milieu as are those of white children related to their cultural milieu. To think, act, feel, and live "white" in a black world which has little use or provides little basis for the use of "white" cognitive, behavioral skills would be a millstone around the neck of the black child. Consequently, he often resists learning these "useless," alien skills. When and if he does later recognize that the learning of such skills is indispensible in the world beyond the narrow confines of his ghetto world, it is often too late or he finds himself in need of "remediation," of having to play "catch-up ball" or not playing at all. For the white middle class individual continuing in school is almost an unconscious process, the school being such an intimate part of white middle class life, but for the black individual it is an exasperatingly conscious process because of the school's lack of continuity with black life.

The black uneducated ghetto parent, understanding little of the requirements necessary for academic success, can be of little help to her child in acquiring the requisite skills to make such success possible. The lack of an educational tradition in the ghetto home adversely affects the parent's ambitions for the careers of her child. Attending a white staffed and controlled school or a black school run according to unmodified "white" standards, compounds this problem and increases the foreignness of scholastic life for many black students.

The discontinuity between black life and school life breeds resistance, hostility, disinterest, etc., in the black child. Much of what is taught in school meets his needs. It would be expecting too much however, of the schools, white schools in particular, to bridge the gap between black life and school life and to provide the black child with the achievement drives which are

185

essentially the products of the child's cultural-familial background. Schools exist not so much to provide goals and motivation for achieving goals as they do to provide the *means* for achieving goals and motivational satisfaction. Motivation to achieve must exist prior to active school attendance. The major task of school is to maintain and advance the motivated student toward his goals.

We do not wish to imply here that schools and teachers are not important in bringing about academic success. It is well known that teacher expectations add significantly to or detract significantly from academic achievements. However, more often than not the school's and the teacher's efforts are vitiated by poor home and community environments. So even if white teachers are "better" or white schools are "better" these two factors are relatively powerless against the forces of cultural-familial traditions in the black community. A poorly or inappropriately motivated student will not learn much even with the best of teachers and facilities.

Attending school for the black child is often a schizoid process. He is called upon to alienate himself abruptly from his culture and he must maintain a precarious psychic balance between a black and white world, belong to neither. It is little wonder that the black student rebels against this neurotic process which demands that he become not-self and shed his identity in order to succeed. School programs which accept black culture as a fact and build their teaching programs around this fact so that the black experience is continuous with black life, yet is adequate enough to prepare the black child to cope in an essentially white world, can do much for the black student, black culture and American culture as a whole.

Implications and Recommendations. This chapter basically sums up what had been discussed in detail in earlier chapters. Therefore the implications and recommendations made at the end of each of those chapters will serve to remedy any problems pointed out in this one. However, we wish to emphasize the following:

1. The responsibility for the socialization and education lies within the black family. Blacks must stop expecting government, integration, remediation and the like to do for their children what they should do themselves. The government and whites know no more about how to socialize or educate your child than you do.

2. If our children are to be "saved" in the full sense of that word, then there must come about a complete cultural revolution in the black community. New values, standards, attitudes, etc., must become common in the commumity. Patchwork governmental programs, school programs, etc., will not succeed in the presence of black cultural stagnation.

3. Socialize and educate your child for mastery and control, to be the best among all peoples and not a servant to any people.

186

4. Remember that if blacks change the socialization of our children they will not perpetuate black behavior of the past and it will change the face of American society forever. But you must be the one who takes responsibility for properly socializing your child. You must provide him with the materials and opportunities which will aid his positive growth toward full manhood and mastery. It will not cost much money , only time.

REFERENCES

1. Bernard, J. *Marriage and Family Among Negros.* New Jersey: Prentice-Hall, 1966.
2. Bowlby, J. *Child Card and the Growth of Love.* Maryland: Penguin, 1973
3. Bronfenbrenner, U. In *Scientific American,* August 1974.
4. Burton, B., & Whiting, J. The absent father and cross-sex identity. *Merrill-Palmer Quarterly of Behavior and Development, 7,* 1961.
5. Coleman, J., et al. *Equality of Educational Opportunity.* Washington, D.C.: U.S. Printing Office, 1966.
6. Crandall, U.C., et al. Children's beliefs in their own control of reinforcement in intellectual-academic achievement situations. *Child Development, 36,* 1965.
7. Hall, C., & Lindzey, G. *Theories of Personality.* (2nd ed.) New York: Wiley, 1970.
8. Harrison, F. Relationship between home background, school success, and adolescent attitudes. *Merrill-Palmer Quarterly of Behavior and Development, 14, 1968.*
9. Hess, R. The transmission of cognitive strategies in poor families: The socialization of apathy and under-achievement. In Allen, U. (ed.), Psychological Factors In Poverty. Illinois: Markham, 1971.
10. Horton, P., & Hunt, C. *Sociology.* (2nd ed.) New York: McGraw-Hill, 1964.
11. Hurlock, E. *Child Development.* (4th ed.) New York: McGraw-Hill, 1964.

12. Janis, L., et al. *Personality: Dynamics, Development, and Assessment.* New York: Harcourt, Brace & World, 1969.
13. McClelland, D.C. *The Achieving Society.* New Jersey: Van Nostrand, 1961.
14. Miller, N., & Gerald, H. How busing failed in Riverside. *Psychology Today, June 1976.*
15. Morgan, C., & King, R. *Introduction to Psychology.* (4th ed.)New York: McGraw-Hill, 1971.
16. Pareek, U. Poverty and motivation: Figure and ground. In *Psychological Factors in Poverty,* Allen, U. (ed.). Illinois: Markham, 1971.
17. Pettigrew, T. (ed.). *Profile of the Negro American. New Jersey: Van Nostrand, 1964.*
18. Radin, N., & Kamii, C. The child-rearing attitudes of disadvantaged negro mothers and some educational implications. *Journal of Negro Education, 34* (Spring 1965).
19. Rotter, J. External control and internal control. *Psychology Today, 5 (1),* 1971.
20. Scanzoni, J. *The Black Family in Modern Society.* Massachusetts: Allyn & Bacon, 1971.

21. Schulz, D. *Coming up black: Patterns of ghetto socialization.* New Jersey: Prentice-Hall, 1969.
22. White, B. L. In Smart, M., & Smart, R., *Children: Development and relationships.* (2nd ed.) New York: McMillan, 1972.
23. Winterbottom, M. The relation of need for achievement to learning experience in independence and mastery. In J. W. Atkinson (ed.), *Motives in fantasy, action and society.* New Jersey: Van Nostrand, 1958.

AN OVERVIEW: LANGUAGE, CULTURAL DETERMINSM AND "BLACK MYTHOLOGY"

WORDS AND BEHAVIORAL TENDENCIES. Language is a system of symbols with a series of fixed rules as to their combination so that understandable communications, verbal and nonverbal, can be facilitated between two or more persons. These symbols may originate by convention and arbitration (signs) or represent organic historical-experiential events in the life of an individual or group (symbols). These symbols and signs and their combinatory formulae communicate not only lexical meaning but carry psychosomatic, personal and interpersonal, subjective and objective, conceptual and emotional, conscious and unconscious meanings. Because language operates on all these levels it has powerful control and determinating influence on human consciousness, cognition, emotions and behavior.

In agreement with Steveson (6), Morris (5), and Brown (2), we believe language, to a large extent, contains words (symbols) which have as their basic meaning a behavioral disposition (this includes certain conscious, cognitive, emotional and, of course, behavioral tendencies).

The meaning of a sign, in the psychological sense required, is not some specific psychological process that attends the sign at any one time. It is rather a dispositional property of the sign, where the response, varying attendant circumstances, consists of psychological processes in a hearer, and where the stimulus is his hearing of the sign. (Steveson, 6).

It seems to be that when one comes to understand a linguistic form his nervous system is partially rewired (in the sense of changes in synaptic resistances or neurone process growth) so that one is disposed to behave appropriately with regard to the form as the contingent circumstances are changed. The disposition has no substantial character other than the structure of the nervous system. It is not a leaning, a beginning, a miniature reaction. It is a response potential. A disposition is discovered by creating various contingencies and observing responses.

Within a linguistic community there are standards (not necessarily formulated) for the usage of an utterance and for total behavior with reference to the utterance. These standards define appropriate behavior, the conventional disposition. A child born into the community does not at first conform to these standards, but he eventually does so and is then said to speak and understand the language... Since I define meaning as the total disposition to make use of or react to a linguistic form, it follows that readiness to use words in accordance with conventions about the parts of speech is a part of meaning. However, it is a part that can be distinguished from reference. (Brown, 2).

Brown relates his concept of meaning as a behavior disposition to the concept of "attitude" as it is used in social psychology. Gordon Allport (1) defines an attitude as "... a mental and neural state of readiness, organized through experience, exerting a directive or dynamic influence upon the individual's response." His definition fully implies a readiness to think, feel and act in a certain direction. In general, social psychologists see attitudes as consisting of at least three components: cognitive, affective and behavioral. Thus, an attitude "predisposes" an individual to think, feel and behave in a certain direction, all other things held constant. It is our contention that words or symbols used in language have essentially some of the same properties.

LANGUAGE AND COGNITIVE STYLE. There exists a reciprocal relationship between the characteristics of a particular set of psychosocial, geophysical and economical circumstances and the particular language which develops out of, reflects, and serves as a medium of interaction with those circumstances. We have indicated that the "restricted code" used by lower-class mothers is related to the restricted aspects of lower-class geophysical, econmical, psychosocial living conditions as compared to their middle and upper-class counterparts. The concreteness, directness and apparently "simplistic" characteristics of lower-class language reflects the concretistic, stark, and apparently "simplistic" nature of lower-class existence. The characteristic linguistic code has been "tailored" to the living situation.

However, there is the other side of the coin — linguistic codes tend to "tailor" the individual's perception of his psychosocial, economical and geophysical environment and his method of dealing with problems in general. Linguistic codes shape, to a certain degree, cognitive style and orientation. We've already indicated how the socialization of the black child affects his cognitive style and orientation. We must remember that a very large segment of the socialization process is carried on in terms of language. The linguistic code is the principle medium of socialization. The linguistic code, be it elaborated and universalistic or restricted and concretistic, through its strong influence on consciousness, feelings and behavior, is a major determing factor in the development and operation of motivational, behavioral and cognitive style and orientation.

The segregated living conditions of blacks has tended to force them to develop a linguistic code particular to those conditions (it matters little in this context whether the code has many similarities to the "standard English," it is the underlying nonverbal, subcultural meanings carried by the code that

191

makes the important difference). Black parents socialize their children in terms of this particular code. Since linguistic codes are used to manipulate consciousness, to direct thought and behavior, as a means of coping and adapting, black children socialized under the regime of a linguistic code which has limited application will develop a motivational, behavioral and cognitive style and orientation which will be maladaptive in the context of the demands placed on them by the larger, dominant white society which operates according to a different linguistic system.

Language has several qualities – psychosomatic, personal-interpersonal, subjective-objective, conceptual-emotional, conscious-unconscious (7). This means that the language used by a people or individual actively influences, both in a temporary and in a relatively permanent way, those aspects of the personality which correspond to these qualities. In other words, what the individual is conscious of, what his unconscious reactions are, how he conceptualizes things, how he feels about things, whether he will deal with them on a personal and subjective basis, or on a basis where the personal and subjective are left out, i.e., objectively, and how he reacts psychophysically, what his body response is, how he controls his body, are instigated, developed, maintained and sustained by language. Therefore, what linguistic code is employed during the socialization process will affect significantly many areas of personality functioning, including the cognitive. The manifest as well as covert behavioral, motivational and cognitive style of the individual or of a people are affected by language usage. Language is used by the individual to manipulate and control his consciousness, feelings and behavior and consequently, his cognitive style and orientation. It is used interpersonally to manipulate and control the consciousness, feelings and behavior of others and consequently, their cognitive style and orientation. These manipulations and controls may have and do have a permanent effect on the individual self or on others; consequently the cognitive style and orientation may be permanently affected (until other intervening forces may modify the original structure). Since names, labels, understandable utterances, and other linguistic constructions tend to direct attention, motivation and behavior toward one segment of functioning and to direct attention, motivation and behavior away from an endless number of other areas of possible functioning (this may be momentary and flitting in nature, such as a "stream of consciousness" or prolonged and concentrated in nature such as approaches compulsive-obsession), and since culture tend to direct attention, motivation and behavior toward one general segment of possibilities, those names, labels, utterances, linguistic constructions and/or cultural directives ultimately leave their stamp on the cognitive style and orientation of the individual or people.

Language, along with cultural-ecological factors, tends to control consciousness and thereby control motives, behavior and cognition. This implies that the so-called "restricted code"(and it is restricted only in a relative sense –restricted with reference to a lesser restricted code) used by the black world, the black lower-class world, especially, tends to instigate, develop, maintain and sustain a "restricted" (when compared to the dominant white code which the blacks are forced to learn if they are to "succeed") consciousness, a consciousness which may be dysfunctional outside of its cultural context (which is the case even with the white code), and thereby effect a "restricted" and possibly dysfunctional motivational, behavioral and cognitive style. The restricted, concretistic, inferiority-complexed, exploited, brutalized, propagandized, insecure, scarcity-oriented, racially segregated, culturally segregated, restricted responsibility/action area of many blacks in terms of national and international policy, execution and influence, and their long history of slavery and discrimination, has given rise to a particularistic linguistic code which reflects these factors as well as the unique world-concept and self-concept which tend to orient their consciousness and thereby their cognition, motivation and behavior toward the immediate (thus restricting and limiting the range of cognition and action, tending to reduce generalized, conceptual, and prolonged and involved sequential thought patterns that go beyond the immediate and the practical); the concrete, "real" and tangible (thus leaving outside the range of cognitive concern and action the theoretical, conceptual, abstract, intangible and thus encouraging exclusive cognitive concern and action with the practical, physically manipulative, applied aspects of things — of course, we must note here that that is the role the middle-class and white society imposes on the lower-class and black society — consequently, the lower class and blacks are literally forced to socialize themselves and their children to adapt to such expectations and enforced impositions).

A vicious circle arises — a restricted linguistic code arises from a restricted sphere of life and the code in turn helps to maintain that restricted life. Relatively small vocabulary, narrowly or culturally restrictedly defined word-symbols and concepts tend to restrict the functional operation and power of cognition to the field or cultural milieu from which such word-symbols and concepts were developed. Linguistic codes and concepts with the motivational, behavioral, cognitive styles they tend to engender or are an organic part of, taken out of context can become dysfunctional for the user. A major problem faced by blacks is not only the tendency to use their own cultural codes and concepts out of context (in a white world), but their misunderstanding of the connectedness of the culture, codes and cognitive, motivational, behavioral byproducts. More importantly, black cognitive, behavioral, motivational confusion and inefficiency displayed by many blacks are in part caused by a misunderstanding and lack of a thorough knowledge of the "white" linguistic code in its deepest subconscious, nonverbal sense and an inept transposition and use of "white" linguistic codes, words definitions, conceptualizations, cognitive styles, etc., within a black cultural milieu

193

which does not provide a proper context for the smooth functioning of such codes, words, etc. Thus, unless the black individual understands and knows how to utilize the "white code, and how to modify and cull that code so that it may be appropriately function in the black cultural milieu, i. e., used to accomplish desired ends efficiently, his behavior, cognition and motivation orientations may be basically dysfunctional despite the fact he may be able to phonetically, syntactically, lexigraphically reproduce the "white" code.

The misunderstanding, misuse of the "white" linguistic code by blacks (and whites for that matter) confuses and therefore limits cognition, particularly when it is demanded that that cognition be expressed in "white" linguistic terms. Those blacks who know the "white" codes thoroughly and who choose to act fully in terms of them, providing there are no other negative barriers placed in the way, have little or no trouble assuming and demonstrating a cognitive style and power equal to or superior to "white" cognitive style and power. It is the differing qualitative characteristics of the black and white linguistic codes, codes engendered by differing power and positional relations, that are in the main responsible for the differing cognitive styles and powers. Because the "betterment" of black life calls for a one-way transition — blacks into white world, blacks come to appear "deficient" in mental, linguistic and behavioral terms. One often forgets that these "deficiencies" are relative and contextual. If the whites were called upon to enter the black world they would be "deficient" mentally, linguistically and behaviorally. Thus, cognitive style and power are relative to other conditions and demands and have little to do with demonstrating "native" or innate cognitive capacity. Culturally conditioned cognitive style and culturally measured cognitive power obscures and virtually makes impossible a true and accurate estimation of innate cognitive capacity.

CULTURAL DETERMINISM. Men in groups the world-over have developed some sort of language. It is apparent that all normal human beings have an innate capacity to learn the language taught them by their culture. This potential for language, then, is a given — comes with the human brain and anatomy. What is not given is the culture, geophysical and other circumstances he is born into. This includes the language spoken by the community. As these things differ so do their reflective languages. The human child is capable of learning any of them, no matter how simple or complex. Thus, we can say first there is the capacity for making and learning words. This capacity will be, and is, shaped by the unique psychosocial, geophysical world that surrounds the individual or group.

Hypothetically, a man possessing a capacity for creating linguistic constructions, if put into a particular geophysical environment, will name objects, relations, etc. peculiar to that environment. He will describe that environment, his interactions with it, events that occur within it, his inner psychological and physical experiences within its confines in terms of words and symbols. If these words and symbols and their referents are shared by others in his vicinity a linguistic community begins to develop. The orderliness of nature tends to (possibly) help systematize the language.

Besides nameing and describing, man also organizes and classifies his experiences. Thus he begins to "see" reality as ordered along certain definite lines, as having some visible and invisible organization. He begins to look at the world and certain things,, events and experiences as fitting into certain categories and classes. As he experiences these things, events and experiences he evaluates them — "good," "bad," "irrelevant," etc.

He also seeks to know the "why" of their existence — how they came about, how they are constructed, what are their purposes, how are they related, what is their ultimate destiny, etc. Thus, he is called upon to create a "mythology" to account for and explain these matters. The mythology "explains" the universe of physical, psychological, social and metaphysical phenomena. According to their circumstances different cultures have developed (and some continue to to do so) their own mythology. A culture may have one mythology (e.g., some "primitive" cultures) or any number of mythologies existing simultaneously (e.g., some "modern" complex cultures). The universe can be looked at and "explained" from any number of view points.

In the sense that we are using mythology here, this would include "scientism" as well as "animism." Whether we perceive the world as filled with spirits and gods or atoms and energy we are still seeking to "explain" it, to comprehend it.

Whether we approach it "objectively," the basic process of trying to systematically explain the world goes on. In this sense, science is as much a "myth" as is religion. However, each myth or point of view brings about very different consequences. The consequences of scientific thinking bring on quite different results from those of religious thinking.

The mythological structure prevailing in a culture or individual, during its lifetime of the mythology, that is, creates new concepts, evaluations, behavioral patterns, etc. These concepts, evaluations, behavioral patterns, etc. tend to fade with the underlying mythological structure that created them. However, some mythological structures may endure unchanged for hundreds of years as in some "primitive" cultures. This lack of change has "petrified" such societies and they would no doubt remain so if no radical changes take place in the environmen, e.g. geophysical changes, social contact with others of differing mythologies (this includes war), or some unique individual (s) bringing about change in the group by developing some new mythology or viewpoint. Some mythological structures may not last but a very short time, as with "fads," styles, fashions (these include modes of behavior), etc. In modern complex societies many mythological structures exist simultaneously, are born and die quickly (taking their vocabularies with them or having new meanings attached to them, or leaving relics of their existence) and others endure for long periods of time (certain religious viewpoints, scientism). Many are mutually conflicting, others relatively harmonious. Thus, mythologies create vocabularies, concepts, ways of thinking, perceiving, feeling and behaving. If the mythology is a predominant one, that is, it is generally accepted by everyone in the social unit, the linguistic, perceptual, affective, cognitive, behavioral, patterns of that mythology is taught to their children and these grow up to be like their mentors (usually their parents). This will remain so until events force changes on the prevailing mythology (s).

Each mythology, whether scientific or religious, subjective or objective, etc. carries with it its own method of dealing with the reality it has created or seeks to explain. The methodology (which includes again methods of cognition, feelings, and behavior as well as the ways of effecting or retarding change in the universe) of a mythology can be self-limiting in that its explanatory schema is so fixed that it does not permit new points of view and the methods so entrenched, particularly if the environment remains relatively constant and unperturbed by outer or inner forces, do not lead to new discoveries, provoke new questions, create new problems that must be solved in new ways, jolt the imagination, etc. Modern, objective, scientific mythologies and methodologies are self-generating in that they do provoke new questions, solutions, new problems, imagination, change in the environment, create new objects, establish new points of view, emphasize change and "progress," etc. New Names, concepts, linguistic constructions, meanings, ways of thinking, experiencing and behaving, accompany these events. Old systems die or are modified and the languages generated by them die also or are modified. Thus, the current language is rich and complex as is the thought, feelings and behaviors of the speakers of that language. The whole process feeds on itself. Whether a mythological methodology is self-limiting or self-generating it is still inextricably tied to a particular geophysical, psychosocial situation and there is a mutual interaction between the method and situation. A physical scientist cannot research the nature of a particular object if that object does not exist, cannot be conjectured or imagined. It must have some kind of reality for him. Thus, the structure or the environment, including its potentials, will tend to limit and shape both mythology and methodology.

Language in its fullest sense (its mythological ground, word-sounds, syntax, grammar, denotations, cannotations, conscious and subliminal meanints, etc.) is the symbolic representation of its mother culture and as such shapes and guides the consciousness-cognitions, affects and behaviors of its speakers. The language in its fullest sense determines how the individuals of a particular culture perceive reality and the methods by which they seek to deal with it. (This view is essentially like that of Whorf's (8), but goes beyond it in that it does not deal principally with etymological but with the subliminal, psychological aspects of language How an individual conceives the universe is not determined by the word-names used by a culture, nor by their lexical meanings, but by the mythological, methodological substrate implied by word-names. Until the individual changes his mythological-methodological substrates, his thinking, feeling and behaving are culturally established in the first place. This does not mean that the individual is "locked" forever in a cultural straitjacket. Nor does it mean that his language is not translatable into other languages. There is nothing about cultural determinism that says the individual is imprisoned in his cultural meanings and is beyond hope of ever escaping. This obviously is not the case, as endless examples of persons who fully assimilate the culture and languages of cultures other than their own native language. As a matter of fact many persons not only assimilate new cultures but forget and become non-functional in their original one.

The cultural mythological structure which guides cognition, perception, affects, and behavior may have their influence on the individual for varying lengths of time, theoretically from seconds to infinite years. The structures can be changed instantaneously (although most of them are not) as soon as an accommodative or assimilative process is indicated as a result of the things we listed above (latter paragraph) as well as creative use of imagination, new ideas and concepts as put forth by others. The structures (or schemas) may be changed slowly for the same reasons (we may say here that the usual tendency is to try and assimilate "news" into the original structures without changing them or to explain the "news" in terms of the original structures. This can lead to a conscious or unconscious denial or misperception of the "news." Many times, though, time and circumstance force modification or abandonment of the old structures). Through imagination the human being can, if stimulated, go beyond his cultural schemas and perceive the world in a new light and think, feel and behave in accordance with this new perception and this can take place during the space of a very short human-to-human, human-to-object, human-to-situational, human-to-experiental interaction.

Hence, this makes translation possible. Despite the fact that at any one time an individual may be guided by cultural determinants, the properties of the human Central Nervous System, which is common to all men, makes it possible for him through imagination, analogies, metaphors, one-to-one translations, and other methods, to translate his language into another or vice versa (though this is not 100% true, it's true enough to make understandable translations possible). Even in the case of imagination, analogies, etc. the cultural structures serve as the basic materials out of which new conceptual garments are fashioned. A man always begins a journey from where he stands. Sharing a common CNS and common earth, humans, despite different languages and conceptual systems can communicate with each other though this may be very difficult at times, because there is enough common ground in reality and in the basic human make-up to make this so.

However, we must caution that cross -cultural translations (we're speaking more in the structural-conceptual sense here) that are intended to change one of the interactant's mythological systems and thereby his perceptions, cognitions, affections and behaviors, to be effective, must be done in a step-by-step fashion, To try and teach a crawling baby to do classic ballet would be ludicrous, utterly frustrating to its instructor and psychologically and possibly physically damaging to the child. At least the child simply would not understand and would react with hostility and possibly regression. To try and teach a "primitive" Einsteinian physics when they have an underdeveloped number system or without first teaching them the appropriate number system beginning "where they are" would lead to similar results. As unnecessary as these examples may be, this sort of teaching without giving full consideration to the cultural background of those being taught taking place in America today.

SYMBOLIZATION. Taken as a whole, socialization represents a process we call symbolization — a process whereby things, events, situations, relations, thoughts, feelings, actions, attitudes and other phenomena are symbolized or represented by things other than themselves and whereby the individual comes to react to these symbols with conscious, affective and behavioral tendencies. The symbol is a sort of shorthand for the thing (s) represented.

A word, which is a symbol, can represent or "stand for" an exceedingly complex phenomena. When used in a language that phenomena can be "packaged" or "miniaturized" in a word to the mutual convenience of the commuicating parties. Symbols, when effective, affect their recipients and users in at least three ways. It makes them conscious or attend certain things (this includes purely "mental" things also) in the universe, a universe that is in a constant state of flux — making particular things and ideations figure and others ground. As symbols shift so does consciousness. Symbols also effect affective reactions in their recipient-users. The Christian cross may conjure up "religious" emotions in its devotees. The words on a telegram —"Your mother is dead"— may bring on intense affective reactions of sadness. Feelings and feeling tones accompany symbols of all types. Finally, symbols effect behavioral tendencies in their recipient-users. Symbols, when perceived, effect some gross body or nervous system reactions.

Symbols that have been conventionalized by a culture and socialized into its members then has three major effects on their behavior. They place them into a certain state of consciousness, emotion or feeling and initiate certain behavioral tendencies. Of course, the same symbol does not initiate the same conscious, emotional, behavioral tendencies invariably. The effect of the symbol, to a certain degree, is determined by the context in which it is embedded. However, it is important to remember that recognized symbols can effectively change or distort contexts. These consciousness, affective, behavioral dispositional properties can effectively "blind" the individual to his surround or other alternatives or contingencies in that surround. They may focus his consciousness (which includes subconscious orientations as well), emotional and behavioral attention in such a way as to make him "fixate" on certain objects ts, qualities, etc. of the environment and oblivious to others, thereby at times making him dysfunctional – causing harm to himself and others.

Language, of course, is a system of symbols par excellence. Language, in its verbal and nonverbal aspects, is probably the most effective and frequently used system of symbols to control and deal with people and the universe. But there are other very important symbols that may at times outweigh words, which also effect consciousness, emotions and behavior. These symbols may be objects, status postions, various forms of prowess, behaviors, privileges, etc. Thus, a man dressed in a priest's garments effects a quite distinct state of consciousness, emotion and behavior in his perceivers (and in his own self-perception) than if that same man were dressed in the rags of a beggar. A change of clothing in this instance, all other things held constant (in terms of the man's personality), effects a change in people's consciousness-affective-behavioral tendencies toward him. Thus, symbols, linguistic and/or nonlinguistic, are important in that they have far-reaching effects on states of consciousness, emotion and behavior. These effects can bring on positive consequences to the symbol-emitter and/or receivers (the effect being functional and adaptive) or they can bring on negative consequences (the effect being dysfunctional and maladaptive).

Acculturation and socialization are to a great extend learning the appropriate symbols, their meanings, their use, and developing the ability to use them effectively. Different cultures and groups may socialize their members to perceive and react to essentially the "same" object, event or experience in very different ways – even when the word-name for that symbol may be the same. Thus, members of these separate cultures, if placed into the alien culture, not knowing the alien culture's meaning of particular symbols, become dysfunctional in that culture. For instance, the word-sound "bad" as used in certain contexts within the black community actually may refer to what whites would call by the word sound ""good." To a black a "bad dude" is a statement of envious admiration. To the unknowing white it may imply a deprecation.

Symbols out of context, out of their organic ground base, if not modified to suit the new or different circumstances can bring about dysfunctional behavior and negative consequences for the user – recipient and his surround, which may include other human beings and his physical environment. This occurs because the state of consciousness, feelings and behavior provoked by the symbols may be inappropriate to the current circumstances. The misuse of, or the out-of-context use of, symbols can lead to various forms of malaadjustment from slight annoyance to blind rage and destructive (including self-destructive) behavior, from minor frustration and anxiety to crippling neurosis and full-blown psychosis.

SOCIALIZATION OF THE BLACK CHILD: With Particular Emphasis on the Black "Ghetto" Child. The principles of socialization as outlined above are operant for the black child as they are for the child of any other ethnic group. However, the peculiar social, economic, political-historical situation of the black child, his socialization, may appear to be incomplete or dysfunctional. It is the negative consequences of his socialization for himself, his community and the nation that concerns us here. Let us make something clear: It is not our thesis that the socialization of the black ghetto child is negative – but that the socialization he receives is incongruent within the larger social context in which he lives, that his socialization does not prepare him to meet the demands of the broader society or establish a positive alternative to it and as a consequence he becomes dysfunctional both within his ghetto culture and outside of it. Through his acculturtive-adaptative attemps to become functional within his restricted environment the black child suffers in all areas of his life and his self-actualization is thereby thwarted or distorted and brings on relatively innocuous or negative consequences to his surround.

The three essential socialization processes we noted earlier – proper performance behavior, the playing of approved social roles, and the development of social attitudes – operate within the black ghetto community but a number of factors negate their possible positive results and make ghetto socialized child dysfunctional. The behavior learned within the ghetto context is usually too restricted or inflexible to be appreciably functional in or out of the ghetto context, approved ghetto roles are not approved by the larger society, have little applicability outside or inside the ghetto, are dysfunctional outside and/or inside the ghetto, and the social attitudes that result from ghetto living, though of some demonstrably positive or survival value within the ghetto   racist context, are in the main dysfunctional in and out of the ghetto.

The way a culture socializes its children is a function of the way it perceives the world at present and the world of its children. That world perception is a historical-experiental product of a people and a mythological structure is built upon that perception. The methods of childrearing, the values taught to the children, etc. are organically connected to the cultural mythology (or world view). The black ghetto situation has come about as the consequences of American racism and the blacks' experience and view of that racism. This, in turn, has resulted in a distorted black cultural mythological structure, on which a basically dysfunctional socialization process (es) is predicated. Within the black ghetto mythologival structure, which at best can be described as ambiguous, functional and dysfunctional socializational processes are tangled into an unhealthy jungle-growth. The methodology and aims of socialization processes are based on a cultural mythological structure. If

200

the mythology is unclear, confused, unrealistic, in a rapid, unorganized, constant state of flux, the socialization of children suffer — they will be unclear about themselves, their goals, unrealistic, confused, emotionally labile or apathetic, suffer problems in human relations, lack knowledge of self, etc. It is our contention that the black experience in America, coupled with the black cultural-mythological situation is responsible for the greater portion of black dysfunctionality.

THE CULTURE OF POVERTY. We have defined culture principally in terms of its functions — as a definer of situations, attitudes, values and goals, myths, legends, and the super-natural, as a provider of behavior patterns and molder of national character. As important as these functions are, they are secondary factors, effects to a far greater extent than they are causes. For these functions are grounded and shaped by a prior system of circumstances and realities. These circumstances and realities include the geophysical, economic, and the psychosocial. The geophysical circumstances refer to physical characteristics of the earth occupied by a particular culture, its geographical characteristics, its natural and man-made resources, their use or nonuse, climate, objects and implements for convenience, work and/or pleasure, physical plants for the maintenance and/or advance of the culture, and its physical vitals such as food, clothing and shelter. The economic refers to the means and medium of exchange of goods and services among members of the culture or between cultures and the availability of these means to individuals of the culture and the culture as a whole. It also refers to the means by which resources, goods and services are allocated among culture members and between cultures. The psychosocial refers to the ways of perceiving, coping, behaving, expressing emotions, thinking utilized by the members of a culture, their modes of relating to and behaving toward each other and the world and the quality of the prevailing societal structure at a given point in time.

The resources provided by a particular geographical region and their utilization by a particular culture helps to shape the attitudes, perceptions, behaviors, and values of the people occupying that region. Iron and the behaviors, attitudes, values, etc. that can be generated by its many potential uses cannot be generated in a culture whose geophysical environment does not provide such a resource. Thus, two different cultures can evolve around the fact that one possesses a particular resource that is lacking in the other. This is true for the presence and availability of, or the absence of or utilization or nonutilization of any number of geophysical resources, characteristics and environment conditions. Generally, on an elementary basis, a culture's economic system is tied to its geophysical circumstances and the psychosocial system to the first two.

As long as a culture's values, aspirations and behavior patterns are firmly rooted in its geophysical possibilities, the means of procuring them and their

201

utilization to satisfy the demands of the values, aspirations and behaviors, other things held constant, that culture may be said to be harmonious. If, however, the opposite is the case, that culture will suffer frustration and some or all of the symptoms of frustration such as displaced aggression, apathy, destructiveness, unrealistic striving, etc. – in general, maladaptive behavior sets in.

The black ghetto culture is one wherein its geophysical circumstances, its economic and psychosocial resources, as now existent, cannot meet the demands of values, aspirations and behaviors which are essentially those based on the larger society which has those resources. Thus, frustration and its attendant symptoms, which we shall discuss at the end of this section.

THE GEOPHYSICAL, ECONOMIC AND PSYCHOSOCIAL ENVIRON-MENT OF THE BLACK GHETTO. It is not necessary to repeat a twice-told tale. By now everyone is familiar with the geophysics of the ghetto. The geophysics are intrinsic to the definition of ghetto as currently used. The catalog of garbage – filled streets, run-down and shuttered stores and burnt-out and abandoned cars and buildings, crumbling apartment houses, deteriorating real estate, rats, roaches, flies, stale smells, etc. are well known to ghetto-dwellers and non-dwellers alike. The overcrowdedness on the streets and in the apartments, the lack of heat and hot warter, lack of basic physical services and upkeep, the general decay of all things physical have been articulated many times. This is the geophysical situation of ghettos, the abundance of all that is rottening, decaying, overused, overcrowded, out-moded and the sparsity of all that is needed, but unavailable; the over-abundance of health-damaging conditions and the absence of wholesome, preventative conditions. The over-abundance of life destroying instruments, objects and establishments and absence of life-supporting instruments, objects and establishments; shelters that don't protect from the ravages of the elements, men and vermin, infestation and disease; physical environments that provide no vistas and scenes that uplift the spirit, but which amply provide a mind-deadening drabness, sameness and unrelieved pictures of poverty and squalor. All these things and more are known by everyone so we will not bother to quote statistics here. This lack of resources or their proper utilization in the ghetto and the overwhelming abundance of adverse circumstances shapes the minds of the inhabitants, forces them to narrow their perspectives, to concentrate on adapting and surviving in those conditions, spends their cognitive talents on the trivialities of a highly fragmented environment and this forces them to take their pleasures where and when they find them, to take them immediately and to constantly seek escape – most by psychobiological means such as alcohol, drugs, chronic sexual involvement, to take from their fellow members through crime, whatever amount of scarce resources they may happen to possess.

The ghetto geophysical environment is a disinvested one – one where all valuable physical resources are either deteriorating or being taken out and none being brought in. Thus, social institutions, talented persons, factories, money, etc. are constantly being withdrawn from the community and impoverishment maintains an uninterrupted and geometrical increase in growth. A geophysical environment of this type cannot be life-supporting, it is life-destructive. A well grounded, harmonious cultural-mythological structure cannot be erected on such geophysical foundations. Frustration and its attendant ills must set in.

THE ECONOMIC. The economic picture of the ghetto is as well known as is the geophysical. Unemployment and underemployment abound and are getting worse. The black ghetto employment situation is worse than that at the height of the American Great Depression, 53% or more of black families are below the poverty level. Thus, basic goods and services are lacking to a great extent in the black ghetto due to the scarcity of means (money) to procure them. What few goods are allocated are done so mainly by social service agencies and the working poor and are allocated unevenly and in quantities too small to have lasting effect. The economic means of escaping the ghetto through physical removal, and other socially approved means, such as through education and training, are available to a relatively small number of residents. The high pricing of goods and services, the shoddiness of materials, the gouging tactics of merchants and landlords, operate to deplete and further decimate the economy of the ghetto. The lack of investment, the outflow of capital, the lack of extension of credit and cash serves to establish an economic environment that is tenuous, unpredictable, poverty-stricken, life-destroying. It adds to and multiplies the effects of the geophysical environment just described. It forces the exploitation of some members of the ghetto society by other members. Criminal behavior is resorted to by those who wish to obtain the scarce economic means possessed by their neighbors. Again, an economic environment of this kind cannot be life-supporting. It cannot meet the demands of values, aspirations and behavior patterns which are borrowed from an affluent larger society. Frustration and its attendant ills must set in.

THE PSYCHOSOCIAL. The psychosocial environment into which the black child is born is confusing and complex. The overall reigning psychosocial environment of blacks in general is grounded in the history and experience of slavery and subsequent racial discrimination. The black child is socialized by persons of this historical-experiential background as well as into the geophysical and economic environments just described. In addition, the ghetto child is exposed to a bewildering and kaleidoscopic array of street scenes, lifestyles, family forms, ethical codes, rules of conduct, human relations and economic practices. This makes it difficult for him to synthesize a code of behavior, appropriateness of emotional expression and organization of thought that is functional in or out of his surround. His lifestyle is apt to

203

be a juxtaposition of incongruent styles he has observed in his home and community. A guiding philosophy of life, a knowledge of goals and their attainment are lacking or is thawarted by experiences occurring during critical periods of his life.

Typically, the ghetto street scene contains many models whose behavior, if imitated or identified with by the child, will lead to a restricted lifestyle or to dysfunctional or possibly criminal behavior. On the streets on any day are men standing alone or in groups idled by unemployment, lack of initiative to seek employment. Others are sitting around makeship tables playing cards, drinking, gambling, talking loud and boisterously.

Some are stooping on sidewalks or in alleys shooting craps or in pool halls shooting pool. There may be a fight where some is cut, killed or brutalized. A woman may be assaulted by her husband or boyfriend. Risque jokes and imprecations are common languages. Sexual conquest is the constant talk of the men and the wolfing of women passersby is the expected behavior of the male who is a "man." The boys, a great number of whom are school dropouts, are playing handball and basketball on the sidewalks or stickball in the midst of ongoing traffic in the streets. Or they are aimlessly wandering around in groups or gangs looking for thrills to break the monotony of their lives.

In the garbage-filled streets roam pregnant teenage girls, dirty, unattended children, prostitutes, pimps, hustlers, muggers, con men, homosexuals. Noise and loud rock music rend the air, the stench of decaying buildings, of the smell of urine waft out onto the streets from darkened hallways where may be lurking dangers of all types. What businesses there are are petty and exploitive, their dusty merchandise peering out from window gates. Others have long departed the neighborhood and left behind a legacy of boarded-up windows or burnt-out shells of buildings. Bars, pool halls, "clubs," dry cleaners and storefront churches and candy stores, that are in reality numbers joints, share the sidewalks.

Runaway husbands and fathers make up an influential minority of the hangers-out on the street corners. ADC and food stamps are the coin of the realm. Literacy borders on the illiterate. There is no pretense of a bookstore in the entire block. The library and school are nestled amid the squadlor like alien and lost things from another world. They have nothing to do with the community.

The relations between persons, though many are close and warm, and there is a general heighty-ho in the air of these once hospitable southerners, are tenous and fragile. Persons and families move often and its really difficult to trust anyone — thus deep, refreshing friendships suffer. Inside the crumbling overcrowded apartments persons and families hide behind doors with many locks and windows shuttered and barred to keep the eyes of the outsiders from "casing the joint" or to prevent burglars from breaking in. The family can't go for a stroll because of the degraded conditions of the streets and people or because no one respects anyone else.

The prevailing psychosogical atmosphere is one of fear — sometimes conscious, sometimes unconscious. Fear of being mugged, assaulted, insulted, witnessing revolting acts and events or of returning to a robbed apartment are prevalent. Chronic tension and anxiety force the inhabitants to be constantly hyperalert — even inside their homes or asleep in bed. The attitudes of distrust and suspicion are the best defensive ones for the ghetto dweller. Consequently, paranoia is a way of life and edgedness a chronic state of being. The police are the colonial military whose main function seems to be that of bullying and oppressing .the local populace and protecting rent-gouging landlords' properties and the properties of absentee, exploitive businessmen. Thus, the individual ghetto member feels unprotected and deserted by the government.

The constant threat of violence and intimidation wraps the community in a heavy, oppressive cloud. The attitudes of unfathomable discontent, undirected, unrelieved hostility, or a constant desire to escape are shared by everyone. A constant state of readiness for confrontation, to flee from it, or to avoid it. For undefinable mixed feelings expressed in unpredictable ways connects all the inhabitants of the ghetto, friend and foe, stranger and stranger alike.

Political apathy and a lack of effective political organization leave conditions unchanged, let them further deteriorate in the ghetto. A general feeling of powerlessness, that the locus of power is not in themselves, that if help and positive change must come it will be from the outside, sap the initiative and creativity of the people. It generates a feeling that if things are to be done, then they must be prayed, cajoled, rioted out of other indifferent people. Thus, bluster, bravado, rank emotionalism, aggressiveness, begging or apathetically waiting for someone else to solve their problems becomes the problem-solving method of the ghetto folk. A lack of self-assertiveness in the political arena becomes the prevailing mode of behavior. This leads to a terrific sense of deprivation, frustration, guilt and shame, lack of direction, powerlessness and creates an immense vulnerability for fads, fashions, economic and intellectual, "religious" and profane exploitation. Escapism becomes the chief means of transcending these things. Some withdraw, others fight, others escape into emotional religious meetings or dance and party their frustrations away, others use drugs of all types and descriptions, too few "legitimately" overcome through education, training, finding a good job, returning "down home."

The black ghetto child is faced with lifestyles of all types and is rarely given the opportunity to choose the most positive one. There are a goodly number of "mainstream" families to choose from. In these, the basic family structure resembles that of the larger society. These are the intact families which may or may not live in relative comfort and which profess a general "middle-class" outlook. Other family types are the kinds — families where the fathers and mothers have formed some type of arrangement other than legitimate marriage. There are the "swingers" — married, with families, and unmarried — to whom "partying" and endless "running-around" is a way of life. Then there are the fugitive-father "street" families usually headed by women without husbands. There are many of these. The children may have the same father, but quite frequently have different fathers. Then there are the "street corner" men and women of the streets. How is a ghetto child to know what is best — who can tell Him? When will he learn? How will he learn?

However, this is not the end. No matter how confusing, man fashions out of a chaotic environment or imposes upon it some type of world-view, philosophy or life or mythology, be they consistent and stable or inconsistent and unstable. These become guides and determinants of his behavior, consciousness, thinking and feeling, until modified or abandoned, which, by the way, does not occur nearly as often as we would like to think. Often, if modification does occur (more often or just as often it does not, especially after maturity — even after 2½ — 3 years), residues or derivatives of the old mythologies linger on and continue to distort and twist the new realities. So, the mythological-worldview forged from or imposed by the ghetto life enchains its members, forms filters and distorts their perceptions and things are seen through "a glass darkly."

The ghetto dweller, however, is not shut off from the world. He is exposed to mass media and its messages get through. The values of the larger society, its lifestyles, power, materiality, etc. are forcefully communicated through T.V. and radio shows, movies, newspapers, magazines, conversation, advertisement, churches, schools, observation, reason and imagination. Many of the values of the so-called white middle-class are held by the ghetto dweller. As a matter of fact, this is the source of the problem — the awareness of a better dwelling place, better life, better people and the inability to get them, the failed or illegal attempts to get them, the being held back from getting them because of discrimination — this, as we shall show later, is the source of the frustration which fathers the ghetto conditions we have described (we are not forgetting racism and the slave experience). The geophysical, economic and psychosocial ground of the ghetto cannot support a white value system that is organically grounded in the white socio-politico-economic infrastructure. Attempts at trying to weld white valurs en masse and unmodified onto the structure of the ghetto produce more problems than they solve. The white lifestyles are constantly held before blacks as symbols of what it means to be a complete, acceptable and loved person. However, the cultural ground of the ghetto, its mythological structure, make striving for these symbols by many of its members doom them to disappointment and frustration. If he achieves them his life will often be empty, insecure, a caricature   of the much vaunted white middle-class life. He will then be a black bourgeoisie — all form and no content.

THE BLACK MYTHOLOGICAL STRUCTURE AND COGNITION

During our discussion of cultural determinism we stated that each culture develops a mythological structure — a structure which perceives the phenomenal and metaphysical worlds after a certain fashion and seeks to explain those worlds in terms of its perceptions. Out of this mythological structure come conceptual, evaluative, behavioral, motivational, cognitive systems and methods for dealing with the mythologized world. We also indicated that the character of the mythological structure is determined by prevailing historical, geophysical, economical, psychosocial circumstances and that cultural mythological structures guide cognition, perception, affects and behavior.

What are the characteristics of the "black" mythological structure? We think this question can best be dealt with in terms of the general relations of blacks to whites. What there is of "black" culture in America has been to a great extent deeply influenced by black-white power relations. We cannot speak of a black culture in the pure sense of the word because circumstances have not been conducive for the development of a black culture relatively uninfluenced by other cultures (in America, the "white" cultures) to warrant the use of the term "black culture" in its fullest sense. There is, however, due to the historical and current negated position of blacks in American society, a black subculture (which we will refer to as black culture from here on out) which has distinctive characteristics and which clearly impresses a cultural character on its members.

Black culture to a significant extent is a reactive culture, i.e., its shape and character to a large extent has resulted from the attempts by blacks to adapt to white power and discrimination (we are aware that "deep structures" of the original African cultures prevail and function among blacks and thereby contribute in their own right to black culture. However, such contributions are not germane to our discussion at this juncture). Black culture literally takes its "cue" from white cultural change and movement. The white culture is generally characterized by large and powerful contradictory value systems (regional systems, such as northeastern vs. southern), fast paced technological changes and a value system which is unstable, unbalanced, heterogeneous, highly fluxed and conflicting. The reactive black culture, because of its dependent relationship to the dominant white culture, multiplies the effects already present in the white structure. It suffers doubly what may be troubling the white culture.

So, black culture suffers from three major problems: It must constantly adapt and cope with a confusing, unstable, but all-powerful white culture on which it depends for its very existence, and it is locked out from sharing to any significant extent in the wielding of power and is generally degraded and discriminated against. The term which we feel would best describe the reactions of blacks to this situation and would at the same time serve as the key explanatory concept for explaining the character of a large segment of black culture, is the term – frustration. Associated closely with this term is the fact and experience of powerlessness. To a marked degree the character and attendant mythological structure of black culture has developed out of the chronic frustration and powerlessness of black people.

Frustration refers to the unpleasant feelings and/or state of mind resulting from the lack of the satisfaction of a desire, the fulfillment of a wish and/or from being or having been delayed, misled from, or blocked from reaching a certain goal or goals, and not possessing the power to satisfactorily compensate for the lost satisfaction or filfillment or to overcome the blocking obstacle (s).

We view the barrier which produced frustration within the black community as the racist white power structure (though there are numerous other factors, but we think that one will find that most of these other factors stem from the over-all racial factor) which prevents the balck community from attaining many of the things it desires. Thus, the black community suffers essentially from frustration and many of its characteristics, both functional and dysfunctional, spring from this situation.

Hilgard, et al. (3) adequately summarizes the concept of frustration when he writes:

The term frustration has at least two different connotations in everyday speech. In one sense it refers to the blocking of motive satisfaction. When progress toward a desired goal is interfered with or delayed, we say that the person encounters frustration. But "frustration"is also used to describe the unpleasant emotional state that results from blocked goal-seeking, rather than the event itself. The individual whose car gets a flat tire as he hurries to catch a plane would probably say he feels frustrated. Here frustration is equated with an internal state. For our purposes, however, we will hold to the meaning of frustration as the thwarting circumstances – the external events, rather than their internal consequences.

Unlike Hilgard, et al., we will here emphasize the internal consequences of frustration. For it is these that are responsible to a significant degree for what we may characterize as black culture. It is pertinent at this point to look at two important effects resulting from frustration as formulated by Janis, et (4):

1. The emotional upset evoked by any source of frustration will interfere with attention, thinking, planning, and other mental processes that make for constructive and imaginative performance

2. When a barrier results in the frustration of aroused motive that is ir-relevant to executing the task, the frustrated person will try to continue the irrelevant activity that is being interefered with instead of working on the original task.

Since frustration is almost endemic to black life in America, the conseque-ences of black children being socialized under such a situation are apparent as indicated by the first paragraph of the above quotation — reduced and dis-torted cognitive, motivational and behavioral functioning as well as dysfunc-tional compensatory functioning. The black child is socialized in a — confused culture and his personal, social and cognitive functioning carry the marks of such a socialization process.

The reactions to frustration are fairly well known — restlessness and tension, aggression (direct and displaced), apathy, fantasy, stereotypy, regres-sion (3), and a good number of others. We will explore some of the reactions to frustration as they apply to the black community.

RESTLESSNESS AND TENSION. If the goals of various motives, wishes, de-sires, etc. are attained and are satisfactory, the organism experiences a period of relaxation and fulfillment. However, if the goals are not attained or are not satisfactory the organism experiences increased tension and restlessness — he feels frustrated. There is little or no direct evidence that blacks, as a group, are more restless and tense than are whites, but experiments in support of the basic assumption can be easily found. The fact that blacks have not achieved the goals they want and fight for daily, would indicate that they suffer the tension of frustration — the tensions that come from confronting a recalcitrant system, the tension created by stigmatization, tension created by rejection, tension created by having many strong needs and drives go unfilled. The riots of the sixties and seventies, the increasing suicide rates and mental illness, physical suffering, the high incidence of essential hyper-tension, all are symptomatic of the extraordinary tension experienced by blacks. Many of the blacks who may not have personally confronted the barriers to their fulfillment, those who have been forewarned by other blacks, still suffer from undirected rage and resentment, "floating rage and resent-ment." This undirected rage and resentment, whether consciously felt or re-pressed in the subconscious, is often discharged into generally destructive channels which often leads to over-reactive aggression against persons and property.

AGGRESSION

The anger and possibly fear resulting from being blocked from desired and needed goals may lead to undirected destructiveness and hostility and/or des-tructiveness and hostility directed at the interfering barrier. Quite often the rage and hostility that for various reasons cannot be directed at the party or parties is directed at more vulnerable parties within reach of the frustrated party. Where the frustrating barrier is attacked this is referred to as direct aggression. There things other than the barrier are attacked, we have what is referred to as displaced aggression. One does not have to go far to gather historical and current evidence showing the direct assault by blacks against furstrating racial barriers through a number of means; slave revolts on sea and land, legal battles, bloc voting, demonstrations, sit-ins, riots, direct one-to-one and group-to-group physical confrontations of black against white, etc. Indirect and displaced aggression is evidenced by the destruction of property owned by whites and acting uncooperatively with white authority whenever possible.

However, the most serious evidence of displaced aggression among blacks is the very high rate within group physical brutality of black against black, the murder and assault of blacks against blacks. The rates of suicide, alcoholism, drug abuse, and other forms of self-destructive behavior that have been well documented are evidence of displaced aggression. Self-abnegation by blacks, self-hatred and group resentment by blacks indicate a situation where, instead of negative feelings, hatred and hostility and resentment being directed at the responsible party (the whites) or in addition to them being directed that way, they are directed toward the self and the group to which one belongs (the black group).

APATHY

Although direct and indirect aggression are frequent responses to frustrating circumstances, apathy, indifference, withdrawal, studied avoidance of the frustrating situation also are frequent responses.   This type of response is most likely to occur when the frustrating barrier appears to be extremely powerful, invincible, or severely punishes attempts at overcoming it. This type of response may also stem from the frustrated party's estimation of his weakness, extreme vulnerability, his fear of punishment and failure. Consequently, the frustrated party gives up and exhibits lack of interest in achieving the blocked goals, indifference to those goals, withdrawal from any effort to achieve those goals. The apathy of the black community has been remarked on in the literature quite frequently. Though the sit-ins, demonstrations, voting practices, etc., by blacks, do point to active concern by many blacks, it would not take long to establish that these active blacks represent a small percentage of blacks. The failure of blacks to progress commensurate to their efforts and education has reduced black interest in that direction for many of them. Their rejection in the political arena and their lack of real influence in that area has tended to make a very sizeable percentage of blacks uninterested in politics and voting.

The overwhelming power of the white power structure and swift and over-reactive tendency to punish black aggression, its control over resources, its

210

sustained degrading of black self-confidence along with other negative factors has produced in a very large percentage of blacks what is referred to as Learned Helplessness. The very strong and largely negative control that the white establishment has over black lives has produced among many blacks such a degree of lack of self-confidence that a large number of them do not believe that their personal and group status can be improved, save through the help of whites. The utter dependence of blacks on whites for their physical existence has generalized to an almost utter dependence on whites for their social, economic, political, educational, cognitive existence. This type of apathy has helped to maintain black subjugation, ignorance, lack of self-knowledge, self-love, self-confidence, self-assertiveness, self-education. The situation has been such that when barriers are down many blacks continue to respond as if the barriers still exist.

FANTASY

The recalcitrance and negative reactivity of the white power barriers has been such that it has driven an extremely large segment of the black community to seek solutions to their frustrations in the realms of fantasy and magical thinking. They may engage in fantasies of having reached their goals, or vicariously identifying with whites, they try to "act white" or pretend that America has no racial problems, only a problem of economics, they may enter into their own fantasy world of dancing, partying, constant sexual play, etc. in order to forget their frustrating circumstances, they may become excessively involved in an integrated world or copy "white" habits and interests to such a degree that they forget their blackness and the frustrations connected with it, they may become fanatical about ideas and philosophies which ignore present realities and that dwell on apocryphal "heavens" or classless societies.

STEREOTYPY

In seeking to win full acceptance and equality in and with the larger white society, blacks have tried nearly every possible means available to them to attain such. They have begged, bluffed, rioted, prayed, sat-in, martyred themselves, fought court battles, etc. Yet, none of these methods singularly or in combination have been very successful. The final outcome has been for many blacks a lapse into stereotypy — "a tendency to exhibit repetitive, fixated behavior" (Hilgard, 3). The flexibility required for efficient problem-solving, the ability to follow new directions, is adversely affected or completely negated by the ensuing reactions to frustrations. The fact that many blacks still seek acceptance and equality, by using the means mentioned above, means which have not worked, the fact that they continue to see acceptance and equality with whites as a preeminent goal, despite the fact that such an acceptance and equality may not be in their best interest, the fact that the majority of blacks still reject black nationalism, black self-determination (as far as is possible), black self-evaluation, the fact that blacks have little or no confidence in their ability to educate their own, as evidenced by their constant battles to get whites to educate their children, the fact that blacks see the whites as having the only power and ability to solve their problems, despite the fact that none of these beliefs have accomplished for them what they have wanted for some four hundred years, indicates stereotyped behavior. The extreme conformity with white values and orientations exhibited by a large and influential segment of the black community, despite the fact that these values and orientations have been counterproductive, the suspiciousness and mistrust of many blacks of other blacks, of separatist and/or nationalist orientation due to the fact that such orientations do not have white establishment approval and to the fact that it represents for many blacks too great a departure from stereotyped, minimally effective approaches, indicates the loss of flexibility and originality in black thinking engendered by paralyzing frustration.

One could wager that if blacks could achieve prosperity, independence, peace, respect, self-love, etc. through a nationalistic-separatist program, a very large segment, the middleclass segment especially, would reject such a possibility even if it meant another four hundred years of trying to become fully integrated with the white community. This continuing preoccupation with whites in general, and integration in particular, has been destructive for the black community in many areas of functioning. For such preoccupation has had the effect of blacks neglecting to use their own economic, educational, organizational resources efficiently. They have literally abandoned the education of their children and lost generations of children to ignorance because their integrationist attempts have left them no time or inclination to teach their children what they thought the whites could teach them.

Because of the utter fixation of blacks on whites, creative, original, innovative, unorthodox, powerful, assertive, non-conformist thoughts, actions and beliefs by blacks (even as indicated in black children) have been ignored, actively discouraged or greeted with indifference. Black children reared under this fixation by their parents grow up to feel neglected, inferior, deprived, hostile, rebellious, conformist, withdrawn, self-hating, ignorant, anti-intellectual, present-oriented, exhibit limited cognitive drive and power, have little group love and desire for group cohesiveness, etc. They grow up to be anything but their true selves and hardly begin to approach their full potential and to use their full abilities.

REGRESSION

The feeling of insecurity brought on by frustration can be such that the individual or group returns to "more primitive " modes of behavior, that is, to modes of behavior characterizing a younger age" (3). Adult behavior implies, in part, autonomy, self-evaluation, self-knowledge, self-love, ingenuity, originality, self-controlled, self-initiated and self-organized behavior, seeing the self as the prime source of feelings of happiness, well-being, etc. The severely frustrated adult may lose these attributes and develop their very opposites, may sink into increasing dependency, intemperate and emotional behavior, behavior not guided by feedback, childishness, lack of self-confidence, feelings of helplessness, a strong need of external supports, a severe reduction in the ability to think like an adult, to use the mental capacity to its fullest and most flexible extent. There may be also a return to fantasy, withdrawal, magical thinking, a tendency to immediately lapse into frustrated behavior at the least sign of an obstacle to be confronted — whether that obstacle represents a math problem or a confrontation involving other persons. There may be an attempt to solve problems by inadequate means. Regressive behavior is quite apparent in the black community. The attempts of the black middle-class to obtain strokes from the white power-structure at any cost, whether by ignominious begging, crying, etc., the riotous, tempestuous, property-destructing, etc. behavior by the black lower-class are evidence for regression. And there is much more. Regressed black parents produce regressed black children. The maladaptive behavior of many black children, the academic "failure" of many black children, point to this state of regression existing in the black community.

OTHER REACTIONS ENGENDERED BY FRUSTRATION (as they relate to the black community)

UNREALISTIC STRIVING — striving uninformed by mature, objective, realistic, evaluation of abilities, capabilities, chances and possibilities. A tendency to strive toward empty, grandiose goals or a tendency toward goals that provide little or no challenge.

AMBIVALENCE — a mixed, love-hate attitude toward the frustrating object and toward things that have been identified with that object. Too many blacks are literally fixated by their ambivalent relationship with the obstructing whites, they wish to be fully accepted and loved by the whites, wish to love the whites, but since these wishes are generally rejected by the whites, the blacks hate them. This hate or hostility basically results from the original desire to love. Consequently, a love-hate or hate-love attitude is developed toward whites by blacks. This abivalence feeds on the black personality itself breeding ambivalence toward the self and the group. A great deal of black anti-intellectualism, rejection of academic behavior by black children, rejection of work requiring prolonged periods of thought and concentration and effort, sacrifice, thankless creative labor, continuing education, etc. develop out of the fact that such behaviors have been identified as "white." Thus, such behaviors are pursued ambivalently, half-heartedly, or rejected outright, engaged in just enough to "get over."

LACK OF SELF-KNOWLEDGE AND SELF-LOVE — since the whites are of such overwhelming importance in the black world, so overwhelming that the black self is dwarfed in comparison, interest in things black, knowledge of things black,suffer severely.Thus the black fails to gain knowledge of himself. Since blacks see the gaining of the love of whites as the only means to their "salvation" they have concentrated on gaining this white love to the detriment of developing a love for themselves. Their behavior and orientation becomes almost completely "other-directed" (others being the whites) and the self diminishes·in importance and interest and as an object of self-love as a consequence.

DENIAL AND EMOTIONAL ISOLATION.— the frustrations of having to deal with frustration may lead the person or group to deny the reality of the frustration or to deny the emotional feelings engendered by frustration. The "happy," continuously "partying," "cool," unemotional, self-centered, self-segregated, noncompetitive blacks fit into this category. They have no "race problem." In fact, they have "no problems" at all.

INABILITY TO TEACH OR PROVIDE USEFUL INFORMATION TO OTHERS — the frustrated individual is usually not in a good position or disposition to help others. His concern with his own problems, his obsession with the frustrating situation and more importantly, the lack of self-confidence and the failure to acquire knowledge, capabilities, etc. severely reduce his ability and desire and know-how and confident willingness to teach others. Frustrations have so shaken blacks until they feel that their children can only be trained to function academically, socially, psychologically, etc. not by themselves but by the frustrating white establishment. Consequently, a large segment of the black community fights endlessly for integration of their children into white secondary schools — in many instances indicating a loss of faith in their ability to give their own children the education they wish them to have.

LEARNING PROBLEMS - we've already amply indicated how frustration adversely affects the learning process

LOW ACHIEVEMENT, LOW EXTENSION, HIGH DEPENDENCY MOTIVATION (already discussed).

Thus, many of the characteristics of black cultural and individual behavior can be attributed to the reactions to frustration and the socialization of the black child by frustrated black parents. These characteristics were born of the generally antagonistic co-existence of an almost completely dependent black group and a surrounding independent, all-powerful, white group. This situation, in turn, generates a particular world-view — mythological —in the black culture, the strength and character of that world-view varying a bit with class. Nevertheless, the world-view touches and influenc very black person who perceives himself as such. The symptoms of low   ve-

214

ment motivation, low extension and high dependency motivation heavily color and becloud the black world-view (mythological structure – his explanatory system which seeks to explain how what he perceives as reality came about, why it came about, what is his place and function and destiny in that reality). The symptoms of frustration, some of which we have just discussed, further confuse and negatively influence the black world-view. The world-view (mythological structure) and its inherent socialization tendencies have produced both adults and children who operate at a cognitive, behavioral, motivational deficit in the context of white society. The language and cognitive style developed from this world-view and the world-reality that does exist become millstones around the necks of blacks who wish to "equal" whites in all areas of functioning, identify themselves with whites, measure themselves positively by "white" standards, values and attitudes. Apparently a large number of blacks hope for these things.

The major problem beside rank racial discrimination against blacks has been, and is now, how can blacks produce persons who are "functional" cognitively, motivationally and behaviorally in a world measured by "white" standards, values and attitudes, given pervasive influence of "black life-culture" on its members and the white power structure which "maintains" that life-culture? Some blacks have opted for changing the structure, becoming fully integrated within, identified with it. For these blacks integration in all areas is the answer and the only one. However, integration has been exceedingly slow and in the meanwhile black children, generations of them, are lost. The other way of removing the "deficit" lies in the direction of the socialization practices of black parents and community leaders.

A change in the latter would bring about changes in the behavioral, motivational and cognitive functioning of black children. The socialization practices would seem a more sensible way since it is more under the direct control of conscious black parents to bring about change in black behavior.

It may appear that the picture we have painted of the black culture in the preceding section is a rather negative and pessimistic one, that the culture is totally described by its frustrations at the hands of the dominant culture. This was not our intention. The large majority of black people in America do not fit the foregoing descriptions though an unacceptably large segment does. The positive, healthy and wholesome attributes and orientations of the black community outnumber substantially its negative ones. It is not difficult to document any number of cases where blacks have maintained their identity, fought frustrating barriers and yet have fully realized their intellectual, cognitive, behavioral, emotional and social potentials. Our emphasis in the foregoing discussion was presented so that those factors which unnecessarily retard the physical, mental and social well-being can clearly be identified and reckoned with thereby removing obstacles in the way of the true realization of the black potential.

REFERENCES

1. Allport, G. W. THE NATURE OF PREJUDICE. New York: Doubleday Anchor Books 1958.
2. Brown, R. WORDS AND THINGS: An Introduction to Language. New York: The Free Press, 1968.
3. Hilgard, E. R., et al. INTRODUCTION TO PSYCHOLOGY. SIXTH EDITION. New York: Harcourt Brace Jovanovich, Inc., 1975.
4. Janis, I. L., et al. PERSONALITY: Dynamics, Development, and Assessment. New York: Harcourt Brace Jovanovich, 1969.
5. Norris, C. SIGNS, LANGUAGE AND BEHAVIOR. New York: Prentice-Hall, 1946.
6. Stevenson, C.L. ETHICS AND LANGUAGE. New Haven: Yale University Press, 1944.
7. Thass-Thienemann, T. THE INTERPRETATION OF LANGUAGE. Vol. 1: Understanding the symbolic Meaning of Language. New York: Jason Inc. 1973.
8. Whorf, B. L. LANGUAGE, THOUGHT, AND REALITY. Cambridge: Technology, Press.

Appendix of Recommended Readings for Black Parents

Beck, Joan How To Raise a Brighter Child: The Care for Early Learning (revised edition) N. Y.: Simon & Schuster — Pocket Books 1975.

Doman, Glenn How To Teach Your Baby To Read N. y. Doubleday — Dolphin Books, 1975.

Engelmann, Siegfried and Therese Give Your Child a Superior Mind: Program for The Preschool Child. N. Y.: McGraw Hill, 1966.

Harrison-Ross, Phyllis and Wyden, Barbara The Black Child: A Parent's Guide New York: Wyden 1973.

Shneour, Elie The Malnourished Mind N. Y.: Doubleday — Anchor Press 1974.

Sparkman, Brandon, and Carmichael, Ann Blueprint for a Brighter Child, N. Y.: McGraw-Hill 1973.